Not the Law's Business

n Examination of Homosexuality, Abortion, Prostitution, Narcotics and Gambling in the United States

Gilbert Geis

Schocken Books • New York

First published by Shocken Books 1979
10 9 8 7 6 5 4 3 2 1   79 80 81 82

Preface copyright © 1979 by Schocken Books Inc.

Library of Congress Cataloging in Publication Data
Geis, Gilbert.
    Not the law's business.

    Reprint with new introd., of the 1972 ed.
published by National Institute of Mental Health,
Rockville, Md., which was issued in series: Crime
and delinquency issues, and as Publication no.
72-9132 of the Public Health Service.
        1. Crimes without victims—United States.
2. United States—Moral conditions. I. Title.
II. Series: Crime and delinquency issues.
III. Series: United States. Public Health
Service. Publication no. 72-9132.
[HV6707.U5G44 1979] 364.1   78-26102

Manufactured in the United States of America

This monograph was one of a series on current issues and directions in the area of
crime and delinquency, sponsored by the Center for Studies of Crime and Delinquency, National Institute of Mental Health.

Preface to the Schocken Edition

Criminal law is sometimes said to provide a telling indication of a society's insecurities. Social systems threatened by religious schism will turn the ferocity of their criminal code against behaviors perceived as heretical and heterodox. Failure to attend worship services regularly and blasphemous utterance are legally interdicted. Communist countries, when they are unsure of the persuasive power of the party line, turn to the criminal law to check the nondoctrinaire. Nervous capitalist nations enact criminal laws to punish acts and attitudes deemed unpatriotic, including activities such as membership in groups professing preference for a different kind of economic or political system. The opposition comes to be defined as a revolutionary force beyond the control of all but criminal penalty.

When conditions are calmer, danger is apt to appear less immediate and less overwhelming. The best result, it is suggested, will come about only after a wide range of ideas and acts are allowed to compete unfettered for support in the open market. There is less hysteria, greater hospitality. The view prevails that orthodoxy is so right that it will inevitably emerge victorious against all comers in a fair fight.

The behaviors dealt with in this book—homosexuality, abortion, prostitution, use of narcotics, and gambling—offer particularly telling insight into how comfortable a society such as the United States is with its orthodoxy. That orthodoxy, written into the American Constitution and the Declaration of Independence, holds out the offer of great liberty, even license, but often at the expense of the well-being and the moral predilections of the majority of the population. The behaviors reviewed here provide a political and ideological Rorschach. They may with justice be deemed by advocates of their criminalization as a threat to the basic fiber of the social structure, or, equally decently, they can be defined as inconsequential, even colorful, variations in the usual tapestry of life. Some of the behaviors, abortion in particular, arouse strong emotions. Sanctioning abortion may be regarded as consenting to murder. On the other hand, permitting abortion under the law can be seen as allowing persons who define the act differently to do as they wish about an unwanted pregnancy. In the case of abortion, the question of "harm" becomes most pronounced and direct, while at the same time, paradoxically, the question lies beyond any possibility of scientific resolution, resting foursquare in the domain of theology and belief.

The common method for grouping the acts considered in this volume is to label them as "crimes without victims." This characterization tends to be more on the order of a polemic exercise rather than a scientifically sophisticated use of nomenclature. For one thing, as the individual chapters try to make clear, each of the acts differs in very distinctive ways from the others so that generalizations about them as a class tend to be misleading or inappropriate. For another thing, very distinctive kinds of activities, with very different kinds of implications, are embraced within each of the larger categories. The term "crimes without victims" obviously carries the implication that an injustice exists, that behaviors are being outlawed though they inflict no harm, at least on those who participate in them directly. Being a "victim" and being "harmed," however, are rather different conditions. Few persons doubt that an individual who has an heirloom stolen by a burglar is a crime victim, though the victim may have tired of the inheritance, and may collect more from the insurance company than the possession was worth to him or her. At the same time, the person who buys heroin in a lethal dosage—though not traditionally thought of as a victim, since participation in the transaction was voluntary— clearly will be harmed. It can be argued that the voluntary act did not extend to the death-dealing quality of the drug, but only to a "normal" dosage. In such terms, the victimization, being inadvertent from the viewpoint of both seller and purchaser, might be regarded as nothing more than an accident, much like what happens to a passerby who chances to get hit on the head by an object dropped by mistake from the top of a high-rise building under construction.

It can be seen that use of the term "crimes without victims" tends to focus attention on the possible harmful consequences of the behaviors being considered, sometimes to the neglect of what appear to be more pertinent characteristics. It is perhaps a truism that living itself—the very process of existing—inevitably and inexorably victimizes, and that individual and group decisions on how to behave and what to tolerate (speed limits, marketing of certain kinds of food products, pollution levels, years of mandatory education) always carry with them units of victimization, that is, statistical likelihoods and certainties related to injury and death for certain numbers of people who might have been spared something and somewhat had other kinds of arrangements been made. Thus the question pointedly arises about each of the behaviors discussed in this book: Why have they been singled out for proscription while other acts, some of them more reprehensible by congruent standards, are tolerated and even encouraged? There are suggestions throughout the book bearing on this matter. Considerations of power, tradition, ethnocentrism, class, and inertia—among others—seem to be notably influential in the processes leading to the criminalization of the categories of behavior considered.

Power seems to be particularly high on the list of forces operating in regard to homosexuality, prostitution, narcotics use, abortion, and gambling. Recent developments in each of the areas tell a pointed story. The behaviors in general—or aspects of them—have been decriminalized if their supporters were prominent and powerful. Abortion on demand within the first trimester of a woman's pregnancy received the imprimatur of the United States Supreme Court. The move was preceded by a well-managed feminist campaign which insisted that control of a woman's body was her own prerogative, not the state's. Prominent women came forth with stories of illegal abortions that they had undergone, degrading and dangerous experiences which were dictated, they said, by the medieval, moralistic, and masculine character of the existing abortion statutes. The battle regarding the proper legal approach to abortion continues today, but a very significant skirmish has been won by the forces favoring decriminalization. It was won largely because the criminal law as it existed aroused the anger of an articulate and important segment of the population whose own interests were involved—not because the argument for decriminalization was necessarily superior to those brought to bear in efforts to decriminalize numbers gambling, heroin use, and homosexuality.

Consensual homosexual activity involving adults also has moved significantly from the realm of outlawed behavior into the territory of permissible action. The development has not, however, been nearly as rapid or as thorough as that for abortion. More than a dozen American states now have decriminalized private homosexuality. But public referenda, most notably one in Dade County, Florida, saw the rejection of demands for homosexual equal rights in areas such as employment and housing. In mid-1978, California voters provided the first major expression of support for homosexual rights when they resoundingly defeated Proposition Six which, if enacted, would have barred any known or admitted homosexual from teaching in the public schools. The campaign against the proposition by homosexual groups and their supporters was well orchestrated. It was pointed out, for instance, that existing laws provided adequate protection against any possible homosexual involvement by teachers with pupils. The election outcome represented an expression of sentiment on a particular issue in a particular jurisdiction, but it also was a significant straw in the wind, representing a triumph, as was true for abortion, for an influential group.

Gambling continues to be decriminalized at a very rapid rate—witness the recent opening of casinos in Atlantic City—because the appeal of "easy" revenue proves irresistible to fiscally troubled jurisdictions. But numbers betting, the king of gambling primarily pursued by blacks and other inner-city residents, remains largely beyond the pale. The operating principle appears to be that gambling is to be legally permissible, but only for those who can best "afford" it.

Meanwhile, prostitution remains criminalized in all states but Nevada, largely, it may be suspected, because former prostitutes (unlike women who have had abortions) usually do not proclaim their earlier status or speak of the degradation imposed by enforcement of the criminal law against prostitution. Prostitutes have no effective lobby and little likelihood of establishing one in the near future. The most notable development in the area of prostitution, in fact, has been the shift to strong advocacy of strict enforcement of the criminal laws against the behavior by feminists once identified with the liberal movement, which traditionally favored decriminalization. The feminists believe that men who patronize prostitutes ought to be apprehended and prosecuted much more often than they now are. They also maintain that allowing prostitution to go unproscribed by criminal law feeds into a chauvinistic ethos, one which defines women as sexual commodities whose favors are to become available to any male who can afford to purchase them. Harm is said to be done to the prostitute herself as well as to the image of women. That prostitutes might prefer other arrangements than criminalization is regarded as an indication of false consciousness, an inability to comprehend adequately the full implication of their behavior.

The story of heroin and marijuana offers the most telling material. Marijuana, once the weed that crazed and corrupted, is now almost universally tolerated, with the typical criminal statute outlawing only possession of such amounts as suppose an intent to sell. Middle class usage of marijuana is widespread. Heroin, however, remains largely a drug used only by persons in the working class, and it remains totally outlawed. The reputation of heroin as the drug that crazes and corrupts continues unchallenged, seemingly because there is no group interested and strong enough that cares to contradict common wisdom, or nobody powerful enough who is suffering much inconvenience from the interdicted status of the drug.

There is no question that the current today continues to run strongly in the direction of decriminalization of the behaviors discussed in *Not the Law's Business*. At the same time, there remains (perhaps even more so than before) a pressing need for careful scrutiny of the consequences of various arrangements for dealing with (or ignoring) the behaviors considered in this book. Such an evaluative task involves a complex kind of monitoring, one taking account of things such as public and political attitudes, crime statistics, and individual and social health and malaise. Information and discussion bearing upon these issues is offered throughout the book, with the aim of providing a background for adequate judgment. The behaviors pose direct questions bearing upon human freedom and social protection. They offer a challenge to clear thinking and intelligent action. It is hoped that the Schocken edition of *Not the Law's Business* will contribute significantly to the continuing debate about the proper legal position our society should adopt toward homosexuality, abortion, prostitution, narcotics use, and gambling.

Gilbert Geis

University of Sydney
February 1979

Acknowledgments

Impetus for this monograph was provided by George H. Weber, Deputy Chief, Center for Studies of Crime and Delinquency in the National Institute of Mental Health. George suggested one spring day that it might be a decent endeavor to attempt to review for the National Institute of Mental Health the current condition of information and law in regard to a number of crimes which, in the usual sense, do not have victims. He and I both thought that the effort might reasonably extend through a summer school recess.

Some years and many typewriter ribbons later, the manuscript has been completed. During the interval, George remained unfailingly helpful, always encouraging, unflaggingly interested. He must be listed as the gentlest of gentlemen, a fine scholar, and a knowledgeable editor. This work owes both its origin and its completion to his continuing enthusiasm.

I want to express my appreciation also to Duncan Chappell of the School of Criminal Justice, State University of New York, Albany, for many helpful suggestions about various segments of the manuscript. My wife, Robley, as she always does, made this work in many ways a joint enterprise, more fun than the puritans would say it ought rightfully to have been.

Most important, I would like to dedicate the monograph to my mother, Ida L. Geis, with love and gratitude.

GILBERT GEIS

Contents

Unless a deliberate attempt is to be made by society, acting through the agency of the law, to equate the sphere of crime with that of sin, there must remain a realm of private morality and immorality which is, in brief and crude terms, not the law's business. To say this is not to condone or encourage private immorality. On the contrary, to emphasize the personal and private nature of moral or immoral conduct is to emphasize the personal and private responsibility of the individual for his own action, and that is a responsibility which a mature agent can properly be expected to carry for himself without the threat of punishment from the law.

Great Britain, Committee
on Homosexual Offences and
Prostitution,
Report (Cmnd. 247, 1957),
p. 24.

x

I. Introduction

This paper deals with the following kinds of behavior:

It deals with acts such as that of the teenager who sits in a theater balcony, quietly smoking a marihuana cigarette. And it deals with acts such as those of a group of young men and women at a "pot" party, giggling a good deal, passing a "joint" back and forth, getting "high," and making what they regard as extraordinarily incisive remarks about the contemporary condition of mankind.

This paper is also concerned with acts such as those of two men, both homosexuals, both in their early thirties, who come together in a "gay" bar, make cautious overtures, reach an agreement, and then go to the apartment of one or the other. In the apartment, by mutual consent, they engage in an act of oral copulation.

This paper is also interested in looking at the case of a 24-year-old woman, already mother of two children, now 5 weeks pregnant, who does not care to give birth to another child. She tries several folk remedies in an attempt to end her pregnancy, all without success. Then, acting on information from a friend, she arranges an appointment with an abortionist. The business is sordid. She arrives at a prearranged meeting place, is blindfolded and taken elsewhere, treated brusquely, and without dignity, and then returned to the rendezvous point. Afterwards, she may be somewhat ashamed, and in fear of a possible hemorrhage or other physical injury. But she is also likely to be very relieved that it is all done with.

This paper also deals with the second party to this transaction, the abortionist. The abortionist may be rather like the surgeon portrayed in a recent novel, who alleges that he turned to abortions because of the agony and feelings of impotence involved in operating on terminal cancer patients. "I started to do abortions," he says. "Nice and easy, everybody happy, like washing the dishes and leaving a clean sink. . . . I loved being an abortionist. I don't believe a 2-month fetus is a human being so no problems there. I was helping young girls and married women who were in trouble. I was making good money. I was out of the front lines. When I got caught I felt like a deserter that has been hauled in . . . ."[1] Or he may be

---

[1] Mario Puzo, *The Godfather* (New York: Putnam's, 1969), p. 375.

1

an untrained "butcher" with only rudimentary knowledge of surgery and medicine, running the constant risk of committing manslaughter. This paper also discusses gambling transactions involving behavior such as that described in the following vignette:

> Joe stands six mornings a week outside a storefront social club in the "Little Italy" area behind Police Headquarters [in New York City]. He is squat. His long gray sweater blends in color with his thinning hair. Housewives on their way to and from the market, men in work clothes, the unemployed and relief clients stop to exchange greetings with a handshake.
>
> A quarter passes hands, or a half dollar, sometimes a dollar bill—but never a slip with a penciled number. If the police were to frisk Joe they'd find no evidence. He carries the number, given orally, into the club inside his head after each encounter. The club interior, where the numbers and amount of play are listed, is forbidden territory to the police without a court-issued search warrant.[2]

There is a certain congruence among the acts noted above. That congruence inheres in the fact that the marihuana smokers, the homosexuals, the abortionist and his client, and the "runner" and the persons wagering—though all are violating criminal statutes—are in each instance committing acts which, in terms of the common understanding of the term, do not have victims. All parties directly concerned have chosen to do what they are doing voluntarily, presumably because they perceive that the benefits to them are apt to outweigh any disadvantages or inconveniences, including the possibility of penalties they might suffer at the hands of the law.

WHO, THEN, ARE THE VICTIMS?

The foregoing should not be taken to mean that there are in fact no victims of the described behaviors, since the term victim may also reasonably be used to denominate someone who suffers any kind of untoward harm because of a set of circumstances either involving called him or bearing upon him. The acts are said to be "victimless" only so because the victimization from them is more remote and/or more arguable than in the case of most other acts defined as criminal. They also involve willing exchanges of desired goods or services, and it is only rarely that a participant will initiate an enforcement action. As Schur has noted, "The combination of a consensual transaction and low visibility makes evidence extremely hard to come by,

---

[2] "Grocers, Barmaids, Pizza Sellers Help Run Game," *New York Times*, June 26, 1964.

and law enforcers are driven to costly and often repressive techniques to obtain evidence . . ." [3]

It is possible to maintain, nonetheless, that harm is done to the
participants of the acts themselves, either in a physical sense (such
as with abortion or use of marihuana) or in a social sense (such as
with gambling, where time and resources might "better" be used to
other ends). The harm may also be said to be inflicted on other citizens who in any one of a number of ways are offended or inconven-
ienced by the acts. It may be argued that such harm, at times, is a
function of an unreasonable sensitivity (or insensitivity) on the part
of the sufferer, such as a citizen who is annoyed by the sight of
homosexual overtures being made in a public park or upset by a
newspaper photograph of a marihuana "orgy" at a rock festival.
But, reasonable or otherwise, the suffering obviously can be real
and painful.

In addition, an act such as abortion can be claimed to represent
the murder of an innocent unborn child. This kind of victimization
may, of course, be said to hang on nothing more substantial than a
semantic twist that defines a fetus as a human being. Such kinds of
definitional disputation are commonplace in regard to the acts under
review and differentiate them from such things as armed robbery
and burglary where there is only rare controversy concerning the
real nature of the injury and the immediate identification of the
victim.

The victim of acts such as homosexuality, prostitution, abortion,
gambling, and drug use may also be regarded as the society at large,
seen as an entity with a well-being that suffers as a consequence of
such acts. It is a hazardous enterprise to attempt to chart the short-
run rise or decline of a social system and perhaps a vainglorious
enterprise to attempt to pinpoint the causes for such social health or
malaise. But there is no gainsaying that retrospective examination
indicates clearly that some societies have prospered while others
have disintegrated, and that such conditions appear to be related in
some manner to official attitudes and responses to various kinds of
behavior—matters condoned or proscribed, encouraged or discour-
aged. Most often, social critics point to what they see as a lesson
from ancient Greece and Rome, and use the fates of these civilizations as polemic hooks upon which to hang objections to current
policies or proposed changes in policies.

A fictional portrait—that of a speech by a general in charge of

[3] Edwin M. Schur, "Victimless Crime," Letter to the Editor, *New York Times*, January 15, 1972.

American counterintelligence—can serve as a stereotype of the kind of thinking which attempts to equate social policy on moral issues and the survival of the society:

> Our people have forgotten the good old-fashioned virtues that have made this nation the greatest and strongest power in human history. Forget your disciplines and morality and you go under; you sink and die. Look at Rome, Athens. But what America has is worth fighting for, by God, and by all the good principles that made our nation great, I intend to fight for the right as long as I draw a breath in my body. All this soft-headed, socialist thinking in our courts and Congress can only lead to our own self-destruction.[4]

In a more academic vein, we may cite the views of J. D. Unwin, put forward in *Sex and Culture* (1934), a study of 80 preliterate societies and a number of historically advanced cultures. Unwin sought to correlate different societies' sexual permissiveness with their energy for "advancement." Virtually all the civilized societies Unwin examined—the Babylonians, Athenians, Romans, Anglo-Saxons, and English—began their historical careers in a "state of absolute monogamy." The one exception was the Moors, where a specific religious sanction supported polygamy. "Any human society," Unwin wrote, "is free to choose either to display great energy or to enjoy sexual freedom; the evidence is that it cannot do both for more than one generation." [5]

The acts being examined in this paper, then, are not in any true sense "crimes without victims," but rather they are consensual acts whose performance poses arguable deleterious consequences for individuals in the society, including participants in the acts, and for the society as a whole.

BY WHAT RULES ARE THE ACTS TO BE JUDGED?

Some consensus is evident among the more preeminent thinkers who have concentrated upon issues such as homosexuality, gambling, prostitution, narcotics use, and abortion regarding the ground rules under which debate shall be conducted. Official action may legitimately be taken against a behavior, they appear to agree, if some substantial harm can be demonstrated to result from it, either to a victim, seen as an involuntary party, or to the society at large and its legitimate interests. The classic statement of this position is that of John Stuart Mill:

---

[4] Edward S. Aarons, *Assignment Peking* (New York: Fawcett, 1969), p. 36.
[5] J. D. Unwin, *Sex and Culture* (London: Oxford University Press, 1934), p. 412.

> The sole end for which mankind are warranted, individually or collectively, in interfering with the liberty of action of any of their number, is self-protection . . . .
>
> The only purpose for which power can rightfully be exercised over any member of a civilized community, against his will, is to prevent harm to others. His own good, either physical or moral, is not a warrant.[6]

The Mill's statement, for all its clarion stress on individual liberty, is more tantalizing than definitive when the attempt is made to employ it as a guide to social policy. The terms "self-protection" and "to prevent harm to others" admit of numerous interpretations, so that honest persons may strongly disagree when confronted by the same facts. Mill does not tell us how serious the harm has to be and how directly tied to the given act before the act may be banned. Would the harm be sufficient, for example, if it could be demonstrated that, say, homosexuality was producing a decline in the population of such a nature that it was leading to inadequate manpower for economic growth and prowess which, in turn, appeared likely to invite conquest by an alien power? First, of course, some agreement would have to be reached regarding the statistical certainty (or intuitive idea of likelihood) necessary for something to "appear likely." Granting resolution of this not insubstantial issue, would the specified facts constitute adequate cause for homosexuality to be outlawed in order to convince its practitioners—and those perhaps contemplating the behavior—of the relative advantages of heterosexual conduct? Or can such an argument be rebutted successfully by a demonstration that the production of more people, presuming the importance of such people for national goals, could be achieved by means other than the legal repression of homosexuality, means such as cash bonuses for families with three or more children? Bonuses, perhaps that might be paid for by a special levy against persons beyond a certain age who have not produced any children?

"Self-protection" and "harm to others," then, can be seen to represent something of a definitional quagmire. Perhaps the most persuasive attempt to provide solid stepping stones out of that quagmire is that of Patrick Devlin who insists that social harm (and inevitably, as a consequence, individual harm) ensues from failure to bring about adherence to a "common morality." Such failure is seen by Devlin as tantamount to a threat to a society's survival. Therefore, to serve Mill's doctrine of self-protection, Devlin maintains, a society

---

[6] John Stuart Mill, *On Liberty* [1859] (London: Longmans, Green, 1892), p. 6. For background see Michael St. John Packe, *The Life of John Stuart Mill* [1954] (New York: Capricorn, 1970), especially pp. 399–406.

has the right to use the criminal law to insist upon conformity to the moral commitments of its majority, as these commitments normally (and rather tautologically) are expressed by recourse to law for their protection. As Devlin puts the matter:

> Societies disintegrate from within more frequently than they are broken up by external pressures. There is disintegration when no common morality is observed and history shows that the loosening of moral bonds is often the first stage of disintegration, so that society is justified in taking the same steps to preserve its moral code as it does to preserve its government and other essential institutions.[7]

Bertrand Russell, writing from another point on the English political spectrum, arrives at essentially the same view as Devlin, concluding, in regard to homosexuality, that it is unjust and unwise to outlaw such behavior today *but* that it might have been reasonable to do so in an earlier time. Russell reasons in the following manner:

> If it were still believed, as it once was, that the toleration of such behavior would expose the community to the fate of Sodom and Gomorrah, the community would have every right to intervene. But where such factual beliefs do not prevail, private practice among adults, however abhorrent it may be to the majority, is not a proper subject for coercive action for a state whose object is to minimize coercion.[8]

Russell's reliance upon public opinion as a definitive source which makes coercive action against a deviating individual legitimate seems a rather curious position, however. Perhaps, though, Russell's inclusion of the phrase "factual beliefs" is meant to indicate that public opinion must be reasonably aligned with as much accurate information as is available at the moment. It certainly seems evident that the social consequences of a behavior system, such as homosexuality, is to a considerable extent an empirical question and that, to be accorded final authority, public opinion, at least under ideal conditions, would have to be founded upon a reasonable reading of available information and a reasonable exercise of logic and inference. Russell presumably believes, if the quoted statement may be taken as representative of his views, that earlier attitudes toward homosexuality were based on the best information available at the time; otherwise, it is difficult to see what extrinsic standards may be

---

[7] Patrick Devlin, *The Enforcement of Morals* (London: Oxford University Press, 1965), p. 13.

[8] Bertrand Russell, *John Stuart Mill* (London: Oxford University Press, 1955), p. 55.

brought to bear to argue tellingly against any current popular belief that is in accord with the law. If, for instance, most people today continued to believe that homosexuality did indeed tend to produce a modern Sodom and Gomorrah, even though a few persons were able to demonstrate quite well with cross-cultural and other data that this need not be so, and probably wouldn't be so, Russell would presumably abandon the field to the uninformed majority. Perhaps, of course, this is a proper tactic: only when the best information has made a discernible impression on public opinion should leverage be exerted on the law to conform with that impression. Perhaps, in fact, this is the only tactic likely to succeed.

The Devlin position is, of course, much less vulnerable, since it takes as given the arguable proposition that a falling away from common morality poses danger to the state. The argumentative difficulty is equivalent to that posed by a position which defines itself in such a manner that the definition precludes any possibility of rebuttal. It may be shown, for example, that in some societies there existed a striking variance between what appeared to be common morality and the state of the law, and that such societies did not disintegrate, but rather flourished. But the counterargument could be that the statutes did not in fact differ markedly from common morality because otherwise that morality would have been strong enough to have reshaped the law. Therefore, there was only the deceptive appearance of a gap, not an actual gap, between common morality and law.

Also, if common morality and law are defined one by the other, then legal support of common morality obviously has not throughout time always proven sufficient to keep a polity alive and well. If common morality and legal structure are different things, then lack of congruence between them—all other things being equal—should be dysfunctional and congruence enabling for a society. But we know of many preliterate tribes in which morality and law appear to be virtually interchangeable, but where the societies themselves have gone under.

All told, then, the matter of making reliable statements about the consequences of discordance between morality and law is obviously a complicated matter, made not much easier by recognition of the fact that the discordance may be of many kinds, involving among other things failure of the law to proscribe morally disapproved behavior (such as, in present times, the general absence of rules requiring that assistance be given to a stranger in jeopardy) and the use of the law to proscribe morally approved or morally neutral kinds of behavior (such as, say, many of the blue laws requiring cessation of business activity on Sundays). The matter is further compounded by the difficulty of measuring the intensity of moral convictions about any given matter and the difficulty of charting the well-being and fate of something as complex as a social system.

It might be noted, finally, that questions can be raised regarding the implicit assumption that failure to continue existing proscription of morally condemned behavior is apt to produce *only* untoward results. Actually, the results are apt to be of many different kinds, and a true measure of their totality almost an impossible task. A hands-off policy toward homosexuality, for instance, may produce all the deleterious consequences claimed for it, but it may also bring about positive consequences that would counterbalance the social disadvantages. In fact, it is possible that failure to change a policy may itself produce those kinds of consequences that are said to be the likely results of the contemplated change. Just as failure to outlaw homosexuality may ruin a society, so too, continuation of laws against homosexuality may, under certain conditions, also ruin the society—at least, to the extent that any policy toward homosexuality is likely to be of such importance as to effect significantly the history of a social system.

This point, obvious enough once enunciated, may be emphasized by reference to the policies of Herbert Hoover when, as President of the United States, he fought against pressures demanding that he take action to alleviate the economic depression gripping the country. "My countrymen," he pleaded, "the fundamental issue is whether we shall go on in fidelity to American traditions or whether we shall turn to dangerous innovations." [9] Hoover insisted that any kind of dole would harm the American character and that relief should remain strictly a local problem. Franklin D. Roosevelt, of course, took a contrary tack following his inauguration. As one commentator notes: "Who knows? Perhaps the country had been saved [by Roosevelt] from rebellion and anarchy?" [10] He might have added, had he wished to make the matter even more teasing: "Who knows? Perhaps the country would ultimately have been better off had the anarchy eventuated?"

Legal coercion, then, the theorists fundamentally agree, may be employed to protect individuals other than the actors from harm and to protect the society from mor(t)al injury, however these mat-

[9] Quoted in Cabell Phillips, *From Crash to Blitz, 1929–1939* (New York: Macmillan, 1969), p. 75.

[10] W. A. Swanberg, book review of Phillips, *op. cit.*, n. 9. *New York Times Book Review*, November 30, 1969, p. 1.

ters may come to be defined. Agreement does not extend, however, to a third possible source of legitimacy for official action—the protection of the individual actor from, as it were, himself. There are those who insist that the state clearly has such a right or obligation, particularly when conditions prevail where an individual is likely to be "exploited," such as in the case of women, sorely needing funds and seeking "any kind of work," though their "interests" are best served if they are restricted to working only a certain number of hours and only in certain kinds of approved industries.

This position is in part summarized by Edmund Burke with the following view:

> Government is a contrivance of human wisdom to provide for human *wants*. Men have a right that these wants should be provided for by this wisdom. Among these wants is to be reckoned . . . a sufficient restraint upon their passions. . . . In this sense, the restraint on man, as well as their liberties, are to be reckoned among their rights.[11]

Mill, among others, takes a contrary position, insisting that a society does not have the right to use coercion upon its members on the sole ground that such action is in their own interest. Such interest, Mill argues, can best be judged by the person himself—and even if the person's judgment is awry in terms of reasonable standards it is better for him and for us that he be permitted to bear the consequences of his voluntarily chosen action, though Mill notes, society may mount whatever other tactics of persuasion it chooses, short of force, to achieve ends it desires to reach:

> [A man] cannot rightfully be compelled to do or forbear because it will be better for him to do so, because it will make him happier, because in the opinion of others, to do so would be wise, or even right. There are good reasons for remonstrating with him, or reasoning with him, or persuading him, or entreating him, but not for compelling him, or visiting him with any evil in case he does otherwise.[12]

A contrary viewpoint underlies a Rhode Island statute, to cite one example, which makes it a criminal offense for a person without a helmet on to ride a motorcycle. The constitutionality of the statute was found by the Rhode Island Supreme Court to reside in its protection of others. The legislature, the Court ruled, can prohibit persons from engaging in conduct which "could conceivably result in

---

[11] Edmund Burke, "The True Meaning of the Rights of Men," in *Reflections on the Revolution in France* (New York: Liberal Arts Press, 1955), p. 68.

[12] Mill, *op. cit.*, n. 6, p. 6.

their becoming public charges." [13] (But may the legislature legitimately prohibit all conduct which could "conceivably" have such a
result and, if not, where should the line be drawn?) A law similar to
that in Rhode Island was ruled unconstitutional in Michigan. There
the court observed: "Under our system of government, the aim is to
leave the subject entire master of his conduct, except when the public good requires some direction or restraint." [14] Helmets for motorcyclists, the Michigan court decided, protect only the individual, not
the society.

Bodies seeking to arrive at a fair balance between social interests
and personal freedom often operate in a manner which can be seen
in the recent work of the British Advisory Committee on Drug
Dependence in its review of marihuana laws. As is usual in this kind
of soul-searching, the Committee first quotes Mill's views on personal liberty and endorses them in the abstract if not literally. Then
the Committee indicates the futility involved in attempting to separate out the rights of the individual as against those of the society
in regard to any given act, since every act has implications for both
the individual and the society:

> . . . it has to be recognized that no hard and fast line can be
> drawn between actions that are purely self-regarding, and those
> that involve wider social consequences. If, generally speaking,
> every one is entitled to decide for himself what he will eat,
> drink or smoke, the fact remains that those who indulge in gross
> intemperance of almost any kind will nearly always become a
> burden to their families, the public authorities or both. Indeed,
> examples of actions which never in any circumstances involve
> social repercussions are by no means easy to find.[15]

The Committee seeks for some general principle—a formula—by
which judgment can be made on the relative social harm of a given
act. Here, too, however, the quest produces only meager rewards:

> Nor can it be said that any consistent principle dictates the
> occasions on which the law at present intervenes to protect the
> individual from himself. Suicidal attempts at immediate and
> total self-destruction are not criminal; yet he who shortens his
> expectation of life by misusing heroin is liable to prosecution.
> Again, everyone over the age of 16 is entitled to ride a motor
> bicycle, although the statistics of self-destruction thereby bear
> eloquent testimony to the lethal character of these machines.[16]

[13] *State ex rel. Colvin v. Lombardi*, 241 Atl.2d 625, 627 (R.I. 1968).
[14] *American Motorcycle Ass'n v. Davids*, 158 N.W.2d 72, 74 (Mich. 1968),
quoting *People v. Armstrong*, 41 N.W. 275, 277 (Mich. 1889).
[15] Great Britain. Advisory Committee on Drug Dependence, *Cannabis* (London:
Her Majesty's Stationery Office, 1968), p. 4.
[16] *Ibid.*

Finally, expectedly, the Committee is forced to conclude that it must judge every case on its own terms, though it makes a final effort to enunciate those items that will be examined before judgment will be rendered:

> Every proposal to restrict the freedom of the individual in his own supposed interests must, therefore, be decided on merits, in the light of the probable severity of any damage that he may inflict upon himself, and of the risk that in damaging himself he may also involuntarily be the cause of injury to others.
> In addition, account must be taken of public attitudes . . . .[17]

It may be seen, therefore, that issues regarding acts such as homosexuality, abortion, prostitution, gambling, narcotic and drug use—the behaviors which concern us—involve a highly interrelated set of elements. The problem arises in trying to determine the consequences of the behaviors and then in trying to determine the proper amalgam that will sustain one judgment as against another.

In schematic form, material bearing on decisions might be viewed in the following manner:

1. The present policies and their effect upon:
   a. The participants in the specified acts;
   b. Other persons; and
   c. The society at large.
2. Alternative policies and their effect upon:
   a. The participants in the specified acts;
   b. Other persons; and
   c. The society at large.

To declare that the issues are fundamentally empirical is not apt to be much more useful than a declaration that present policies represent "the will of God" or "the will of the people," and that therefore they ought to remain inviolate until the possessor of that stipulated "will" sees fit to signal a change. Empirical though the major ingredients may be, there exist no empirical techniques at this time which would allow definitive answers to be reached on the relevant items necessary for an unchallengeable decision. And, even if the necessary empirical data were to become available, there are no preordained standards by which matters of value may be resolved. For instance: Are four more deaths a year of unhelmeted as against helmeted motorcyclists, half of whom put survivors on public relief, enough to support a law requiring helmets? Or six? Ten? 40?

The point may be illustrated by the contents of a debate regarding

---

[17] *Ibid.*

wiretapping, prior to relaxation in 1969 of the proscription against use of evidence obtained from wiretapping. On one side of the question, a police chief puts forward the following justification for wiretapping:

> When these organized mobs are operating with their accustomed secrecy there is no technique known to police science by which their criminal activities can with certainty be detected and the criminal brought to account. One of the most effective techniques for such work—wiretapping—is banned under federal and California state law.
>
> When wiretapping cannot be carried on, the most efficient method of suppressing crime and ferreting out criminal activities is to keep the men known to be engaged in these activities under close surveillance. This is not only more costly than any police department can afford, but in the vast majority of cases, it is impossible. The most effective substitutes for constant and close surveillance are to have an undercover agent inside the organization, which is extremely difficult to achieve and very hazardous, or to have some means of overhearing what is said, whether by listening at transoms, outside windows, down a ventilator shaft or by dictograph.[18]

The heart of the police chief's polemic for wiretapping appears in the following statement:

> If society chooses, for reasons of its own, to handicap itself so severely that it cannot or will not deal effectively with the criminal army, it is doubtful that free society as we now enjoy it will continue.[19]

A counterargument regarding wiretapping has been presented by a law professor who believes that all taps which invade the privacy of the individual and which are exploratory dragnets should be prohibited. The professor flays wiretapping as a form of expedient police and public morality and asks why, if wiretapping is to be permitted, we do not open up for police surveillance the religious confessional and the public mails. Contrary to the view that a society which will not protect itself by certain methods may cease to be free, he believes that a society "which countenances [such] practices ceases to be free." [20]

Neither debater, we would assume, would disagree with the other's conclusion if the two together were able to settle on a version of facts

---

[18] William H. Parker, "Surveillance by Wiretap or Dictograph: Threat or Protection?", *California Law Review*, 42 (December 1954), pp. 734–735.

[19] *Ibid.*, p. 738.

[20] Richard C. Donnelly, "Comments and Caveats on the Wire Tapping Controversy," *Yale Law Journal*, 63 (April 1954), p. 806.

other than the one they employ. If, indeed, American society surely would go under without an authorized regimen of wiretapping, presumably the law professor would be willing to allow such procedures, at least under certain specified conditions and with various kinds of controls against their further abuse and arbitrariness. If, however, authorized wiretapping opened the door to totalitarian procedures which transformed the essential nature of American society, a society able to struggle along, though with some loss, without wiretapping, we may presume that the police chief would yield on his position.

Suppose, however, that the themes of both positions are in fact correct—that without wiretapping, American society will be unable to exist as a free society and that with wiretapping it will cease to exist as such a society. Then which position should be favored? Or is it a matter to be resolved by turning attention to other alternatives which, while less valuable, also pose less threat?

In any event, it seems very clear that even the most tentative steps toward resolution of controversial matters of public policy must rest upon a blend of fact with a valuation of such fact, and must include consideration of alternatives when the diametric choices appear equally unsatisfactory.

The first part of such an undertaking—the mustering of relevant facts—relates to what might be said to be a state of sociological grace that could be called "interested indifference." The second part involves interpretation of the connection between the facts and present or proposed policies.

It seems essential in this regard that the present writer's preconceptions be indicated, because these will surely bear upon, subtly or otherwise, his method and some of his conclusions. That bias is in line with the so-called "libertarian" position enunciated by Mill: The burden of proof bearing upon any social policy inhibiting human choice, it is believed, must rest with those who support the policy, and the burden that they bear should be a heavy one, perhaps one as imposing as the criminal law's demand for proof "beyond a reasonable doubt" or the Supreme Court's standard of "clear and present danger."

On the other hand, I have been convinced that the reading of history by Will Durant is likely an accurate one, "that nations are born stoic and die epicurean." [21] It is possible, of course, that cyclical theories of history are sound ones and that any tamper-

---

[21] Will Durant, *Our Oriental Heritage* (New York: Simon and Schuster, 1954), p. 259.

ing with an epicurean trend is merely a finger in the dike, momentarily staying an inexorable tide. If so, American society is already doomed. Even if an epicurean trend is reversible, however, it does not follow that it should by all means be reversed. Under certain conditions, certain societies (like certain people) are, unfortunately, better off dead, at least if we can maintain that there are values whose preservation is more important than the survival of people or societies.

So, again, we are confronted with a dilemma. If American society is permitted to establish epicurean manners, it will, if the Durants are correct, be moving along the road to its own doom. If not, it will at times be undermining basic principles for which it stands—such as those favoring a freedom of choice. The present writer, facing this seemingly insoluble dilemma, will opt for an uneasy compromise. It is essential, I believe, for American society to protect itself, as best it may, against its own dissolution or dismemberment—since I believe that it has much in it well worth protecting—but that protection may only be had under rather strict conditions which involve permitting the free sway of epicurean behavior unless or until such time that such behavior clearly threatens the existence of others or of the society or, under more demanding kinds of standards, the individual participants themselves.

The rationale for such a viewpoint is this: Durant's view and my support of their view may be inaccurate readings of the world's history. Pending much better information, speculations such as ours cannot be employed to support coercion of behavior deemed to be epicurean and therefore destructive of a society. The danger, of course, is that if the Durants are correct, the point of no-return may long have passed before its existence is noted. But, then, no one has ever doubted that the use of democratic principles is a highly dangerous way to run a government.

It is against such a background then, that we will examine, in turn, homosexuality, abortion, gambling, narcotic and drug usage, and prostitution. We will first attempt to determine the causes and backgrounds of the behaviors, and then to indicate their apparent impact upon participants, others, and on the society at large. These items set in place, we will examine the possible consequences of alternative social policies, and, finally, we will present some views on what seem to be the reasonable methods for dealing with the issues at hand.

II. Consensual Adult Homosexuality

Headlines and titles of mass media discussions of homosexuality encapsulate the attention and controversy that surrounds such activity in the United States today. "A 4-Million Minority Asks for Equal Rights," a feature story in the *New York Times* magazine section is titled.[1] *Time* summarizes its eight-page report on homosexuality with the following banner head: "The Homosexual: Newly-Visible, Newly-Understood." [2] For the *Wall Street Journal*, the pertinent elements of its review of homosexuality are headlined as: "The U.S. Homosexuals Gain in Trying to Persuade Society to Accept Them." For a subhead, the *Journal* uses: "With a Growing Militancy, They Battle Discrimination on Social, Legal, Job Lines." [3] A pulp magazine, selling on newsstands throughout the country, asks: "Homosexuals . . . Should We: Doctor Them? Jail Them? Leave Them Alone?" [4]

This, then, is one of the conditions of homosexuality in its contemporary American setting: It has become a phenomenon much attended to, with many of its more articulate practitioners and their supporters aggressively seeking relief from what they believe to be untoward oppression and discrimination.

The roots of such concern and agitation are planted in diverse soils. For one thing, there has been growing evidence that homosexuality is a choice, not a disease, evidence that has undoubtedly encouraged homosexual practitioners toward more assured and forceful pleading of their case. Attention being devoted to homosexuality today is also probably a function of an ever-increasing frankness, even bluntness, about sexual behavior, a phenomenon marked by both honesty and prurience. Discussions of homosexuality are also likely a product of emerging concerns with overpopulation, so that homo-

---

[1] Webster Schott, "A 4-Million Minority Asks for Equal Rights," *New York Times Magazine*, November 12, 1967, pp. 45ff.

[2] "The Homosexual: Newly-Visible, Newly-Understood," *Time*, October 31, 1969, pp. 56–67.

[3] Charles Alverson, "U.S. Homosexuals Gain in Trying to Persuade Society to Accept Them," *Wall Street Journal*, July 17, 1968.

[4] Daniel Russell, "Homosexuals . . . Should We: Doctor Them? Jail Them? Leave Them Alone?", *Master Detective*, 78 (September 1969), pp. 46–47, 57–59.

sexuality may now, if one so chooses, be regarded as a possible social boon in controlling a potential social disaster. Finally, attention to homosexuality appears to be a product in considerable part of the press for equality by and for many minorities and oppressed segments of the society—be they blacks, women, the poor, or the sexually different.

Homosexual behavior seems to occur most often in systems which are sexual but one-sex: that is, systems which share in a general encouragement toward sexuality, but do not provide much opportunity for such encouragement to be expressed in heterosexual ways. Traditionally, military and naval personnel, prison populations, and private school pupils have been regarded as members of groups likely to manifest a heavy involvement in homosexual behavior. Winston Churchill is said to have remarked of the traditions of the Royal Navy just before the First World War: "What are they? Rum, sodomy, and the lash." [5] In addition, homosexuality is said to flourish disproportionately in metropolitan areas, in large measure because of the anonymity afforded by such areas and because of the enhanced opportunities to meet a variety of potential sexual partners. A recent newspaper survey of homosexuality in New York City, for instance, noted the presence of "what is probably the greatest homosexual population in the world and its increasing openness" and regarded this situation as "the city's most sensitive open secret." The ecology and culture of New York's homosexual population was said to include the following items:

> [I]dentifiable homosexuals—perhaps only half the total— seem to throng Manhattan's Greenwich Village, the East Side from the upper 40's through the 70's, and the West 70's. In a fairly restricted area around Eighth Avenue and 42nd Street there congregate those who are universally regarded as the dregs of the invert world—the male prostitutes—the painted, grossly effeminate "queens" and those who prey on them.
>
> In each of these first three areas the homosexuals have their own restaurants and bars—some operated for them under the contemptuous designation of "fag joints" by the organized crime syndicate.
>
> They have their favorite clothing suppliers who specialize in the tight slacks, shortcut coats and fastidious furnishings favored by many, but by no means all, male homosexuals.
>
> There is a homosexual jargon, once intelligible only to the initiate, but now part of New York slang. The word "gay" has been appropriated as the adjective for homosexual.[6]

---

[5] Quoted in *Time, op. cit.*, n. 2, p. 64.

[6] Robert C. Doty, "Growth of Overt Homosexuality Provokes Wide Concern," *New York Times* (western edition), December 27, 1963.

Concern with homosexuality as a defined social problem in considerable measure may be a function of the emergence of the behavior from underground conditions to the public appearance and mass media attention marked by the quoted newspaper report. It would be interesting, in this connection, to determine the extent of public awareness of homosexuality and the intensity of convictions regarding it, matters neglected in the usual kinds of surveys which request only an expression of an attitude of approval or disapproval. It would be interesting to know, for example, whether public opinion concerning homosexuality results from views built upon actual experience with homosexuals and homosexuality, either in the past or on a continuing basis, or whether such attitudes are largely abstract matters, traceable not to experience, but to general feelings, perhaps not so deeply and strongly held, which might readily be changed (in either direction) by exposure to homosexual activity or propaganda. Certainly, it seems likely that a considerable segment of the public has only the vaguest ideas about the reality of the homosexual world and homosexual behavior, though its views might be rather more substantial than those of the scatterbrained young girl in Bruce Jay Friedman's play, *Scuba Duba:*

> You know, a lot of people believe massages are a homosexual thing. I don't. But I don't even believe homosexual relations really exist. Certainly not between two men. Why would they bother? There are so many other things they could be doing. I don't think it's ever really happened. Maybe in Germany once or twice in the thirties, but that was the only time. I think it's something made up to play a big joke on society. A couple of fags made it up.[7]

In any event, the mounting campaign for homosexual equality and the growing freedom of homosexual identification will undoubtedly produce a significant impact on public attitudes and public responses to the behavior. It is not true, however, that familiarity inevitably produces friendliness, any more than familiarity necessarily breeds contempt. The result of the growing openness and frankness of homosexual advocacy will in large measure depend upon the attractiveness and persuasiveness of the proponents and their views, as well as the mesh between such aims and the values, commitments, aspirations, and flexibility of those who make or influence the making of policy decisions in the United States.

---

[7] Bruce Jay Friedman, *Scuba Duba* (New York: Simon and Schuster, 1967), pp. 44–45.

EXTENT OF HOMOSEXUALITY

By far the most reliable and most often-cited figures on the extent of homosexuality in the United States are those reported in the 1950's by Alfred Kinsey and his associates in their survey of male and female sexual behavior. Four percent of the American white males, Kinsey noted, are "exclusively homosexual throughout their lives after the onset of adolescence," a figure far in excess of previous estimates which had been based either on intuition or extrapolation from more selective samples. Approximately half as many women as men were reported by Kinsey to be exclusively homosexual. In absolute figures, therefore, the exclusively homosexual male population could be put at 2.6 million persons and that of women at 1.4 million. In addition, between 30 and 45 percent of American males were said to have experienced some overt homosexual contact to the point of orgasm since adolescence.[8]

It is estimated that no more than 10 percent of the homosexual population is readily recognizable in terms of the stereotypes of homosexuals held throughout the society. Of the remainder, as one description puts it: "Their wrists are rigid, their 's's' well-formed, they prefer subdued clothes and close-cropped hair, and these days they may dress more conservatively than flamboyant straights." [9]

ETIOLOGY OF HOMOSEXUALITY

The explanation of homosexuality constitutes one of the more controversial scientific questions of the day. Some persons maintain that homosexuality is a "normal" form of behavior, but the difficulty here is that the word "normal" itself has aroused much philosophical and legal debate, so that acceptance of one or another definition of normality will lead to one or another interpretation of the behavior being judged. Some persons, for instance, maintain that sexual acts that result in reproduction constitute the only type of normal sexual behavior. By this criterion premarital petting and various marital sexual techniques other than genital-to-genital intromission without recourse to birth control techniques are defined as abnormal.

Other persons insist that normal and abnormal can best be understood by reference to theological writings and prescriptions. Such a position precludes debate, at least so long as there is agreement on the nature and meaning of the theological doctrine under review,

---

[8] Alfred C. Kinsey, Wardell B. Pomeroy, and Clyde E. Martin, *Sexual Behavior in the Human Male* (Philadelphia: Saunders, 1948), pp. 650–651.

[9] *Time, op. cit.,* n. 2, p. 62.

which sometimes is no easy matter. As one theologian has noted, disputation can arise concerning the relative importance of diverse biblical injunctions: "Before attributing too much to [the Biblical sanctions against homosexuality]," Roger L. Shinn observes, "anybody might ask about many other verses of scripture, more explicit and emphatic in the original, they have *not* shaped our culture." [10]

Further debate may center on the extent to which theological doctrines should be translated into criminal rules solely on the basis of their religious underpinning. It may be maintained that such translation unjustly forces individuals who do not accept the concepts to refrain from activities which they regard as moral and blameless. A contrary view would maintain, of course, that as a traditionally Christian nation we have a duty to insist on standards of normality as these are defined in the dominant theological system.

A third position regarding "normal" behavior concentrates on comparisons between behavior in humans and behavior in infrahuman species. The assumption in this approach is that forms of sexual conduct found among chimpanzees, for instance, are "normal" forms which have only come to be labeled "perverted" through social interpretations. It is notable, in this respect, to observe, as Seymour Halleck does, that "almost any kind of sexual behavior humans can think of has some phylogenetic and ontogenetic basis." [11] Somewhat similar to this approach is that which examines behavior from a cross-cultural perspective. Proponents of this view maintain that if societies can be found in which all or most members engage in certain forms of sexual behavior then logic is stretched unreasonably by defining such behavior as abnormal for the human species.

Agreement on a proper definition of "normal" does not, however, insure that further agreement may be had on proper interpretations of the behavior under review. Most zoologists, for instance, find homosexuality rife in the animal kingdom, and presume that it therefore represents a reasonable arrangement for all species. Desmond Morris, however, viewing the same evidence, takes exception to such a view. Wild animals, he tells us

. . . under normal conditions in their natural habitats . . . do not mutilate themselves, masturbate, attack their offspring, develop stomach ulcers, become fetishists, suffer from obesity,

---

[10] Roger L. Shinn, "Homosexuality: Christian Conviction & Inquiry," in Ralph W. Weltge (editor), *The Same Sex: An Appraisal of Homosexuality* (Philadelphia: Pilgrim Press, 1969), p. 45.

[11] Seymour L. Halleck, *Psychiatry and the Dilemmas of Crime* (New York: Harper and Row, 1967), p. 178.

form homosexual pair-bonds, or commit murder. Among human city dwellers, needless to say, all of these things occur.[12]

There is considerable agreement (though not consensus) among students of the subject (Morris included) that homosexuals are products of their environment, usually products of early indoctrination into the behavior. Even here, however, disagreement can be found. There are schools of thought, for instance, that maintain that endocrine imbalance, hormonal disturbances, and/or physical characteristics of the opposite sex cause homosexual behavior. It has been stated categorically that the origin of homosexuality is "always constitutional or biological, never environmental or acquired."[13] Finally, some Freudian theorists have put forward the viewpoint that all human beings are "latent" homosexuals, carrying within themselves a repressed drive toward the behavior, but this thesis appears to have as much value as others which might insist that all persons are "latent" murderers or "latent" capitalists.

Eclectic opinion is inclined to the view that there are different types of homosexuals, produced by different conditions. Most support appears to lie with the explanatory views of Kinsey, who first notes that it is more difficult to understand why "each and every individual is not involved in every type of sexual activity"[14] than it is to understand homosexuality. Kinsey then offers the following interpretation of homosexuality:

> The inherent physiological capacity of an animal to respond to any sufficient stimulus seems . . . the basic explanation of the fact that some individuals respond to stimuli originating in other individuals of their own sex—and it appears to indicate that every individual could so respond if the opportunity offered and one were not conditioned against making such responses. There is no need of hypothesizing peculiar hormonal factors that make certain individuals especially liable to engage in homosexual activity, and we know of no data which prove the existence of such hormonal factors. There are no sufficient data to show that specific hereditary factors are involved. [Our] data indicate that the factors leading to homosexual behavior are (1) the basic physiological capacity of every mammal to respond to any sufficient stimulus; (2) the accident which leads an individual into his or her first sexual experience with a person of the same sex; (3) the conditioning effects of such experi-

---

[12] Desmond Morris, *The Human Zoo* (New York: McGraw-Hill, 1969), p. 8.

[13] Herbert Greenspan and John D. Campbell, "The Homosexual as a Personality Type," *American Journal of Psychiatry*, 101 (March 1945), pp. 682–689.

[14] Alfred C. Kinsey, Wardell B. Pomeroy, Clyde E. Martin, and Paul H. Gebhard, *Sexual Behavior in the Human Female* (Philadelphia: Saunders, 1953), p. 451.

ence; and (4) the indirect but powerful conditioning which the opinions of other persons and the social codes may have on an individual's decision to accept or reject this type of sexual contact.[15]

Psychiatric writers, though they might give some credence to the Kinsey postulation, are likely to insist that certain kinds of family constellations are fundamental in producing homosexuality. Chief among the psychiatric theorists has been Irving Bieber, who believes that parents with emotional problems can be an important cause of homosexuality. They are said to leave their child without adequate identification with the parent of the same sex and with an ambivalent feeling toward the parent of the opposite sex. Examining homosexuals whom he had under psychiatric treatment, Bieber observed that a large number came from families where the father was hostile, aloof, or ineffectual, while the mother was, in his terms, C.B.I. (close-binding, inappropriately intimate). The only protection against such a mother, Bieber maintained, was an adequate father:

> We have come to the conclusion that a constructive, supportive, warmly related father precludes the possibility of a homosexual son; he acts as a neutralizing, protective agent should the mother make seductive or close-binding attempts.[16]

At the same time, Bieber's wife, a psychologist, reported that she had found many of the same family constellations, although in reverse, for female homosexuality.[17] This finding was disputed, however, after an intensive reworking of the Bieber material, by Ralph E. Gundlach and Bernard F. Reiss, who insisted that the roots of lesbianism, wherever they lay, did not reside in a "mirror image" of the family style reported by Bieber. The researchers found only three responses among the answers of their subjects to hundreds of questions about their parents' behavior which distinguished between lesbians and heterosexuals. Twelve percent of the lesbians, compared to 27 percent of the heterosexual women, reported that their father made the family decisions. Twelve percent of the lesbians, compared to 24 percent of the heterosexuals, said they had spent a good deal of time with their mothers. And 35 percent of the lesbians, compared

---

[15] *Ibid.*, p. 447. But see Robert C. Kolodny, William H. Masters, Julie Hendryx, and Gelson Toro, "Plasma Testosterone and Semen Analysis in Male Homosexuals," *New England Journal of Medicine*, 285 (November 18, 1971), pp. 1170–1174.

[16] Irving Bieber, *et al.*, *Homosexuality: A Psychoanalytic Study* (New York: Basic Books, 1962), p. 311.

[17] Tony Bieber, "The Lesbian Patient," *Medical Aspects of Sexual Behavior*, 3 (January 1969), pp. 6–12.

with 4 percent of the heterosexual women, expressed fear of or aversion to the sexual organs of men.[18]

At first, many homosexuals seized upon the postulates of psychiatrists such as Bieber to turn the blame and opprobrium they believed their behavior received away from themselves onto circumstances over which they could not have had any control. This pattern persists to an extent today, but what is becoming more common is a militant stance which insists that the psychiatric formulations are tautological, and that they derive from a highly selective sampling process, one founded upon experiences with patients in therapy. As Wardell Pomeroy, one of Kinsey's associates, has indicated: "If I were to base my views on heterosexuality upon the patients I see, I would have to conclude that it is a totally sick and archaic institution."[19] The debate between social and psychiatric explanations of homosexuality and its implications has been summed up in the following terms:

> There is a school of psychiatric thought that believes homosexuality is a sickness capable of being cured and thus that efforts to help homosexuals live with their condition are misguided. But the great majority of sex researchers holds that homosexuality is not a disease but is a deep-rooted sexual orientation. Because more and more people are now accepting this latter view, homosexuals are winning ground in their efforts to improve their lives.[20]

Perhaps the greatest challenge to the psychiatric views regarding the importance of family structure and functioning in the etiology of homosexuality has been the lesser amount of homosexuality found among blacks. "One would suspect," says Dr. Richard Sallick, a National Institute of Mental Health psychiatrist, "that looking into American Negro society you would find a greater incidence of homosexuality because of its predominantly matriarchal quality. But apparently it's not true. Instead there appears to be a greater amount of sexuality in all its forms."[21] In essence, then, the psychiatric judgment appears to be what philosopher Ernest Nagel has called a "pseudoexplanation":

> . . . the premises simply rebaptize the facts to be explained by coining new names for them. The classical example of such pseudoexplanation is the butt of Molieré's satire in which he

[18] Ralph H. Gundlach and Bernard F. Riess, "Self and Sexual Identity in the Female: A Study of Female Homosexuals," in *New Directions in Mental Health* (New York: Grune and Stratton, 1968), pp. 205–231.

[19] Wardell B. Pomeroy, "Homosexuality," in Weltge, *op. cit.*, n. 10, p. 13.

[20] Alverson, *op. cit.*, n. 3.

[21] Quoted in Schott, *op. cit.*, n. 1, p. 69.

ridicules those who explain the fact that opium induces sleep by invoking the dictum that opium possesses a dormative virtue. A less obvious illustration, sometimes found in popular expositions of science, is the explanation of the law that the velocity of a body remains constant unless the body is acted on by an unbalanced external force, because all bodies possess an inherent force of inertia.[22]

Rather than such pseudoexplanations, available data seems firmly to support the view of the Kinsey researchers and others, such as John L. Hampson, quoted below, who have taken similar positions:

We conclude that an individual's gender role and orientation as boy or girl, man or woman, does not have an innate, preformed instinctive basis as some theorists have maintained. Instead the evidence supports the view that psychologic sex is undifferentiated at birth—a sexual neutrality one might say— and that the individual becomes psychologically differentiated as masculine or feminine in the course of the many experiences of growing up.[23]

HOMOSEXUALITY CROSS-CULTURALLY

Historical and cross-cultural materials strongly support theories stressing the social basis of homosexual activity. Preliterate societies run the gamut in terms of their condemnation or approval of homosexuality. In some preliterate groups, such as the Swanis of Africa, all men are expected to engage in homosexual activity, and those who do not do so are regarded as "peculiar." [24] In ancient Egypt, homosexual practices were apparently condoned for members of the families of Pharaohs.[25] Many early civilizations, such as that in Greece, apparently regarded homosexual affection as the most noble of all forms of love. Ruth Benedict has noted that "Plato's *Republic* . . . is the most convincing statement of the honorable estate of homosexuality in Greece," [26] a situation traced by Freud to the fact that children were raised by male slaves.[27] The Old Testament inveighs against homosexuality with a reference to sodomy as an "abomination" (*Leviticus* 18:22) for which it decrees the death

---

[22] Ernest Nagel, *The Structure of Science: Problems in the Logic of Scientific Explanation* (New York: Harcourt, Brace, and World, 1961), pp. 36–37.

[23] John L. Hampson, "Determinants of Psychosocial Orientation," in Frank A. Beach (editor), *Sex and Behavior* (New York: Wiley, 1965), p. 119.

[24] Clellan Ford and Frank A. Beach, *Patterns of Sexual Behavior* (New York: Harper, 1952), pp. 131–132.

[25] Stephen Schafer, *Theories in Criminology* (New York: Random House, 1969), p. 65.

[26] Ruth Benedict, *Patterns of Culture* (Boston: Houghton Mifflin, 1934), p. 263.

[27] David Abrahamsen, *Who Are the Guilty?: A Study of Education and Crime* (New York: Rinehart, 1952), p. 187.

penalty (*Leviticus* 20:13). Roman law punished homosexuality by confiscation of half of the goods of an offender in the patrician classes and banishment of an offender of the lower classes.[28]

The relationship between the prevalence or absence of homosexuality, as well as lenient or harsh treatment of it, and the vitality of a society—a key issue—is almost impossible to read with any clarity from historical records. Both Greece and Rome fell before invaders, but Elizabethan England, in which homosexuality was common and where an atmosphere of "wholesale permissiveness" prevailed, saw, in the words of one commentator, "not only one of the most robust literary and intellectual outpourings the world has ever known, but also the groundwork for Britain's later imperial primacy." [29] In fact, the roster of homosexuals who made their mark in history, a *Who's Who* often recited by homosexual advocates, is not unimpressive:

> Socrates and Plato made no bones about their homosexuality. Catullus wrote a love poem to a young man whose "honey-sweet lips" he wanted to kiss. Virgil and Horace wrote erotic poems about men; Michaelangelo's great love sonnets were addressed to young men, and so were Shakespeare's. There seems to be evidence that Alexander the Great was homosexual and Julius Caesar certainly was—the Roman Senator Curio called Caesar "every woman's man and every man's woman." So were Charles XII of Sweden and Frederick the Great. Several English monarchs have been homosexual . . . . About some individuals of widely differing kinds, from William of Orange to Lawrence of Arabia, there is running controversy which may never reach a definite conclusion. About others—Marlowe, Tchaikovsky, Whitman, Kitchener, Rimbaud, Verlaine, Proust, Gide, Wilde, and many more—there is no reasonable doubt.[30]

CONSEQUENCES OF HOMOSEXUALITY

Homosexuality is outlawed in all American states except two— Illinois (since 1962) [31] and Connecticut (since 1971).[32] Statutory

[28] Jon J. Gallo, *et al.*, "The Consenting Adult Homosexual and the Law: An Empirical Study of Enforcement and Administration in Los Angeles County," *UCLA Law Review*, 13 (March 1966), p. 647.

[29] *Time, op. cit.*, n. 2, p. 65.

[30] Byran Magee, *One in Twenty: A Study of Homosexuality in Men and Women* (New York: Stein and Day, 1966), p. 46.

[31] Illinois Revised Statutes, chap. 38, §11–2 (Deviate Sexual Conduct), and §11–3 (Deviate Sexual Assault) (1961). Cf., Charles Sheedy, "Law and Morals," *Chicago Bar Record*, 43 (May 1962), pp. 373–378; "Deviate Sexual Behavior Under the New Illinois Criminal Code," *Washington University Law Quarterly* (April 1965), pp. 220–235.

[32] Public Act 828, 1969; Connecticut General Statutes, §53a–75–80 (Special Pamphlet 1972). Cf., "Private Consensual Homosexual Behavior: The Crime and Its Enforcement," *Yale Law Journal*, 70 (March 1961), pp. 623–635.

penalties against the behavior run from mild to severe, though in practice, as we shall see, their exact stipulations make comparatively little difference because few acts of homosexuality are prosecuted under sodomy laws—the most serious designation for homosexual behavior—but rather almost all homosexual charges are broken down into various kinds of misdemeanors, such as lewd and lascivious behavior, loitering, and soliciting. Suffice it to note for the moment, though, that homosexual behavior is in violation of criminal law, and that homosexuals therefore may be subjected to criminal penalties. Because of this, and for other reasons, including theological proscriptions and, perhaps, esthetic objections and personal fear, a large segment of the society and its official apparatus do in fact consider homosexuals to be "queer."

What are the consequences of this situation?

Impact on Homosexuals

It is difficult to separate out the consequences upon an individual of being a homosexual in a society proclaiming the virtues of heterosexuality as contrasted to the consequences of being a homosexual in a society that imposes various kinds of restrictions and handicaps, including criminal penalties, upon the practice of homosexuality. It is possible, for instance, that removal of legal bans would make no difference in terms of such things as the homosexual's self-concept so long as the social definition denigrating homosexuality prevailed. On the other hand, the interrelationship of the two items—legal and social—cannot be overlooked: changes in one may likely produce changes in the other.

Evidence bearing on the relationship between the practice of homosexuality and self-esteem is far from conclusive, in part certainly because homosexuals are of many kinds and their adjustment to the world about them depends upon many things, including their own strengths and the success they have had in achieving things that they have come to value. The firmest conclusion must be a negative one: that homosexuality per se does not inevitably lead to malfunctioning or malaise. The most persuasive demonstration of this point derives from the work of Evelyn Hooker. She administered a battery of projective tests to a sample of 30 homosexuals drawn from the general community and the same battery to a matched sample of 30 heterosexual males. Two expert judges, knowing nothing about the individual subjects, examined their test results and experienced great difficulty in distinguishing between the homosexual and the heterosexual protocols. Hooker reports that neither judge was able to do better than guess: "In seven pairs both judges were incorrect; in twelve pairs, correct; and in the remaining eleven they disagreed." [33]

A vignette of the life of a homosexual man indicates in some detail the manner in which such a person could adjust to society more or less on his own terms:

> Charles Eliott, 40, owns a successful business in Los Angeles. In the den of his $60,000 house he has a bronze profile of Abe Lincoln on the wall and a copy of *Playboy* on the coffee table. Wearing faded chinos and a button-down Oxford shirt, he looks far more subdued than the average Hollywood male; he might be the happily married coach of a college basketball team—and a thoroughgoing heterosexual. In fact, his male lover for the past 3 months has been a 21-year-old college student. He says: "I live in a completely gay world. My lawyer is gay, my doctor is gay, my dentist is gay, my banker is gay. The only person who is not gay is my housekeeper, and sometimes I wonder how she puts up with us."
>
> Eliott has never been to an analyst; introspection is not his forte. Why did he become homosexual? "Well, my mother was an alcoholic; my brother and I ate alone every night. I was the person who always went to the circus with the chauffeur. But I wouldn't say I was exactly sad as a child. I was rather out-ward going." He went to prep school at Hotchkiss, and on to Yale. There he discovered his homosexual tendencies.
>
> Eliott returned home to Chicago to run the family business; to maintain his status in the community, he married. It lasted 5 months. After the divorce he married again, this time for 2 years: "She began to notice that I didn't enjoy sex, and that finally broke it up. I don't think she knows even today that I am a homosexual."
>
> It took 10 years to make Eliott give up his double life in Chicago for the uninhibited gay world of Los Angeles. He avoids the gay bars, instead throws catered parties around his pool. "I suppose most of my neighbors know," he says. "When you have 100 men over to your house for cocktails, people are going to suspect something. Now that I no longer try to cope with the straight world, I feel much happier." [34]

Perhaps, though, the ambivalence that many homosexuals mani-fest in regard to their situation shows most clearly in a recent poll in which 83 percent of a sample of 300 male homosexuals indicated that they would not want a son to follow in their sexual path. Only 2 percent answered in the affirmative, while the remainder said that they would leave the choice up to the hypothetical son. On the other

---

[33] Evelyn Hooker, "The Adjustment of the Male Overt Homosexual," in Hen-drik M. Ruitenbeek (editor), *The Problem of Homosexuality in Modern Society* (New York: Dutton, 1963), pp. 141–161.

[34] *Time, op. cit.,* n. 2, p. 62.

hand, an overwhelming 97 percent of the respondents said that they would not want to change their own behavior, even if a change were easy to accomplish.[35]

The evidence on the other side of the issue, which insists that homosexuality inevitably takes an adjustment toll (or that it is a function of an original inability to adjust) is summed up in a line from *Boys in the Band*, a popular off-Broadway play that deals with homosexual mores. "You show me a happy homosexual," one of the characters says, "and I'll show you a gay corpse." [36]

A similar verdict, also in connection with the theater, is entered by Stanley Kauffmann, a critic, who places the onus for homosexual difficulties on social attitudes. "Conventions and puritanism in the Western world have forced them to wear masks for generations, to hate themselves, and thus to hate those who make them hate themselves." [37] Kauffmann further insists that such a situation has produced unfortunate results for the society, making it a victim of its own prejudices, so that homosexual playwrights, for instance, feel obligated to invent a two-sex version of the one-sex experiences that they have themselves had.[38] It has been argued, for instance, that plays such as *Who's Afraid of Virginia Wolfe?* and *A Streetcar Named Desire* would make more sense if performed by all-male casts since this is the structure in which their authors conceived them.

The phenomenon of homosexual self-hate, mentioned by Kauffmann as a product of social ostracism and scorn, has been portrayed as well by James Baldwin, who sees it in the following terms:

> He knew that he had no honor which the world could recognize. His life, passions, trials, loves, were, at worst, filth, and, at best, disease in the eyes of the world, and crimes in the eyes of his countrymen. There were no standards for him except those he could make for himself. There were no standards for him because he could not accept the definitions, the hideously mechanical jargon of the age. He saw no one around him worth his envy, did not believe in the vast gray sleep which was called security, did not believe in the cures, panaceas, and slogans

---

[35] Randolphe Wicker, quoted in Doty, *op. cit.*, n. 6.

[36] Mart Crowley, *The Boys in the Band* (New York: Farrar, Straus and Giroux, 1968), p. 178.

[37] Stanley Kauffmann, "Homosexual Drama and Its Disguises," *New York Times,* January 13, 1966, sec. 2.

[38] *Ibid.* See also William Goldman, *The Season: A Candid Look at Broadway* (New York: Harcourt, Brace, and World, 1969), p. 238, and note that Kauffmann's piece was partly responsible for costing him his job, according to Turner Catledge, *My Life and The Times* (New York: Harper and Row, 1971), p. 244.

which afflicted the world he knew; and this meant that he had
to create his standards and make up his definitions as he went
along. It was up to him to find out who he was and it was his
necessity to do this, so far as the witchdoctors of the time were
concerned, alone.[39]

Finally, the extreme view of homosexual inadequacy appears in a
report by the Committee on Public Health of the New York Academy
of Medicine, which declares flatly that "homosexuality is indeed an
illness" and that "the homosexual is an emotionally disturbed individual who has not acquired a normal capacity to develop satisfying
heterosexual relationships." The report of the medical group notes
that "overt homosexuality may be an expression of fear of the
opposite sex and of inability to accept adult responsibility, such as
marriage and parenthood." Homosexuals, it declares, are victims
of "arrested development," the consequence of "neglect, rejection,
overprotection, and overindulgence" by parents. Efforts should be
directed toward treating homosexuals in order to overcome this
disability and to involve them in heterosexual activities, the report
recommends.

The report also deplores the tendency by homosexuals to define
their behavior as "a desirable, noble, preferable way of life." With
some sarcasm, the Academy authors observe that homosexuals "claim
that it is the perfect answer to the problem of population explosion."
The doctors had gained "an impression" that homosexuality was on
the increase, though they granted that such a conclusion might have
been the result of a growing openness in discussions regarding
homosexuality:

> Many plays and books are having homosexual characters, and
> more homosexuals seem to have taken to writing autobiographies.
> Furthermore, the homosexuals seem to have become more for-
> mally organized, with a central office and a magazine of their
> own.[40]

The adjudication of the issues posed above in regard to the psychological state of the average homosexual does not seem to pose
many difficulties for questions concerning the proper legal attitude
toward the behavior. It seems self-evidently clear that the question
is itself out-of-order, that, ill or otherwise, maladjusted or not,
homosexuals are making an adaptation of choice. Mill's dictum is
preeminently to the point here. Society may choose to persuade the
homosexual to change his ways, on the ground that to do so would

---

[39] James Baldwin, *Another Country* (New York: Dial, 1962), pp. 212–213.
[40] New York Academy of Medicine, Committee on Public Health, "Homosexuality," *Bulletin of the New York Academy of Medicine*, 40 (July 1964), p. 576.

be in his best interests. If the homosexual elects to accept the invitation, reasonable methods may be used to achieve the outcome both he and the treatment forces have agreed upon. But it seems clear that if the homosexual decides not to change his orientation it cannot be insisted, by the use of forceful coercion, that it is to his own best interests to do so. For one thing, such a viewpoint is not necessarily and certainly not demonstrably true; for another, it is unjust. The point has been precisely summarized by Roger Shinn, a theologian. "Morality," he writes, "is not a valid pretext for cruelty." [41]

This is not to maintain that we will not discover other reasons for continued criminal action against the homosexual, reasons, perhaps, of a social nature. These, however, must make their case unaided by questionable psychiatric harangues against homosexuality.

There are a few additional consequences of homosexuality that bear upon the practitioner that might be considered before reaching a determination of the mechanisms suitably adapted for dealing with homosexuality. Many of the items bear not only on the homosexual, but also on the quality of social life. That homosexuality may handicap an individual from obtaining the kind of employment he desires, for instance, can be regarded as (1) a consequence of homosexuality bearing on the individual; (2) a benefit to heterosexuals—something of a reward, in fact—who gain a competitive advantage; (3) a benefit to persons who prefer not to deal with homosexuals; (4) a disadvantage to the society which loses a certain amount of talent, and perhaps distinctive talent which cannot be adequately reproduced by heterosexuals; and (5) an advantage to society which accrues from having heterosexual viewpoints in ascendancy. To weigh each of these items, as well as innumerable others which we have not delineated here, is a task of utmost difficulty, and very likely in all an impossible task.

In the area of employment, homosexuals are categorically excluded from military service. Given the nature of public sentiment today, this may, for some persons, be regarded as an advantage rather than a handicap for homosexuals, and there are many reports of young men pretending to be homosexuals in order to avoid the military draft. If discovered while in military service, homosexuals will be given dishonorable discharges, even though allegations have not been made that they committed homosexual acts in the course of military assignment.[42]

---

[41] Shinn, *op. cit.*, n. 10, p. 45.
[42] See Colin J. Williams and Martin S. Weinberg, *Homosexuals and the Military: A Less than Honorable Discharge* (New York: Harper and Row, 1971).

In regard to civilian employment, Gebhard reports that 16 percent of the homosexuals he interviewed had employment difficulties because of their homosexuality, including 9 percent who lost jobs because they were homosexuals.[43] In many States a male convicted of a homosexual offense is not allowed to teach in the public schools, the theory being that it would be dangerous to place young boys under his influence. But, as Wardell B. Pomeroy points out, little thought is given to the dangers of exposing young girls to the influence of heterosexual teachers.[44] Homosexuals have in the past also been barred from civil service employment. The justification for this policy was put in the following form by John W. Macy, Jr., former Chairman of the Federal Civil Service Commission:

> Pertinent considerations here are the revulsion of other employees by homosexual conduct and the consequent disruption of service efficiency; the apprehension caused other employees by homosexual advances, solicitations, or assaults; the unavoidable subjection of the sexual deviate to erotic stimulation through on-the-job use of common toilet, shower, and living facilities; the offense to members of the public who are required to deal with known or admitted sexual deviates to transact government business; the hazard that the prestige and authority of a government position will be used to foster homosexual activity, particularly among the youth; and the use of government funds and authority in furtherance of conduct offensive both to the mores and the law of our society.[45]

Macy's views have, however, in large measure been repudiated by the Federal Appellate Court in Washington, D.C., with the declaration that a governmental agency could not dismiss an employee without first providing proof that his homosexuality would clearly interfere with the efficiency of the agency's operation.[46] The Court's ruling led the New York Civil Service Commission to reinterpret its ban on homosexuality as a categoric bar to employment. The New York Commission now requires that a determination be made of "the personal qualities reasonably considered indispensable to the duties of the position," and then "whether the applicant's condition

---

[43] Unpublished study, cited in National Institute of Mental Health, Task Force on Homosexuality, *Final Report* (October 10, 1969), p. 22.

[44] Pomeroy, *op. cit.*, n. 19, p. 11.

[45] Quoted in Lewis I. Maddocks, "The Law and the Church vs. the Homosexual," in Weltge, *op. cit.*, n. 10, p. 101.

[46] *Norton v. Macy*, 417 Fed.2d 1161 (D.C. Circ. 1969) ; *Scott v. Macy*, 349 Fed.2d 182 (D.C. Circ. 1965). But see *Anonymous v. Macy*, 398 Fed.2d 317 (5th Circ. 1968).

is inconsistent with the possession of these qualities to the extent of rendering him unfit to assume the duties of the position." [47]

Examining this and other evidence, the Task Force on Homosexuality, reporting to the National Institute of Mental Health in October 1969, recommended that there be "a reassessment of current employment practices and policy relating to the employment of homosexual individuals with a view toward making needed changes." The Task Force noted that "discrimination in employment can lead to economic disenfranchisement, thus engendering anxiety and frustrating legitimate achievement motivation." The Task Force granted that certain homosexuals might not be suited for certain jobs, but called for more careful statements regarding such relationships rather than across-the-board disqualification of homosexuals. [48]

It was also noted by the Task Force that homosexuals might not be suitable for sensitive positions involving Government security because of the risk of blackmail, though "changes in our present laws concerning homosexuality may ultimately eliminate this." [49] In this manner, the Task Force pointed to the circular nature of the blackmail alarum: By peremptorily discharging homosexuals, agencies make them notably susceptible to blackmail; they then use this special susceptibility, which they have created, as the ground for refusing to hire homosexuals. Benjamin Karpman, a psychiatrist who was a leading critic of the government policies in regard to homosexuals, called them "baseless, stupid, political, and productive of nothing except glorious encouragement of blackmail which, in the light of abstract morality, is the worst and most contemptible of possible crimes." [50]

Several blackmail scandals involving homosexuals have provided details on their particular vulnerability. In 1966, for instance, the District Attorney's office in New York City disclosed that eminent educators, including a number of college professors and at least two deans from eastern universities, prominent theater personalities, and officers of the armed forces—all homosexuals—had been the victims of an extortion ring that operated throughout the United States for nearly 10 years. So brazen was the operation that in one instance two gang members, posing as New York detectives, walked into the Pentagon and walked out with a high officer in the armed services. The officer, whom they shook down for several thousand

[47] "City Lifts Job Curb for Homosexuals," New York Times, May 9, 1969.

[48] National Institute of Mental Health, op. cit., n. 43, pp. 20–21.

[49] Ibid., p. 21.

[50] Benjamin Karpman, The Sexual Offender and His Offenses (New York: Julian Press, 1954), pp. 462–463.

dollars, committed suicide the night before he was scheduled to testify before a grand jury. All told, more than a thousand victims had paid millions of dollars in extortion money, with some individuals paying as much as $20,000 to the ring members. Yet only a small number had been willing to sign complaints for the District Attorney's office.

The modus operandi of the extortion ring was described in the following terms:

> With about 25 members, the ring worked with what were called decoys or "chickens," and phony policemen. The decoy would lure the victim to a hotel room, usually from a midtown bar, and get him into a compromising situation. Then one of two things would follow.
>
> A bogus policeman would break in and threaten the victim with arrest and exposure unless he paid off or the decoy would assault the victim and steal his money and credentials. The credentials would then be sent to bogus policemen who would shake down the victim at a later date.[51]

The following year—in 1967—additional details of the ring's operations were announced. The list of victims was expanded to include a member of Congress, an admiral, a general, a British producer, and two well-known American singers. At least 30 persons had been arrested for participating in the extortion game. On the basis of their investigations, the law enforcement officials issued the following general warning:

> Extortion of money from well-known persons who are homosexual or bisexual is a persistent problem. We want to alert these people who come from all walks of life that such extortion schemes exist and we want to impress upon them that New York detectives are not part of this disgusting racket.[52]

It is noteworthy that the Sexual Offences Act in Great Britain, which lifted the ban under criminal law against consensual adult homosexuality in private, also provided that any person subject to blackmail as a homosexual would not be identified in court, but would appear as "Mr. X." [53] Impetus for this provision in the legislation had come from the report of a former British Attorney General that 95 percent of the blackmail cases he had handled were related to homosexuality.[54]

---

[51] Jack Roth, "Nationwide Ring Preying on Prominent Deviates," *New York Times*, March 3, 1966.

[52] Jack Roth, "Blackmail Paid by Congressmen," *New York Times*, May 17, 1967.

[53] "The Crimes Against Nature," *Journal of Public Law*, 16 (1967), p. 191.

[54] Edwin M. Schur, *Crimes Without Victims: Deviant Behavior and Public Policy* (Englewood Cliffs, N.J.: Prentice-Hall, 1965), p. 82.

Other hazards of the homosexual role include periodic beatings and robbery, many carried out on the assumption that the victim will not be willing to resort to law enforcement agencies for assistance. William Simon and John H. Gagnon note that "the proportion of homosexuals who report having been robbed (frequently after being beaten) is over 25 percent, and the number who have been blackmailed is almost 10 percent." [55] The conclusion of an article examining the social position of homosexuals takes note of this situation. "The homosexual," it observes, "still lives on the edge of catastrophe." [56]

That catastrophe in its most marked form for some 10 percent of the active homosexual population involves an arrest for violation of the criminal law. The most penetrating study of the operation of the legal process in regard to homosexuality is that conducted by law students at the University of California, Los Angeles. They found that no homosexual was sentenced in the city during 1967 as a felon, with virtually all defendants pleading guilty to charges that were reduced to misdemeanors, for which they were either placed on probation or given jail terms. A breakdown of characteristics of the persons involved in the cases investigated by the U.C.L.A. research team showed that almost 80 percent of the defendants were Caucasians, and that a large majority—274 of 493—had been arrested in public restrooms. The remainder of the arrests took place in vehicles (108), private residences (24), jail (18), public parks (17), and steambaths (11), with 26 additional arrests occurring either in an idiosyncratic site or not being listed on official records. Some 345 of the 493 persons arrested for felonious involvement in homosexual activity showed no previous criminal record, while 86 had at one time been arrested for sexual crimes and one for a crime of violence. None of the 493 had ever been arrested for an offense involving children.[57]

The manner in which homosexuals are handled, at least in Los Angeles, can be seen to represent a considerable dilution of statutory dictates, a process rather ubiquitous not only for this offense but throughout the American system of criminal justice.[58] In part, however, the more benign treatment of homosexuals probably reflects differences in attitudes between policemen and judicial authorities.

[55] William Simon and John H. Gagnon, "Homosexuality: The Formulation of a Sociological Perspective," in Weltge, op. cit., n. 10, p. 18.

[56] Schott, op. cit., n. 1, p. 44.

[57] Gallo, op. cit., n. 28, pp. 643–832.

[58] See, e.g., Donald J. Newman, Conviction: The Determination of Guilt or Innocence Without Trial (Boston: Little, Brown, 1966).

Policemen, generally recruited from the lower social classes, tend to consider homosexual acts particularly unnatural and reprehensible, while the attitudes prevalent in the upper social levels, from which judges tend to be drawn, show more tolerance toward deviate sexual behavior. As the *Journal of Public Law* has noted, "the more restrained view of many judges may act to frustrate or mitigate the severity of statutory provisions and the arbitrary nature of some police arrests." [59]

The statutes themselves—classified as sodomy offenses—call for an extraordinarily wide range of penalties in the United States. There have been reported cases of sentences of more than 20 years for homosexual acts in private among adults, though some States, such as New York, no longer allow penalties of more than a year for sodomy offenses. In addition, in recent years there has been some movement by the courts away from the imprecise language in which the laws against homosexuality are set forth. Thus, in December 1971, the Florida Supreme Court struck down the State's 103-year-old statute outlawing "crimes against nature," a phrase that embraces homosexuality. Persons of common intelligence, the court said, ought to be enabled to know what it was that they were prohibited from doing; the existing law, it found, was marked by "vagueness and uncertainty in its language." The misdemeanor law against "unnatural and lascivious acts" was allowed to stand, however, supported by the court's belief that through its use "society will continue to be protected from this sort of reprehensible act." [60]

In other jurisdictions, the statutes differentiate among the ingredients of the homosexual behavior, in the manner that New York did prior to the recent change in its law:

> In each of the last 4 years (1959–1963), 1,000 to 1,200 men have been arrested in New York for overt homosexual activity. Most—about two-thirds—were arrested under the disorderly conduct statute for soliciting male partners.
>
> Spokesmen for the Mattachine Society, a homosexual group, complain bitterly against alleged entrapment of homosexuals by plainclothes policemen sent into homosexual haunts. The homophile groups have won some support from civil rights groups in their campaign to outlaw the uncorroborated testimony of an arresting officer as proof . . . .
>
> Any sexual contact between persons of the same sex is punishable under the sodomy statute. If the action involves any use of

---

[59] "The Crimes Against Nature," *op. cit.*, n. 53, p. 174.

[60] *Franklin v. State,* 257 So.2d 21 (1971). Sodomy penalties are listed in Gilbert M. Cantor, "The Need for Homosexual Law Reform," in Weltge, *op. cit.*, n. 10, p. 84.

force or threat of force or if one of the participants is a minor, sodomy is a felony. There have been about 250 such arrests in recent years, with about two-thirds of them coming to indictment and trial.

In all other cases, notably acts between consenting adults, sodomy is a misdemeanor. There have been an average of 120 arrests here annually under this section, most often for acts in public.

First Deputy Police Commissioner John F. Walsh says the Police Department has limited itself to an effort to suppress solicitation in bars, public lavatories and Turkish baths and any approaches to minors by homosexuals. No attempt is made, he says, to enforce the theoretical ban on private homosexual conduct between consenting adults.[61]

Among the large countries of the world, none punishes sodomy more severely than the United States and the Soviet Union, and a large number of jurisdictions do not include the offense in their criminal law. Certainly, few jurisdictions are as remorseless as Yemen, where in August 1966, a 60-year-old municipal employee was sentenced to be beheaded in public for homosexuality. A religious court had first sentenced the offender to death in the traditional manner, decreeing that he be taken to the highest point in the city and thrown from it. Some consideration had, in fact, been given to dropping the offender's body from an airplane. This was ruled out as too expensive, however. Then, when the headsman failed to arrive on time, the matter was concluded—before 6,000 spectators—by having an Army officer empty his eight-shot revolver into the man's head.[62]

In Japan, there is neither legal nor ethical objection to homosexuality, though "extreme homosexual relations are regarded as somewhat puzzling."[63] Sweden lifted its general ban against homosexual behavior in 1944, though homosexuality is still punished if the act is directed against (a) an adolescent under 18 years of age, or (b) an adolescent who is 18 or more, but not yet 21, provided the act has involved exploiting either the inexperience of the adolescent or his or her position of dependency. Sweden also provides legal sanctions against an official of an institution who commits a homosexual offense against an inmate.[64]

[61] Doty, *op. cit.*, n. 6.

[62] "6000 Witness Public Execution of Homosexual," *Los Angeles Times*, August 1, 1966 (AP).

[63] Yushi Honde, quoted in Karpman, *op. cit.*, n. 50, p. 557.

[64] Sten Rudholm,, "Swedish Legislation and Practice Concerning Sexual Offences," in Cambridge [University] Department of Criminal Science, Faculty of Law, *Sexual Offences* (London: Macmillan, 1957), p. 455.

Prison sentences for homosexuals, in whatever country, tend to evoke a great variety of analogies from writers on the subject. One, for instance, has noted that putting homosexuals in prison is much like "putting an alcoholic in a brewery for therapy." [65] Martin Hoffman observes that "putting a homosexual in prison is like trying to cure obesity by incarceration in a candy shop," [66] while a Federal judge was moved to the following prose regarding the matter:

> Putting Perkins into the North Carolina prison system is a little like throwing Brer Rabbit into the briar-patch. Most doctors who have studied homosexuality agree that prison environment, including close, continuous, and exclusive contact with other men, aggravates and strengthens homosexual tendencies and provides unexcelled opportunity for homosexual practices.[67]

The exploitation of homosexuals in prison is testified to by a wide range of writings. A vivid recent example occurred in the summer of 1969 during a psychodrama session held by the National College of State Trial Judges for judicial and correctional personnel and attended by a number of prison inmates. At one point in the enactment a new prisoner pleads with a correctional officer for protection from sexual assault. The officer promises that he will be segregated and guarded if he discloses the names of those who have harassed him.

Prison inmates watching the session interrupted at this point to protest against its inaccuracy, pointing out that there was no method in use by which a homosexual could be kept from exploitation or revenge from other prisoners. "It's a jungle," one man, who was serving a life term, insisted. "Why, I could get to the man three times a day because I bring food to the cells. I could dash a pot of hot coffee into his face . . . anything." Later, the inmates argued for inauguration of conjugal visiting programs, used then only at the Parchman Prison in Mississippi to alleviate homosexual pressures in institutions. "Even a monkey in the zoo has a mate," one convict said.[68]

Conjugal visiting, a pattern under which wives are permitted to have sexual intercourse with their incarcerated husbands, had never been sanctioned in the United States until recently with the exception of Parchman, though, according to Austin MacCormick, a lead-

---

[65] J. Tudor Rees and Harley V. Usill (editors), *They Stand Apart: A Critical Survey of the Problems of Homosexuality* (New York: Macmillan, 1955), p. 6.

[66] Martin Hoffman, *The Gay World: Male Homosexuality and the Social Creation of Evil* (New York: Bantam, 1968), p. 89.

[67] *Perkins v. North Carolina*, 234 Fed.Supp. 333, 339 (West. Dist. No. Car. 1964).

[68] Homer Bigart, "A Playlet About Prison Homosexuality is Disputed by Convicts in Audience," *New York Times*, June 17, 1969.

ing authority on American prisons, there was some surreptitious conjugal visiting in several other institutions.[69] Ruth Cavan and Eugene Zemans have noted that "conjugal visits are not compatible with the mores of the United States since they seem to emphasize only the physical satisfactions of sex," but they point out that home leaves and family residence in prison colonies, both of which offer emphasis on the whole complex of married life and family relationships, might contain rehabilitative potentialities.[70] The conjugal visiting program at Parchman was enacted into law in 1956. It involves some 500 married women and a number of common-law wives who visit their husbands in separate apartments on the prison grounds from 1 to 3 p.m. each Sunday and from 1 to 5 p.m. every third Sunday. It is sometimes said that since the program involves less than a third of Parchman's 1,630 inmates it only intensifies the monastic feelings of the majority. It has also been said that the conjugal visiting program diverts attention from basic deprivations in Parchman. The prison is run almost exclusively by trusties, prisoners themselves, and is said to be marked by homosexuality, bribery, and brutality, despite recent improvements.[71] Persons denying these allegations maintain that the conjugal visiting program has enthusiastic inmate support and represents one of the most progressive and encouraging innovations in American penology.[72]

Some states require that homosexual offenders register with the police in the jurisdictions where they reside or through which they pass regularly. Such registration often involves being fingerprinted and photographed and contains a rule that the exoffender cannot change his residence without notifying the authorities within a specified period.[73] For homosexuals, the registration statutes tend to be seen as nothing other than untoward harassment; for law enforcement officers they are sometimes regarded as a method for becoming aware of homosexuals within the jurisdiction in the event that an offense occurs that appears to be of homosexual origin. In

---

[69] Austin McCormick, quoted in Morris Kaplan, "Experts See Many Causes for Rash of Prison Riots," *New York Times*, August 29, 1955.

[70] Ruth S. Cavan and Eugene Zemans, "Marital Relationships of Prisoners in Twenty-Eight Countries," *Journal of Criminal Law, Criminology, and Police Science*, 49 (July–August 1958), p. 139. See also Zemans and Cavan, "Marital Relationships of Prisoners," *Journal of Criminal Law, Criminology, and Police Science*, 49 (May–June 1958), pp. 50–57.

[71] Douglas Kneeland, "Mississippi Prison, A Symbol of Horror, is Reforming Quietly," *New York Times*, February 14, 1968.

[72] Columbus B. Hopper, *Sex in Prison: The Mississippi Experiment with Conjugal Visiting* (Baton Rouge: Louisiana State University Press, 1969).

[73] See, e.g., California Penal Code §290 (Deering 1971).

practice, it seems likely that the registration statutes offer little law enforcement aid and are most often used to provide a charge (that is, failure to register) against an offender who is wanted for other reasons which cannot as readily be sustained.[74]

Homosexuality as It Bears on Others

The rather direct impact of homosexuality upon persons other than its participants can be found in a number of regards. The homosexual law, for instance, inevitably affects police operations and court procedures. Homosexuality also has an impact upon those solicited for homosexual acts and those aware of the behavior who either approve it or are distressed by it. It is these forces, then, that we will consider here—the special agencies of the society concerned with homosexuality and, most particularly, the members of the society as a unit, seeking their own advancement and pleasure through the agency of the polity, as it both permits them to do as they wish and keeps others from doing that of which they disapprove.

Cesare Bonesana, Marquis de Beccaria, perhaps the most influential writer in the history of criminal law, indicated in 1764: "No lasting advantage is to be hoped for from political morality if it is not founded upon the ineradicable feelings of mankind." [75] How, by this standard, does homosexuality fare?

The most comprehensive recent poll of public opinion is that by Louis Harris, conducted in 1969. Harris put the following question to a cross section of 1,895 households in the United States and compared the results to a similar survey conducted in 1965:

> America has many different kinds of people in it. But we would like to know whether you think each of these different types of people is more helpful or more harmful to American life or don't they help or harm much one way or the other?

Sixty-three percent of the respondents indicated that they believed that homosexuals were more harmful than helpful to American life. The rather curious wording of the question insists, however, that interpretations be made cautiously regarding precisely what it was that the respondents had in mind when they answered. Some might have believed, for instance, that homosexuals ought to be jailed, though they could have thought that homosexual behavior was not harmful to what they were using as their concept of "American life." Others might have supplied the same answer—not harmful—with a very different rationale for it.

---

[74] See *Lambert v. California*, 335 U.S. 225 (1957).

[75] Cesare Beccaria, *On Crimes and Punishments* (*Dei Delitti e delle Pene*) [1764], trans. by Henry Paolucci (Indianapolis: Bobbs-Merrill, 1963), p. 10.

It can be noted, however, that the 63 percent "harmful" response is seven percentage points below the response of 70 percent from 1965. In fact, except for "beatnicks" (up from 52 to 54 percent), all the remaining behaviors surveyed showed a decrease in adjudged harmfulness—prostitution down from 70 to 67 percent, young men with long hair and beards from 52 to 43 percent, and women who wear bikini bathing suits from 36 to 24 percent.[76] The Harris Poll result, it might be noted, is contrary to that of an Australian poll taken at about the same time which indicated that "a much larger percentage of the population oppose the liberalization of the laws relating to homosexuality than those relating to abortion and prostitution." [77] It may be that the different nature of the question put to the two groups is responsible for the disparate results, though the Australian conclusions tally with those from a poll conducted by CBS–TV which showed that "two out of three Americans look on homosexuals with disgust, discomfort or fear, and one out of ten regards them with outright hatred. A majority," the reported results showed, "considers homosexuality more dangerous to society than abortion, adultery, or prostitution." [78]

Other information available refers to the views of particular groups in American society toward homosexuality. There is the intuitive opinion of Lawrence LeShan, a research psychologist, that "young people make no value judgments about homosexuality. They have the attitude that there are many different ways of loving," he maintains, "and that it's no one's business. They are a tremendously moral generation. They care only about how people feel about each other." [79] The difficulty here, of course, is the tendency to generalize from extremely unrepresentative samples and in so doing misrepresent the view of the total membership of the stipulated group. Considerably more reliable are the results of a poll of medical doctors regarding their opinions of homosexuality. As reported by *Modern Medicine*, 67 percent of 27,741 doctors included in the survey were in favor of allowing consensual acts between adult homosexuals to take place without interference by the criminal law.[80]

---

[76] "Public Tolerance is Little Changed," *New York Times*, October 21, 1969.

[77] Paul R. Wilson and Duncan Chappell, "Australian Attitudes Toward Abortion, Prostitution and Homosexuality," *Australian Quarterly*, 40 (June 1968), pp. 7–17.

[78] "Homosexuality," *Time*, October 24, 1969, p. 82.

[79] Quoted in Enid Nemy, "The Woman Homosexual: More Assertive, Less Willing to Hide," *New York Times*, November 17, 1969.

[80] "Modern Medicine Poll on Sociomedical Issues: Abortion—Homosexual Practices—Marihuana," *Modern Medicine*, 37 (November 3, 1969), pp. 18–25. Cf., Donald W. Hastings, "Interpretative Summary of Poll on Sociomedical Issues," *ibid.*, pp. 26–30.

Both of these results—LeShan's intuitive portrait of at least a
highly visible segment of the youth of today and the medical response—seem to indicate that homosexuality is likely to be regarded
more tolerantly by persons with greater amounts of training and
education and by younger rather than older persons. If so, the
results bode well for changes in public attitudes toward homosexuality with the passage of time. But the larger, more comprehensive
surveys show quite unequivocally that there now exists a considerable
and deep feeling of opposition to homosexual behavior, which would
very likely manifest itself in a strong reaction against attempts at
the moment to change legal attitudes toward the behavior.

There are at least two other major areas in which the existence
of homosexuality tends to have an impact upon the performance
and well-being of other persons. One is in regard to police activity;
the second concerns the prosecution of homosexual acts.

The police role in apprehension of homosexuals has been sting-
ingly castigated as, among other things, an ill-advised use of manpower. Martin Hoffman writes, for instance:

> I would argue further that putting out as decoys police officers
> who are young, attractive, and seductively dressed, and who
> engage in enticing conversations with homosexuals is itself an
> outrage to public decency. Since practically no homosexual
> arrests involve complaints from anyone, it is a very good question
> just why public funds are being expended for this purpose.[81]

In support of his view, Hoffman quotes the conclusion of the law
students from U.C.L.A. who surveyed patterns of enforcement of
statutes against homosexuality and decided that "empirical data
indicate that utilization of police manpower for decoy enforcement
is not justified." [82]

In addition, the impact upon witnesses, especially young witnesses,
of court proceedings involving charges of homosexuality has been
sharply criticized. "The mental stress caused in a child by the inquisi-
tion in a court of law may be much more harmful than the seduction
itself," Michael J. Buckley observes, adding: "Permanent harm may
be caused to a minor when he has to repeat his evidence in one court
after another. If a case is adjourned from a lower to a higher court
weeks or months may elapse between the hearings, and throughout
the period child witnesses have to keep in their minds the sordid
incident and all its objectionable details." [83]

[81] Hoffman, op. cit., n. 66, p. 85.
[82] Gallo, op. cit., n. 28, p. 795.
[83] Michael J. Buckley, Morality and the Homosexual (Westminster, Md.: Newman Press, 1960), p. 112.

INVESTIGATION AND LAW REFORM IN
GREAT BRITAIN

Developments in Great Britain regarding homosexuality and public and legislative response to it provide instructive case history material for speculation regarding possible future events in the United States, though it is always a difficult enterprise to attempt to translate British findings into American terms. Persons citing British experience with narcotics, gambling, unarmed police and similar matters rarely get beyond the first cry of outrage from their opponents that the situation in England is no ways translatable to America because of distinctly different conditions prevailing in the United States.

The thoroughgoing review of national policy regarding homosexuality undertaken in Britain was largely a result of agitation concerning the apparent rise in the behavior, combined with a concern on the part of some about the stringency of penalties. Prosecutions for homosexuality in England and Wales had risen from 299 a year in the 1935–40 period to 1,686 in 1952. The penalty for sodomy was life imprisonment, and for attempts to commit "unnatural offenses," 10 years. The popular press clamored for even more severe penalties to attempt to reduce offenses, while the conservative press, represented by the *Sunday Times*, asked for an inquiry into the subject, and the liberal journals called for reform of the law. Kingsley Martin, for instance, editor of the *New Statesman and Nation*, wrote of homosexuality: "It is a social evil, but its bad effects are greatly aggravated by our stupid, savage, and out of date criminal laws." [84] In addition, religious leaders, represented by the Moral Welfare Council of the Church of England, called for an inquiry into homosexuality, insisting that the state had a duty to protect young persons from homosexuals.[85]

The reaction of governmental authorities to the growing social agitation indicates clearly the ambivalence involved in the issue and the potentiality for change, given a panorama of competing views.[86] Thus, Sir David Maxwell Fyfe, the Home Secretary, responding to

---

[84] "Homosexuality Rise is Troubling Britons," *New York Times*, November 2, 1953; Kingsley Martin, "Society and the Homosexual," *New Statesman and Nation*, 46 (October 31, 1953), p. 508.

[85] "Homosexuality Study is Asked in Britain," *New York Times*, December 11, 1953.

[86] As the *New York Times'* London correspondent reported: "Since the *Sunday Times* brought the problem into the open . . . that newspaper and other newspapers and weeklies have received hundreds of letters. The subject, once taboo, has become a major topic of public and private discussion. *Ibid.*

questions, told the House of Commons that punishment of homosexuals contained a protective element that was highly necessary "because homosexuals in general are exhibitionists and proselytizers and a danger to others, especially the young." At the same time, Sir David granted that there existed another problem, namely "the validity of the right given to the state to take cognizance of immoral private actions between adult male homosexuals." [87]

As a result of the public debate, the British Government appointed a committee, headed by Sir John Wolfenden, vice chancellor of Reading University, to look into both homosexuality and prostitution. Reporting in 1957, 3 years after its constitution, the committee recommended heavier penalties against streetwalkers on the ground that their loitering and soliciting were an affront to public order and decency. Homosexuality, on the other hand, the committee believed, was a matter of morals, and not of law when practiced privately by persons 21 years of age or older and "should no longer be a criminal offense." The committee said that it had found no evidence supporting the view that homosexuality is "a cause of the demoralization and decay of civilizations." [88] In short, the Wolfenden Committee thought that private, adult, consensual homosexuality was "not the law's business." [89]

Parliamentary reaction to the controversial report suggests generalizations about workable methods for transforming law in the face of public attitudes which are apt to resist such change rather intensely. As Leo Abse, a Member of Parliament, has noted in regard to debates on the Wolfenden Report recommendations, they "helped to make our country a little more rational. Persistent educational campaigns of this kind assist both the nation and its leaders to gain insights and to come to terms with sexuality and aggressions." [90] When Parliament began reviewing the Wolfenden proposals, newspaper polls showed strong public opposition to those regarding homosexuality. Thus, the *News Chronicle* Gallup Poll indicated 47 percent of the public was against the Wolfenden recommendation, 38 percent for it, and 15 percent without a firm opinion. The division in a *Daily Mirror* survey was almost even, with 6,144 against and 5,561 in favor. The opponents of change were said to be "bitterly opposed to homosexuality" and to regard its practice as

---

[87] *Ibid.*
[88] Great Britain, Committee on Homosexual Offences and Prostitution (Cmnd. 247, 1957), p. 22.
[89] *Ibid.*, p. 24.
[90] Leo Abse, "The Sexual Offences Act," *British Journal of Criminology*, 8 (January 1968), p. 87.

"abhorrent." Nonetheless, reports said that "the debate has been conducted on a high plane and . . . has demonstrated that Britons are profoundly concerned about the moral and legal questions involved." "This concern," it was reported, "extends beyond those immediate questions and to the whole problem of the apparent weakening of moral values in today's society." [91]

The prediction that nothing would be done for a time about homosexuality, in part because the Government was "having sufficient trouble on other political fronts without risking a controversy that might alienate more voters," [92] proved perceptive. In mid-1959, however—2 years after the Wolfenden Report had been filed—Parliament approved the Street Offences Act, increasing severely the penalties against streetwalkers so that thoroughfares in London and other major cities were soon reported to be clear of prostitutes. In 1960, following the first Parliamentary discussion of the homosexuality recommendations in the Report, the House of Commons overwhelmingly rejected a motion with a 213 to 99 vote that the homosexual recommendations be supported by statute. [93] Increasing support of the Report's proposals by church authorities, however, began to exert particular suasion as the movement for reform gained momentum, despite this initial setback. Leaders of the Anglican, Methodist, and Roman Catholic churches of Britain all publicly approved the Wolfenden recommendations, arguing that it was futile to attempt to make sins into crimes without further justification, and that such actions aroused contempt both for law and for morality. [94] When the issue again came up in Parliament in 1965, Dr. Arthur Ramsay, the Archbishop of Canterbury, spoke in favor of reform, noting carefully that he was not condoning homosexual acts, but only asking that they be placed in the realm of private moral responsibility. The Labor Government, after providing the means for consideration of the measures, indicated that it would not introduce a bill of its own, since it regarded the issue as moral rather than political, but would permit a "free" vote, that is a vote unrestricted by demands of party-line discipline. [95] Two weeks later, in

---

[91] Thomas P. Ronan, "Report on Sex Problems Stirs British Debate," *New York Times*, September 22, 1957.

[92] *Ibid.*

[93] "Easing of Homosexuality Laws Opposed by British Parliament," *New York Times*, June 30, 1960.

[94] See, e.g., Derrick S. Bailey, *Homosexuality and the Western Christian Tradition* (London: Longmans, 1955); Buckley, *op. cit.*, n. 83.

[95] Gloria Emerson, "Parliament to Study Reform of Penalties for Homosexuality," *New York Times*, May 13, 1965.

a surprise vote of 94 to 49, the House of Lords approved in principle
a bill removing from criminal law all penalties for homosexual conduct by consenting adults in private. The surprise arose from the
reputation of the House of Lords as "maintainer of the conservative
tradition of stiff-lipped old Britain." There was special drama in the
debate in the House of Lords when the 35-year-old Marquess of
Queensbery rose for his maiden speech in the House. It had been
his great-grandfather who had denounced Oscar Wilde as a homosexual in 1895, an accusation which resulted in Wilde's going to
prison in the most notorious case ever brought under the laws that
the present bill sought to repeal. The Marquess himself favored the
reform in 1965.[96] A second surprise, however, temporarily derailed
the proposed law reform as the House of Commons, shortly after
the favorable action by the House of Lords, refused permission, by
a vote of 178 to 159, to allow a private member's bill repealing homosexual bans to be introduced. The move has relevance to the American experience, since it was regarded as an instance in which
members of the House of Lords, as hereditary holders of their position, felt able to act freely while the elected members of the House
of Commons felt more restrained because of their political vulnerability. In fact, nearly half of the House of Commons' membership
abstained or remained absent from the vote. Under House provisions,
the motion to allow introduction of the bill was brought up under
a special procedure permitting just one 10-minute speech on each
side. The comments in opposition to the idea are worth noting: "The
vast majority of our people," Sir Cyril Osborne, a conservative,
said, "consider sodomy to be wrong, unnatural, degrading, and dis-
gusting, and I agree with them." [97]

A year later, however, the House of Commons voted 164 to 107
(with more than 350 abstentions or absences) to approve the Wolfenden recommendations regarding homosexuality, thus providing a
numerical index of the progress made in garnering support for this
viewpoint. The 1960 vote had been 213 against to 99 for the measure,
while that in 1965, as noted, had been 178 against to 159 in favor.
Now it had swung to 164 in favor to 107 in opposition. Public opinion polls indicated a shift in voter attitudes as well. By the time of
the approval by the House of Commons, nearly two-thirds of the
population was indicating its support of the suggested approach. In

---

[96] Anthony Lewis, "Lords Vote to Ease Homosexuality Ban," *New York Times*,
May 25, 1965. Cf., H. Montgomery Hyde (editor), *The Three Trials of Oscar
Wilde* (New York: University Books, 1952).

[97] Anthony Lewis, "Commons Blocks Bill to Ease Curb on Homosexuality,"
New York Times, May 27, 1965.

the House of Commons, opposition continued to be led by Sir Cyril Osborne, who told the members that he was "rather tired of democracy being made safe for the pimps, the prostitutes, the spivs, and the pansies, and now the queers." The Home Secretary, Roy Jenkins, speaking as an individual, not for the Government, argued in favor of the bill:

> The great majority of homosexuals are not exhibitionistic freaks but ordinary citizens. Homosexuality is not a disease but is more in the nature of a grave disability for the individual, leading to a great deal of loneliness, unhappiness, guilt and shame.[98]

Dissolution of the Parliament for the British general elections in March 1966, automatically put an end to the chances of the homosexuality reform measure for enactment, though it had passed the House of Lords and through two of three readings in Commons by this time. Most noteworthy in the elections was the defeat of Humphrey Berekely, a conservative from Lancaster who had sponsored the reform measure in the House of Commons, a defeat believed to be at least partly due to the electorate's response to his position.[99]

Finally, late in 1966, the Parliament put final approval on the recommendations made 7 years previously by the Wolfenden Committee, agreeing that consensual homosexuality in private would no longer be a criminal offense. However, the penalty of life imprisonment was retained for a homosexual offense against a boy under the age of 16. In addition, new legislation provided that an act of gross indecency against a youth between the age of 16 and 21 could be punished by 2 years in prison.[100] The new law, it may be noted, is not without definitional difficulties. A sleeper on a night train to Scotland, for example, has been labeled a "public place." [101]

LAW REFORM IN THE UNITED STATES

In the United States, essentially the same views as those now adopted in Great Britain are found in the 1955 draft of the Model Penal Code of the American Law Institute, whose commentary notes

---

[98] Anthony Lewis, "Commons Endorses A Measure to Reform Homosexuality Law," *New York Times*, February 12, 1966.

[99] Clyde H. Farnsworth, "2 Reform Bills Advance in Lords," *New York Times*, May 11, 1966.

[100] The Sexual Offences Act, 1967 (1967, c. 60), Halsbury, 3d ed., Vol. VIII, pp. 577–582.

[101] Schott, *op. cit.*, n. 1, p. 49.

that "this area of private morals is the distinctive concern of spirit-ual authorities." The Code drafters also maintained that homosexual laws are marked by capricious enforcement and a diversion of police energies from more violent kinds of offenses.[102]

Only two States have responded to the recommendation in the Model Penal Code regarding abolition of statutes outlawing homo-sexuality. Since 1962, Illinois has permitted all but what is called "deviate sexual behavior," defined as acts involving force, or young and immature persons, or those which disturb the peace because of their open and notorious character.[103] The impact of the change in the Illinois statute, however, according to all observers, has been virtually nonexistent. Martin Hoffman, for instance, noted in 1967 that "homosexuals in Chicago have had somewhat more trouble with the law since the enactment of the new penal code than have homo-sexuals in San Francisco during the same period of time." [104] During a recent 12-month span, nearly 100 arrests were made for public solicitation in Chicago's Loop area; in the absence of sodomy laws, homosexuals note, the police invoke nuisance and loitering statutes against them.[105] In fact, it is believed that removal of sodomy laws in Illinois has caused the police to become more intense in their pur-suit of homosexuals under the solicitation laws: "We're worse off now than before," one of the leaders of the homophile movement maintains.[106]

Connecticut has been the only State to follow Illinois' example to date. Its new penal code, which went into effect on October 1, 1971, not only liberalized homosexual laws, but removed fornication between unmarried consenting adults from the criminal code and reduced the penalty for adultery to a misdemeanor. Dropped from the penal code totally was the offense of "lascivious carriage," defined as "conduct which is wanton, lewd or lustful and tending to produce voluptuous emotions." [107]

OTHER FOREIGN DEVELOPMENTS

Similar reforms to those in Connecticut and Illinois inaugurated abroad include the revised Canadian criminal code, which, in regard

---

[102] American Law Institute, Model Penal Code, Tentative Draft No. 4, §207.5, Comments, pp. 277–278 (1955).

[103] Cf., n. 31 material.

[104] Hoffman, op. cit., n. 66, p. 95.

[105] Schott, op. cit., n. 1, p. 47.

[106] Foster Gunnison, Jr., "The Homophile Movement in America," in Weltge, op. cit., n. 10, p. 119.

[107] Cf., n. 32 material and John Darnton, "Hartford Supports Homosexuality Bill," New York Times, June 2, 1970.

to homosexuality, was described by Prime Minister Pierre Elliott Trudeau as taking the "government out of the bedrooms of the nation." The Canadian legislature also changed the law so that an offender could no longer be kept in preventive detention simply because he might commit a further sexual offense, even though the offense would not likely cause harm to anyone else.[108]

In West Germany, the legislature in May 1969, matched the Canadian procedure by removing consensual homosexuality from the criminal statutes, which had not been revised since 1871. The German measure also dropped penalties for adultery and those which could have been used against parents who permitted their children to engage in extramarital sex relations. Gustav Heinemann, West Germany's president-elect and a former justice minister, explained some of the motivations for the legal changes in a brochure titled "Progress in Penal Law: Demand of Our Time":

> A penal code which brands people as criminals only because of abnormal sexual qualities encourages hypocrisy, snooping and blackmail. Thus it must be welcome that the Bundestag has been called on to abolish offenses such as homosexuality.[109]

Under the new German penal code, the so-called "active" partner in a homosexual act must be over 18 years of age, and the "passive" partner over 21 for the act to be classified as "consensual." [110]

NEW DIRECTIONS

Measures enacted in recent years by Illinois and Connecticut and the trend of legislation abroad clearly indicates the direction in which legal attitudes toward homosexuality are moving. It would be most useful to have available ongoing opinion surveys concerning the changes in public thinking which have—or have not—accompanied the legislative shifts. Certainly, two things appear obvious from our review of available materials: First, that there has been enough of a change in the ideas of legislators, or at least in their willingness to translate such ideas into law, to have given impetus to the passage of several liberalized laws regarding homosexuality. Second, it appears quite evident that, at least in the United States, there exists

---

[108] Jay Walz, "Broad Criminal-Code Changes Voted by Canadian Commons," *New York Times*, May 16, 1969.

[109] "Homosexuality Laws Eased by W. Germany," *Los Angeles Times*, May 11, 1969 (AP).

[110] Ralph Blumenthal, "Bundestag Votes Penal Reform: Ends Most Sex Crime Penalties," *New York Times*, May 10, 1969.

a deep core of feeling against homosexuality and against laws permitting its practice.

It is not possible to determine what effect a change in law, and
possibly one in attitudes, might have upon individual homosexuals.
It appears likely that some of the more sordid things connected
with the behavior—things such as blackmail—would be apt to
decrease, perhaps markedly. The self-hatred of the homosexual might
also be lessened, though it may be doubted that the "deviant" label
attached to the behavior, and presumably introjected by many of its
practitioners, would evaporate very quickly by reason of nothing
other than a change in statutory penalties.

It may be argued that it matters not whether a change in the law
would lead to an increase or a decrease in the amount of homosexual
behavior, once a judgment is made that the behavior should be permitted in a democratic society. But concern might exist regarding
the involvement of more persons in homosexual behavior than the
society might be willing to tolerate, presuming it is willing to tolerate present numbers. It should be noted, first, that the laws themselves are undoubtedly provocative of a not inconsiderable number
of homosexual acts, an item often not sufficiently attended to in
debates about the impact of legal sanctions on human action. Oscar
Wilde noted, for instance, that enactment of an 1885 law in England
which proscribed homosexual "indecencies," even if practiced in
private, provided further reason for him to engage in the behavior:
"It was like feasting with panthers, the danger was half the excitement," Wilde wrote.[111]

The truth of the matter regarding expansion of homosexual activity probably has its roots not in legal tolerance or legal prescription
of the behavior but in the social arrangements of the society itself.
Certainly, there has been no decline in the glorification (if that is
the correct word) of heterosexual activity by the advertising media
in the United States. That the incessant blaring of the necessity of
sexual activity and sexual success does not convince at least a segment of the society—the homosexual segment—is a fitting and ironic
testament to the power of advertising to undermine its own message
by its very ubiquitous and shrill nature. That is, it may be that
heterosexual stimuli become so omnipresent and pervasive that homosexual acts are resorted to as an escape from an otherwise compelling
but unobtainable and now anathema act. But availability of heterosexual outlets also seem to be on the increase. All told, it seems

---

[111] Oscar Wilde, *De Profundis* [1905], in *Complete Works* (Garden City, N.Y.:
Doubleday and Page, 1923), Vol. XI, p. 93.

unlikely that either personal or cultural pressures toward heterosexuality will decrease or that they will not have a continuing strong tendency to generate the behavior they glamorize.

But answers to the question of whether homosexuality will increase or decrease, absent its sanctioning through law, probably lie most fundamentally within the social system and its constituent elements. In this respect, the analysis of Charles Winick seems very sound. Winick maintains that American society is moving toward the production of a "new people," individuals who are most basically "desexualized," that is, persons who less and less identify strongly with either masculine or feminine roles. Winick enters a number of observations about this process, indicating first that cross-cultural evidence insists that societies of the kind that he believes the United States is becoming are apt to have low rates of homosexuality. He notes, for instance:

> The decision to have fewer children may represent one of the ways in which some people respond to confused sex roles. Others may run away into a reaction formation, e.g., an excess of sexual activity. Relatively few are likely to move toward homosexuality, which is not likely to be fostered by our society's blurred sexual identification. Societies with little or no homosexuality, like the Arapesh, Lepcha, and Mundugumor, have blurred goals of masculinity and femininity.[112]

Winick suggests that, rather than an increase in homosexuality today, we are likely witnessing the first phases of its decline, that it is more tolerant attitudes which provide the "illusion of numbers." He indicates, finally, that defeminization of women by itself will more readily permit males who might otherwise enter into homosexuality to find satisfaction in heterosexual relationships:

> Homosexuality could also be declining because of the mannish aspects of women's appearance. A fashionable woman of today could sport a hard, boyish Vidal Sassoon haircut and a crash helmet, with a chinstrap framing her colorless face. Her pants suit would minimize the display of breasts and buttocks. A relationship with such a woman could displace or sublimate homosexual impulses, especially now that oral and anal sex are achieving heterosexual popularity.[113]

Another author to observe that the repeal of statutes outlawing homosexuality is likely to have negligible effect on the extent of the behavior is Richard Sallick, a psychiatrist with the National Insti-

---

[112] Charles Winick, *The New People: Desexualization in American Life* (New York: Pegasus, 1968), p. 325.
[113] *Ibid.*, pp. 326–327.

tute of Mental Health. Sallick notes that the proportion of homosexuals in Europe is almost exactly the same as in the United States
and observes that: "Some people fear that if the taboos against
homosexuality were removed everyone would want to become homosexual. Nonsense. Most people can't be made to want homosexual
experience." [114] The argument might be carried somewhat further by
noting that the absence of bans against heterosexuality have hardly
been adequate to induce homosexuals into the behavior; so, too, a
reverse trend is unlikely to produce a flight into homosexuality,
unless it is suggested that homosexuality is a preferred mode of
behavior, avoided only because of the fear of legal retaliation. We
would regard this as a very doubtful thesis.

NIMH TASK FORCE ON HOMOSEXUALITY

In October 1969, a Task Force on Homosexuality, appointed 2
years earlier by the director of the National Institute of Mental
Health, submitted a report urging the United States to follow the
lead of Great Britain and abolish laws forbidding private homosexual relations among consenting adults. The group noted:

> Homosexuality presents a major problem for our society
> largely because of the amount of injustice and suffering entailed
> in it, not only for the homosexual but also for those concerned
> about him.[115]

Three members of the 14-person group expressed reservations
regarding the proposed legal changes saying that "consideration of
social policy issues should be deferred until further scientific evidence is available." The remainder, however, after calling for the
establishment of a Federal Center for the Study of Sexual Behavior,
insisted that social reforms should include, not only statutory change,
but also training of mental health professionals and law enforcement personnel, broader programs in sex education, and the collec-
tion and dissemination of information on sexuality. The report also
called for deeper exploration of therapeutic techniques for homosexuals who are interested in treatment. In the area of the law, the
Study Group made the following recommendation:

> Although many people continue to regard homosexual activi-
> ties with repugnance, there is evidence that public attitudes are
> changing. Discreet homosexuality, together with many other
> aspects of human sexual behavior, is being recognized more and

[114] Quoted in Schott, op. cit., n. 1, p. 70.
[115] National Institute of Mental Health, op. cit., n. 43, p. 4.

more as the private business of the individual rather than a subject for public regulation through statute. Many homosexuals are good citizens, holding regular jobs and leading productive lives. The existence of legal penalties relating to homosexual acts means that the mental health problems of homosexuals are exacerbated by the need of concealment and the emotional stresses arising from this need and from the opprobrium of being in violation of the law.[116]

On the other hand, the Study Group noted, there was no evidence that the statutes were serving to reduce or prevent homosexuality—though it might equally well have pointed out that the opposite was equally true, that there was no evidence that they were not serving such a purpose. Given this condition, it was believed desirable that "statutes covering sexual acts be recast in such a way as to remove legal penalties against acts in private among consenting adults." It was further urged that ongoing studies be begun to deal with the legal and social implications of such a change with respect to both homosexual and heterosexual behavior.[117]

THE RELIGIOUS VIEWPOINT

It is quite clear that there exists no consensus among the major religious bodies regarding the necessary relationship between theological dictates and secular law. It is evident that some of the most forceful opposition to changes in homosexual statutes arises from religious sources and is buttressed by theological doctrine. On the other hand, some of the most effective advocacy of statutory liberalization has arisen from religious leaders. Epitomizing this movement is the stand of a group of the most influential Quakers in Great Britain who, in a 70-page report, "Towards a Quaker View of Sex," have appealed for a more tolerant view of sexual variation.

The report, as one summary notes, "rejects almost completely the traditional approach of the organized Christian church to morality, with its supposition that it knows precisely what is right and what is wrong, that this distinction can be made in terms of an external pattern of behavior, and that the greatest good will come only through universal adherence to that pattern."

The report does not represent the official view of the British Society of Friends, but was published by the Society and written by a group of 11 persons of whom six were Society elders. The report holds that there has to be a morality of some sort to govern sexual

[116] *Ibid.*, p. 18.
[117] *Ibid.*, p. 19.

relationships, but it concludes that "sexuality, looked at dispassionately, is neither good nor evil—it is a fact of nature." The report adds:

> It seemed to us that morals, like the Sabbath, were made for man, and not man for morals, and that as society changes and modes of conduct with it, we must always be searching below the surface of human behavior, to discover what is in fact happening to people, what they are seeking to express, what motives and intentions they are satisfying, what fruits, good or bad, they are harvesting.

Homosexual affection, it was held, is not morally worse than heterosexual affection and should be judged by the same standards. An act that expresses true affection between two individuals and gives pleasure to them could not be said to be sinful merely because it is homosexual.[118]

In summary, it seems evident to the present writer—perhaps because his predilections have led him to select out and emphasize those materials most favorable to his view—that the most persuasive arguments regarding homosexuality lie on the side of those who would see the law altered. Such alteration would not only eliminate the sodomy statutes but also laws, such as that against solicitation in Illinois, if such solicitation is no more aggressive than that now tolerated for heterosexual persuasion.

It also seems clear that there is no substantial evidence that legal—and, hopefully, in the longer run, social—toleration of homosexuality is apt to impose harm upon the homosexual participants, upon others, or upon the social structure that all involved would not be able to handle adequately. A democracy, after all, is a society that permits the greatest possible freedom to minorities. In regard to homosexuality, as well as in regard to matters similar to it, the remark of Henry Luce to a group of college students seems notably pertinent: "The most important question of our age," he said, "is: Can democracy be the religious principle of the coming world?"[119]

---

[118] "Quakers Propose a Wide View of Sex," *New York Times*, February 19, 1963.

[119] John K. Jessup (editor), *The Ideas of Henry Luce* (New York: Atheneum, 1969), p. 305.

III. Criminal Abortion

Distinctions between homosexuality, which we have just considered, and criminal abortion, which we will now consider, are fundamental in gaining an understanding of the differing character of debates about the two subjects. In homosexuality, for instance, we have a pair of persons, both of whom may be either male or female, engaging in an act from which they derive certain satisfaction. Were they not to take part in the act, however, the consequences need not be overtly self-evident. They might, arguably, suffer some untoward agitation, even a severe breakdown, but such a consequence is rather subtle, in the sense that its relationship to homosexual frustration is not directly discernible. It is also a problematic outcome, since we presume that numerous "homosexuals" are able to control such impulses without untoward consequences.

Failure of the pregnant female to undergo an abortion, on the other hand, has consequences that are immutable and may be long term. Birth of the child is likely to begin a long period of parenthood, with quite stringent imperatives associated with it. If the child is put out for adoption, social and personal definitions of this course may leave deep scars. Failure to engage in homosexuality, therefore, can be seen as no more than an omission; failure to be aborted is apt to set up an elaborate chain of consequences and demands which fall upon the pregnant female.

Sexual roles are quite different in abortion than in homosexuality. The gender of the abortionist is irrelevant to the act; the gender of the person being aborted is unvarying. Thus, at once, the idea of sexual discrimination is introduced, since laws against abortion bear most directly only upon women. That item is compounded by the fact that abortion laws are written and administered almost exclusively by males. Equally important is the fact that abortion is a considerably more limited act than homosexuality. Women are apt to be aborted only once, and certainly at most only a few times, during the course of their lives. In addition, the satisfaction they obtain from the act is social rather than sexual, and is hardly an untainted blessing. Women undergoing abortions may suffer from the same guilt as homosexuals in the face of social definition of their behavior as "bad." They may on occasion also suffer physically.

Though the pain of abortion usually is not severe, there is always the danger, absent in homosexuality, that the act may result in permanent injury or death.

And, finally, there is the problem of the object of the abortion—the fetus. It may be argued with some conviction that homosexuals are behaving in a manner affecting none but themselves. It cannot be argued altogether convincingly that abortion is only the business of the woman being aborted and the person performing the abortion. There hovers about the abortion transaction questions and feelings related to that bit of protoplasm which is being extracted. The fetus may or may not be human; this is a matter of definition which, like any matter of definition, may be resolved by changes in social mores. After all, it is just as possible to maintain that sperm are viable "human" entities and that their spillage in masturbation is unconscionable and should be declared criminal. But masturbation, however sinful, is not regarded as criminal, any more than the use of birth control techniques is so viewed. (Peripheral exceptions are Indiana [Stat. Ann. 10–4221, 1956] and Wyoming [Comp. Stat. 6–98, 1957] which consider it a crime to "entice, allure, instigate or aid" a person under 21 to masturbate.) Opponents of any relaxation of abortion laws maintain, of course, that given the play in the proper definition of "human," any slippage is apt to have subsequent further consequences. Allow a fetus to be aborted legally, they insist, and you have entered a wedge for the killing not only of unwanted fetuses, which are now defined as nonhuman, but also of infants themselves who can by later extension of this idea also be declared as nonhuman, before they have, say, reached their first birthday. Such reasoning represents what is usually a passionate but rather fruitless kind of debate. Changes in social definitions often do set eddies in motion which spread outward. But the rote extrapolation from changes is a feckless enterprise. First, a change may represent the last movement of its sort along the continuum being considered; second, a change may produce an antithesis; and third, the later predicted consequences, if they come about, may not in their time be as grim as they would appear to be at the point at which they are being used as horror tales to hold in check the more limited contemplated change.

We need only repeat then, in summary, the observation that abortion is a quite different act from homosexuality and from the acts we will subsequently review—gambling, prostitution, and narcotics offenses. Conclusions about any of these events do not necessarily apply to the remainder, though it is not unreasonable to anticipate that the common element of these behaviors—the possible absence in each of them of documented social harm of such a magnitude that it threatens the existence of the social order—may dictate social responses of a similar general nature to all of them.

MATTERS OF DEFINITION

Virtually all writing and debate about abortion concentrate upon the expectant mother. In most States, however, criminal sanctions relate not to the woman being aborted, but to the person who performs the abortion. In the States where both parties are criminally liable, the practice is to prosecute only the abortionist, and then most often only when the aftereffects of his act have caused injury serious enough to bring the "victim" to the attention of medical authorities. It is she who, under such conditions, is sometimes persuaded to testify for the State against the abortionist. Therefore it is not the labeling of an aborted woman as a felon, or the penalties which might follow her apprehension, which are relevant, but her forced involvement in an act that contains many squalid and dangerous elements. In fact, when a 23-year-old Florida girl was convicted for submitting to an abortion in late 1971, she was believed to be the first woman in the English-speaking world to have been so dealt with by the criminal justice system. She was sentenced to a 2-year term of probation, and given 1 week to leave Florida and return to her relatives in North Carolina.[1]

There is, in addition to the unlikely possibility of arrest, the inhibiting effect of the laws. Unlike the case of homosexuality, it is presumed that in abortion numerous persons who might engage in the activity are deterred from doing so by the definition of the behavior as criminal and the consequent limitation of opportunities conducive to having abortions easily.

By definition, abortion involves the premature delivery or expulsion of a fetus before it is capable of sustaining life. The gist of the criminal offense of abortion lies in the intent to commit the act and the artificial means used to procure fetal expulsion. In some States (though the matter is still legally controversial), it is a crime to advise a person to undergo an abortion, if such advice is heeded. Statutes also vary regarding the legal consequences to the abortionist if his patient dies. Largely because of the consensual nature of

---

[1] " 'Get out of Florida'—Abortion Penalty," *Los Angeles Times*, October 16, 1971 (AP) ; Marlene Cimons, "Woman Faces 20-Year Term for Having Florida Abortion," *Los Angeles Times*, September 30, 1971 ; Jon Nordheimer, "She's Fighting Conviction for Aborting Her Child," *New York Times*, December 4, 1971.

the act, the abortionist may be tried in some States only for manslaughter; in others, a murder charge will lie. Penalties run a wide range for abortion, from 1 year in Kansas to 1 to 20 years in Mississippi. In some States, there is a requirement that the woman must be pregnant before an abortion charge will stand, but in most of the states the actuality of her pregnancy makes no legal difference.

If all women submitting to criminal abortions in the United States were apprehended and convicted, the female crime rate would come much closer to matching that of the male, and prevalent generalizations about the crime proneness of the sexes would have to be thoroughly altered. The same point, of course, may be entered with regard to other statutes—such as frequenting a prostitute—which also are not enforced, but which involve acts committed primarily by males.

The rapidity of alterations in public attitudes and official policies in regard to abortion has been extraordinary. This substantiates the idea that social change can be brought about with dramatic suddenness, given the right combination of latent social forces as these forces blend with public events, which may be either planned or fortuitous. In 1965, Samuel Kling could note in response to the question: "What are the prospects for reform of our obsolete and inconsistent abortion laws?" that such prospects were "at the moment not very promising." [2] Just 5 years later, Hawaii had enacted a law permitting abortion on the demand of the pregnant female, leading the *New York Times* to observe editorially that this new act "dramatically illustrated" the "revolutionary change in public attitudes toward abortion." [3] Even the director of the Planned Parenthood-World Population Association, himself a leading fighter for abortion reform, was taken aback by his own success. "The progress that's been made is fantastic," Alan Guttmacher noted. "Nobody could have dreamed this degree of progress." [4]

It is not easy to pinpoint those exact reasons which led to abortion becoming so intensely debated a proposition and which presaged the sweeping changes that occurred in the abortion laws of various States. Certainly the enhanced vigor—punning, one might call it the "increased virility"—of the feminist movement played a very large role. That movement itself probably had deep roots in an affluence which afforded increased opportunity for women to achieve outside

---

[2] Samuel G. Kling, *Sexual Behavior and the Law* (New York: Pocket Books, 1969), p. 14.

[3] "Legalizing Abortion," *New York Times*, March 3, 1970.

[4] Quoted in Louise Cook, "Move for Abortion Reflects U.S. Mood," *Los Angeles Times*, March 20, 1970 (AP).

the home. Also, as with homosexuality, revived Malthusian fears of overpopulation disaster led abortion to be redefined in some instances as an attractive resolution of a severe problem. Birth control pills, which allowed even more calculating interference with conception than previous methods had offered, called into question the necessary inviolability of the birth process once it had gotten underway, since it could have, so casually, been prevented before it began. The public nature of birth control also brought into the limelight cognate, once taboo, subjects. Inserting a diaphragm or using a condom are private processes. Birth control pills, however, lie on the kitchen counter, and are gulped down with the orange juice at the family breakfast. As Robert Hall, a gynecologist, has observed:

> The climate for accepting even a discussion of the abortion issue has been enhanced by the progress made in birth control. Five years ago birth control was a dirty word. Now it's socially acceptable, and that means abortion can be discussed as well.[5]

The declining hold of theological orthodoxy on the minds and allegiances of Americans also contributed significantly to the rise of agitation demanding abortion law reforms. Church leaders were taking the position—made prominent during the British debates on homosexuality—that religious morality which was translated into unenforceable criminal law tended to discredit both the law and the morality. The fact that the Catholic Church, the major opponent of liberalized abortion laws, has come under ideological siege on a broad range of fronts in recent years also meant that it had fewer resources to devote unrestrainedly to the struggle over abortion.

These considerations provided the background for the growing intensity of debate regarding abortion in the United States. In addition, cumulative experience in foreign countries with less severe restrictions on abortion than those prevailing in the United States provided a comparative bank of information with which to rebut allegations about hypothetical consequences of changes in American laws, as well as at times information to undergird Cassandra-like warnings about the outcome if America were to duplicate foreign procedures in regard to abortion.

It was a single sensational case, however, which thrust the abortion issue into public awareness. The case—that of Sherri Finkbine, an attractive Arizona television performer, already mother of several children—involved the use by a pregnant woman of a drug, thalidomide, that appeared "likely" to cause her to give birth to a deformed

---

[5] Quoted in Edward Edelson, "Abortion—An Endless Debate," *New York World-Telegram*, March 19, 1965.

child. Once the issue had been raised, it was but a short polemical jump from matters of physical deformity to those of psychic aberration, and from concern with the baby's well-being to concern with the mother's. Inevitably, then, the fundamental question appeared: Should the state have any right at all to dictate that the pregnant woman had to carry her child to term?

THE SHERRI FINKBINE CASE

Abortion became a national news item in the United States in 1962 when the media were able to concentrate on the dramatic ingredients of a single case. In Phoenix, Arizona, Mrs. Robert L. Finkbine, a 31-year-old mother of four, well-known in the city as Sherri Chessen, the star of "Romper Room," a television show for youngsters, requested a therapeutic abortion on the ground that she had taken thalidomide during the course of her pregnancy and that, because of this, there was a considerable likelihood that her child would be born deformed. Thalidomide had been synthesized by Chemie Gruenthal in West Germany, and was reported to have no ill effects when tested on animals. It was first marketed under the name *contergan* as an anticonvulsant, but was shortly found to be of little value for this purpose. Soon thereafter, however, contergan became West Germany's "baby sitter," the most popular sleeping potion on the market. The drug was widely exported and sold under a variety of brand names before it began to be linked to phocomelia babies, infants born with deformities of the extremities. Some 1,000 babies were born deformed in Great Britain between 1958, when the drug was introduced, and late 1961, when it was withdrawn from sale after tests on rabbits established that more than half of their litters contained deformed young. Nearly 4,000 deformed babies were reported in West Germany as a result of the use of contergan by expectant mothers early in their pregnancy. In December 1970, after a two-and-a-half year trial, a settlement was reached awarding $19,000 each to the surviving 2,000 deformed children, and providing a total of $1.6 million to 800 adults claiming nervous disorders as a consequence of their use of thalidomide.

The drug was prohibited from sale in the United States because Dr. Frances O. Kelsey of the Food and Drug Administration had not been satisfied regarding the thoroughness of the testing program conducted by its distributor. Nonetheless, some 1,200 American doctors had been sent samples of thalidomide for distribution to their patients.

Mrs. Finkbine's husband had secured thalidomide in Britain while he was there chaperoning a group of high school students on a European tour. His wife had taken the drug during a bout of nausea. Later news on the possibility of it's affecting her unborn child dictated her decision to seek a therapeutic abortion. In Arizona, which operated under a 1901 statute allowing abortion only when the health of the prospective mother is threatened, a hospital review committee concluded that the Finkbine situation met this requirement. The Phoenix City Attorney, however, indicated publicly that he would prosecute any person involved in the proposed abortion of Mrs. Finkbine.

At first, Mrs. Finkbine planned to fly to Japan to seek her abortion, but she had difficulties securing a visa. At the last minute she shifted her destination to Sweden, where her case was presented to a Committee on Abortion, consisting of a gynecologist, a psychiatrist, and a female member. The panel normally reviews some 4,000 cases annually, rejecting about 40 percent of them. In Mrs. Finkbine's case, the decision was affirmative, and the abortion thereafter routine. Afterwards Mrs. Finkbine was told by doctors that examination of the fetus indicated that she would have given birth to a deformed child. Subsequently in the United States, 17 deformed babies were born to American women who during their pregnancy had taken thalidomide obtained from foreign sources.[6]

Reactions to the Finkbine events were intense and varied. The Vatican radio, without mentioning the case specifically, declared that "homicide is never an act of goodwill. Love always chooses life, not death." [7] The day after Mrs. Finkbine's abortion, the same source was more specifically denunciatory: "Crime is the only possible definition of what happened yesterday at Caroline Hospital in Stockholm, Sweden. Morally, objectively, it is a crime, and all the graver because it was committed legally." [8]

American public opinion was somewhat more undecided about Mrs. Finkbine's decision. A Gallup Poll conducted less than a month after her abortion had put this question to a nationwide panel:

---

[6] See: "Mother Loses Her Plea for Immunity Against Prosecution in Arizona," *New York Times*, July 31, 1962 (AP) ; "Mother Now Seeking Abortion Out of Arizona, Maybe Abroad," *New York Times*, August 1, 1962 (AP) ; "Britain Bars Payment," *New York Times*, July 31, 1962 ; Marjorie Hunter, "1,229 U.S. Doctors Got Thalidomide," *New York Times*, July 31, 1962 ; Werner Wiskari, "Mother Awaits Swedish Verdict," *New York Times*, August 13, 1962 ; "Drug is Defended by German Manufacturers," *New York Times*, August 4, 1962.

[7] "Vatican Decries Abortion," *New York Times*, August 4, 1962 (AP).

[8] "Vatican Sees 'Crime' in Finkbine Abortion," *New York Times*, August 20, 1962.

As you may have heard or read, an Arizona women recently had a legal abortion in Sweden after having taken the drug thalidomide, which has been linked to birth defects. Do you think this woman did the right thing or the wrong thing in having this abortion operation?

More than half the sample thought that Mrs. Finkbine had done the right thing. Thirty-two percent thought her wrong, while 16. percent either had no opinion or would offer none. Protestants outnumbered Catholics considerably in condoning the abortion—by 56 percent to 33 percent. Men and women were about evenly divided— 50 percent of the women and 54 percent of the men declaring that Mrs. Finkbine had done the right thing.[9] American public opinion, at least in terms of this specific case, seemed rather evenly divided, and in one sense this balance could be regarded as a presage for legislative action: there were votes to be had by advocacy of a view favored by so many constituents. On the other hand, there remained the tradition of inertia in American politics to be overcome: it would not do to make enemies gratuitously. The public opinion poll had not indicated any intensity of feeling among the respondents, and it could well have been that the opponents felt very strongly about the matter, while those in favor were relatively lukewarm. For another thing, it is a legislative axiom that moral issues are better left dormant, absent a heavy groundswell of reform sentiment. In regard to abortion, the absence of such a groundswell was obvious in 1962.

Nine years later—by 1971—the abortion situation in the United States had changed almost unbelievably. A dozen States had liberalized their abortion laws and two States—Hawaii and New York— had inaugurated programs under which women could have legal abortions on demand if their pregnancy had not gone beyond a certain time. In Maryland, a similar law had been enacted by the legislature, though it was vetoed by the Governor. In addition, a Wisconsin district court had declared that the State's abortion law was unconstitutional in a decision filled with ringing rhetoric: "We hold that a woman's right to refuse to carry an embryo during the early months of pregnancy may not be invaded by the state . . . . When measured against the claimed 'rights' of an embryo of 4 months or less, we hold that the mother's right transcends that of the embryo," the court declared.[10]

---

[9] George Gallup, "Public Gives Its View on the Finkbine Case," *Los Angeles Times*, September 12, 1962.

 [10] *Babbitz v. McCann*, 310 Fed.Supp. 293, 301 (East. Dist. Wisc. 1970).

The implications of these changes are what concern us here. What does the drive toward abortion on demand mean for those persons immediately involved; that is, the pregnant woman and her family? What about the unborn child and its legal rights, and the legal rights of others who might come to be defined as expendable, such as the retarded and the crippled? What about the dangers to the society? Will freer abortion represent an inroad into the governance of the United States under traditional principles of religion and morality which will lead to a decrease in the strength of the society? Will, on the other hand, changes in abortion practices bring forth a society in which children, because they are now desired, will be more cherished? And, if so, what are the implications for a society in which children are cherished?

These are but a number of the questions necessarily involved in determination of public policy on abortion. Answers of varying reliability can be gathered from examination of experience with abortion both in the United States and in foreign jurisdictions. Using such information as undergirding, we may then attempt to generalize about the relationship of abortion practices to a number of items of social importance upon which they bear.

COLORADO'S PIONEERING STATUTE

The first major reform in abortion laws in the United States was enacted in Colorado in 1967, passing both houses of the legislature by a 2 to 1 majority. The new Colorado law allowed abortion for a variety of reasons, including pregnancy which had resulted from rape and incest, cases in which there was suspected deformity, and those in which it was judged that termination of the pregnancy was necessary to protect the life or health of the prospective mother. To obtain an abortion a woman had to receive approval from a committee of doctors in a certified hospital.[11] To the legislators opposing the law, which took effect on April 25, 1967, it seemed destined to make Colorado "the abortion mecca of the world,"[12] a prophecy unfailingly voiced by the opposition in every State that has changed its abortion laws.

Reports by those who sponsored the Colorado law indicate considerable disappointment with the operation of the program. By August 1967, only 45 abortions had been performed, in part undoubtedly because of attitudes such as that expressed by a Denver psychia-

---

[11] Colorado Revised Statutes §40-2-50 (1953). Cf., Luis Kutner, "Due Process of Abortion," *Minnesota Law Review*, 53 (November 1968), pp. 1–28.

[12] "Colorado Assays its Abortion Law," *New York Times*, June 9, 1968.

trist, who noted the criteria he employed to evaluate an application
for an abortion:

> We are being very careful and discriminating . . . . Some
> women who have come to us have gotten pregnant for important
> emotional reasons they're not even aware of. To grant them an
> abortion might do more harm than good.[13]

The arrogance of the psychiatrist's presumed insight and his presumption in second guessing applicants can be taken as epitomizing
the grounds upon which the advocates of "abortion on demand"
refuse in other States to compromise and accept the Colorado approach to legal abortion.

It is now granted that the new Colorado abortion law has made
little indent on the number of criminal abortions, though it is
believed that the law has made the illegal abortionist cut his prices.
A year after the new act had gone into effect, some 289 abortions
had been performed, plus a number of others which came under the
law but were not reported to the authorities. This compared with
37,273 live births for the same period. Statistics for the first 14
months of the legislation showed a total of 338 abortions, 100 of
which had been undertaken for nonresidents of the State, though,
on the advice of the Colorado Medical Society, hospitals were
refusing to accept rape or incest cases from out of State on the
ground that to do so would involve legal judgments that physicians
were not qualified to make. More than half of the cases—195 in
all—and virtually all those of nonresidents, had come under the
"mental health" clause of the new act. Thirty-two abortions had
been performed for medical reasons, 33 on rape victims, 20 on persons who had had German measles. In 56 instances, no official explanation was offered on the official form.[14]

By mid-1969, total disenchantment had set in with the operation
of the Colorado statute. The legislator who had led the fight for its
enactment noted that "abortion reform is a political product purchased in the political marketplace, paid for with political dollars,
and often with political lives." That bit of legislative lore off his
mind, the lawmaker was categoric in his denunciation of the law he
had sponsored: "We have," he said, "replaced one cruel, outmoded

---

[13] Abraham Heller, quoted in Jane E. Brody, "Abortion: Once a Widespread
Problem, Now a Public Debate," *New York Times*, January 8, 1968. Cf., Abraham
Heller and H. G. Whittington, "The Colorado Story: Denver General Hospital
Experience with the Change in the Law on Therapeutic Abortion," *American
Journal of Psychiatry*, 125 (December 1968), pp. 809–816.

[14] Jim Hyatt, "Colorado's Cautious Use of Liberalized Statute May Spur
Similar Laws," *Wall Street Journal*, August 18, 1967.

law with another one." [15] Illegal abortions were believed to still be in the range of 8,000 to 10,000 a year in the State. There had been 768 legal abortions performed in the 2 years following the new act, but only one out of 13 applications for such abortions had been approved. The Colorado law was said to be legally cumbersome, to involve unnecessary medical red tape, and to have pushed the operation beyond the reach of the poor. It had also been found that the staff members at hospitals tended to look down on abortion patients, making them feel uncomfortable, unwanted, and in some way unclean.[16] In its third year of operation the Colorado program showed no improvement. It was estimated that 19 out of 20 persons were being turned down for legal abortions by the committees at the hospitals, and that the average price for a legal abortion had risen to about $500. The total number of legal abortions had increased from 497 in 1968 to 946 in 1969, but this figure hardly made a dent in the illegal rate.[17]

THE CALIFORNIA EXPERIENCE

Passage in 1967 of the Therapeutic Abortion Act made California the second State to change its abortion law drastically. The California action, given the size and prominence of the State, was of outstanding importance in the nationwide drive for abortion reform. The new California law allowed abortions up to the 20th week of pregnancy with the approval of a majority of a hospital board reviewing the application. The protection of the mental health of the woman was the major ground allowed for legal abortion. Requests for abortions following rape or incest had first to be forwarded to the district attorney in the county where the act was alleged to have taken place. If the district attorney vetoed the request only a successful appeal to the State Supreme Court could reverse his decision.[18]

The California law does not allow potential deformity of the child to constitute a basis for legal abortion. Governor Ronald

---

[15] Richard Lamm, quoted in Lynn Lilliston, "Abortion Reform Bill 'Falls Short,' " Los Angeles Times, May 13, 1969.

[16] Richard D. Lyons, "Colorado Abortion Law Assessed," New York Times, December 8, 1969.

[17] Robert D. McFadden, "Flaws in Abortion Reform Found in 8-State Study," New York Times, April 13, 1970.

[18] California Health & Safety Code §§25950–25954 (Deering 1971). See also Brian Pendleton, "The California Therapeutic Abortion Act: An Analysis," Hastings Law Journal, 19 (November 1967), pp. 242–255; Zad Leavy and Alan F. Charles, "California's New Abortion Act: An Analysis and Guide to Medical and Legal Procedure," UCLA Law Review, 15 (November 1967), pp. 1–31.

Reagan, in opposing such a provision, had insisted that "a crippled child has a right to live." The Governor's position reflected in part fierce activity by a Catholic member of the State Board of Medical Examiners who, under the earlier law, sought to keep doctors from aborting women who had contacted rubella (German measles) during their first 3 months of pregnancy. Nationwide estimates are that of some 82,000 women with such a condition during the 1963–65 period, some 15,000 gave birth to deformed children. In California, women who had the measles told hospital abortion review boards that they would kill themselves rather than go through with the births. On this basis, arguing that the operation was to save the life of the mother, some boards had given permission for legal abortions. This had resulted in action against nine doctors by the State Board, and reprimands to eight of these. The appellate court had reversed the verdict against one of the eight who had appealed the administrative rebuke. Then the subject became moot with passage of the new abortion law.[19]

Omission of potential physical deformity as a ground for legal abortion was regarded by some as a "tragic" decision. Dr. Edward Overstreet of the University of California Medical Center in San Francisco thought the omission particularly unfortunate because diagnostic techniques had now reached a point where doctors were able to determine with considerable accuracy the likelihood of birth defects. "It is now possible," Overstreet noted, "by means of trans-abdominal puncture and a sampling of amniotic fluid before the 16th week of pregnancy to determine the presence of severe metabolic diseases in the intrauterine infant." [20]

Criticisms of the California abortion law during its initial years in operation echoed those leveled against the new Colorado statute. Hospitals were differentially permitting access to their facilities, and almost invariably favoring persons of means as opposed to those less affluent. Nor were the provisions of the act being interpreted similarly in the different parts of the State. Fifty percent of the legal abortions were being performed in the San Francisco area, for instance, though only 16 percent of the State's live births occurred there. In Los Angeles, on the contrary, there were 23 percent of the abortions, though the area recorded 60 percent of the State's live births.[21]

---

[19] Keith Monroe, "How California's Abortion Law Isn't Working," *New York Times Magazine*, December 29, 1968, pp. 10–11, 17–20.

[20] Lynn Lilliston, "Victorian Hangover Seen in Attitudes on Abortion," *Los Angeles Times*, May 14, 1969.

[21] "Abortion Experts, Saying Women Should Decide on Birth, Ask End to Curbs," *Los Angeles Times*, November 24, 1968.

Flagrant cases of rejection of applications for legal abortion also began to be noted. A couple with two idiot children had applied for an abortion and been denied; later, their third child, also severely mentally defective, was born. A raped woman's application was vetoed by a district attorney who insisted that the father could have been her own husband. All told, there were 2,035 legal abortions during the first half of 1968, after the law had received a brief shakedown period, a figure nowhere near the estimated total of 100,000 illegal abortions.[22] Eighty percent of these—91 percent in regard to white women—were granted on the ground of a mental health danger inherent in the pregnancy.[23] But each day seven to ten women were being received at the Los Angeles County Hospital suffering from attempts at self-abortion with coat hangers, knitting needles, and gasoline. Fees for legal abortions were running from $600 to $800, and there was a reported instance of a 15-year-old girl being charged $1,800. Hospitals worked carefully to stay within self-adopted abortion "quotas" in order to avoid the possibility of being defined as "abortion mills." [24]

In 1968, the first full year the new law had been in effect there were a total of 5,030 abortions under its provisions. This figure rose to 15,339 during the following year and had increased to 62,000 in 1970.[25]

Estimates of the impact of the new California law were uniformly deprecatory. It was noted, for one thing, that there continued to be approximately 80,000 illegal abortions in the State.[26] In part, such illicit operations were the clear consequence of tight interpretations given to the conditions under which legal abortions would be performed. In November 1970, for instance, the California Court of Appeals ruled that unmarried pregnant girls under the age of 21 could not obtain therapeutic abortions without parental consent if they were still under parental control. In Los Angeles, officials at two hospitals estimated that they were seeing about ten such cases each week, and the head of Harbor General Hospital told the court that it was his opinion that "many of these girls have and will in the future turn to self-induced or unprofessionally performed criminal abortion outside of the hospital." [27]

[22] Monroe, *op. cit.*, n. 19, p. 10.

[23] Lynn Lilliston, "Aspects of Abortion Law Cited at Seminar," *Los Angeles Times*, May 30, 1968.

[24] Monroe, *op. cit.*, n. 19, p. 19.

[25] "1970 State Abortions Hit 62,000," *Los Angeles Times*, July 23, 1971 (UPI).

[26] McFadden, *op. cit.*, n. 17.

[27] Gene Blake, "Court Tightens Abortion Rules for Unwed Girls," *Los Angeles Times*, October 26, 1970. The ruling was reversed by *Ballard v. Anderson*, 484 Pac.2d 1345 (1971).

On the other hand, there was some good news in regard to what might have been the number of illegal abortions in California or, perhaps, the manner in which they were now being performed. In September 1970, a University of California medical school professor reported to the convention of the American Academy of General Practice that the statewide death rate attributable to abortions had dropped from eight per 100,000 in 1967 to three per 100,000 in 1968.[28]

It was obvious, however, that the new law had done little to remove the onus upon a woman to become a supplicant pleading for a favor from medical authorities. One woman, for instance, deplored the necessity for psychiatric approval of her request for a legal abortion: "I feel I don't have to be declared nutty to make up for the fact that my diaphragm didn't work," she noted. Instead, she went to Mexico City for an abortion, saying that she would not go through the "humiliating experience" inflicted upon women in California.[29] In all, the verdict on the early phases of the operation of the new California statute tended to find it unsatisfactory.

> The reasons for the persistence of illegal abortions are not difficult to locate. Legal abortions are still rare because they cost so much, because of the ambiguities in the law, because of the legal and organizational and financial pressures from those opposed to any kind of liberalized abortion practices.[30]

NEW YORK: ABORTION ON DEMAND

Colorado's liberalization of its abortion law signaled the first breakthrough in the United States against aged statutes on the subject. The California reform represented the movement of a heavily populated State into the then thin ranks of jurisdictions which have revised their abortion laws. The immediate effect of the California reform was more symbolic than meaningful in regard to fundamental matters such as the number of illegal abortions taking place. The drive in New York State, culminating in the enactment of a statute which allowed abortion as a matter to be determined between the physician and his patient,[31] represented by far the most significant assault on traditional abortion law in the history of the country. How abortion on demand came about in New York merits documentation because it focuses on many of the funda-

---

[28] Gary Stewart, quoted in "Deaths from Abortions," *Los Angeles Times*, September 30, 1970.

[29] "Abortion and the Changing Law," *Newsweek*, April 13, 1970, p. 56.

[30] Monroe, *op. cit.*, n. 19, p. 18.

[31] New York Penal Law §125.05 (McKinney 1971).

mental arguments employed for and against such reform. What has happened subsequently in New York is noteworthy because it foretells the probable consequences of similar legislation, if enacted elsewhere.

The original abortion statute in New York had gone into effect in 1830, and it took 139 years—until 1969—for the first significant attack to be made on it. The 1969 reform bill, however, did not progress beyond the State Assembly, where it was introduced, largely because of a passionate last-minute appeal by a legislator who movingly told of his own polio deformity when he was 13-months old. He insisted that children who might be born with handicaps similar to his deserved the right to live.[32]

Paradoxically, this same legislator had altered his position by the following year on the ground that his constituents had persuaded him of their support for changes in the law. The 1970 bill was sponsored, interestingly enough, by a woman Catholic (rather than a male Jew, as had been the case in 1969). She insisted that a distinction had to be made between the proper place of law and the true role of religion in regard to abortion:

> I think we must once and for all realize that the law is not the end-all of our ethical behavior. I think the purpose of the law must be to resolve social differences, to preserve the society, to strike the balance. It must not be a substitute for a moral code or individual ethics.[33]

It was suggested that the Catholic Church, the most intense foe of reform, actually was more opposed to amendments to the statute which followed the line taken in Colorado and California than it was to total abandonment by the State of its involvement with abortion. "Repeal is a more acceptable idea to Catholics than reform," one legislator noted, "because it takes the State out of the position of deciding who shall be born and who shall not." [34] There was further argument that the movement of the courts into the abortion issue would result in judge-dictated policies rather than those which might better be achieved through legislative debate and action. In California, the law in force prior to the reform enactment—a law similar to that in New York—had recently been struck down by an appellate court on the ground that it was "too vague for a physician to under-

---

[32] William E. Farrell, "Opponents of Abortion Law Gather Strength in Legislature," *New York Times*, January 26, 1970.

[33] Virginia Spring, "Miss Krupsak Backs Abortion Repeal," *Albany (N.Y.) Times-Union*, February 18, 1970.

[34] Jane E. Brody, "States Are Planning for Repeal of Abortion Law," *New York Times*, March 12, 1970.

stand clearly." Specifically, the court held that the California statute had violated "the fundamental right of a woman to choose whether to bear children" and her "right to life," a right which was placed in jeopardy "because childbirth involves the risks of death." [35]

The proposed New York legislation would permit abortion on demand up to the 24th week of pregnancy. Opponents of the measure insisted that it threatened the total fabric of the society. "If this bill passes, our society will be filled with childless families and society as we know it will perish and succumb," one legislator insisted.[36] Dispute often rose to an intense pitch. As the vote approached, demonstrators paraded outside the State Capitol. Opponents chanted, "Down with Murder," while proponents countered with, "Down with Bigots." Included among the bill's opponents was a mother of seven children, one of whom had been born defective. "I had a birth defective baby," the mother told newspaper reporters. "She is moderately hard of hearing, but God help me if I had ever killed her because of my German measles." [37] During the height of the legislative debate an elderly woman in the gallery had to be quieted by police, according to the newspapers:

> "Murderers," she called out, her thin voice quivering in the still chamber. "You are murderers, that's what you are. God will punish you. You are murderers." [38]

In the final moments before the vote, the majority leader, tears welling in his eyes, read from what pretended to be the diary of an unborn child. For December 28, the "diary" noted: "Today, my parents killed me . . . ." The majority leader, too moved, could go no further.[39]

Passage of the reform measure was achieved in a suitably dramatic manner. The final vote resulted in a tie, and it was well known that the Speaker would cast his ballot against the bill. Then an upstate legislator, a 55-year-old Jewish attorney, got the floor and reversed his vote. "I realize, Mr. Speaker," he declared, "that I am terminating my political career, but I cannot in good conscience sit here and allow my vote to be the one that defeats this bill. I ask that my

[35] *People v. Belous*, 458 Pac.2d 194, 199 (Calif. 1969).

[36] Bill Kovach, "Abortion Reform Has Only a Fighting Chance," *New York Times*, March 22, 1970.

[37] Nancy Hartnagel, "Abortion Outstorms Clouds," *Knickerbocker* (*N.Y.*) *Union Star*, March 24, 1970.

[38] Bill Kovach, "Abortion Reform is Voted by Assembly, 76 to 73," *New York Times*, April 10, 1970.

[39] Howard Clark, "Abortion Reform Passes Senate by Vote of 31 to 26," *Schenectady* (*N.Y.*) *Gazette*, April 11, 1970 (AP).

vote be changed from 'no' to 'yes.' "[40] The legislator later told reporters that he had switched position to keep "peace in my family," and that his son, a rabbi, had called him a political "whore" for opposing abortion reform.[41] The legislator proved an apt political prognosticator. A few months later he was denied renomination in his heavily Catholic constituency.

In signing the bill, the Governor offered some opinions on the forces that had brought it to fruition. "Women's liberation played an important part," he suggested. The Governor also thought that a powerful force behind the measure had been the wives of legislators.[42] Other persons suggested that events such as rising welfare costs and growing illegitimacy rates had led to passage of the abortion measure, as had increased concern in the United States with child abuse and child neglect.[43]

I have also been told the following by a person who is conversant with the legislative details of the 1971 New York bill, and who wishes to remain anonymous: ". . . one reason why the *repeal* bill was let out of committee and onto the legislative floor was that our opponents thought that seeing that *reform* had been defeated in the previous session, so far-out a measure as outright repeal wouldn't stand a ghost of a chance. At that point they had lost the battle but they didn't know it because we kept some of our voting strength secret, and they were disarmed and taken unaware."

The New York "abortion on demand" measure became law on July 1, 1970. The experiences of New York with the law as time passes will undoubtedly play a very large role in dictating the direction that the remainder of the Nation will take in regard to abortion. For one thing, New York City, where most abortions will occur, is the national headquarters of the mass media—the radio and television networks, the news magazines, and the wire services—so that events there are inevitably better attended to than they are elsewhere in the country. The ability of New York to handle the new statute with comparatively little friction could encourage other jurisdictions; its failure to do so without intense controversy, or

---

[40] Kovach, *op. cit.*, n. 38.

[41] Francis X. Clines, "Pressures on Assemblymen Over Abortion Measure Were Personal and Powerful," *New York Times*, April 11, 1970. Cf., Clayton Knowles, "Man Whose Vote Passed Abortion Law Honored," *New York Times*, May 3, 1971.

[42] Bill Kovach, "Governor Signs Law on Abortion," *New York Times*, April 12, 1970.

[43] Jane E. Brody, "Abortion Laws Gaining Favor as New Statutes Spur Debate," *New York Times*, November 22, 1970.

with dire results, would warn off those States contemplating changes in their statutes.

To date, the New York law cannot be said to have brought about thoroughgoing changes in patterns of abortion. Extrapolations from available figures indicate that by the middle of 1971, the first year of the law's operation, 115,000 legal abortions will have been performed in the State. This figure, however, remains inexact because many physicians have not been filing the legally required fetal death certificates with the authorities. Estimates are that about 40 percent of the legal abortions have been done on women from outside of New York State.[44] All told, the 115,000 legal abortions in New York should constitute more than half of the Nation's total of such operations in 1971. The national total—about 250,000 predicted for 1971—compares with 18,000 legal abortions just 3 years earlier.

It seems likely that a large number of the abortions in New York have been performed to date on women who would not otherwise have terminated their pregnancy. The abortion law has put a new and subtle pressure upon relatively affluent women who unexpectedly become pregnant to justify why they should have this child, and many such women who would have borne the child now are undergoing legal abortions.[45] Hospital data support this supposition with figures showing that the number of lower-class patients appearing with sequelae from poorly performed illegal abortions has not declined significantly since implementation of the new law in New York.

Techniques for legal abortion were also becoming more refined with practice. "D and C," dilation of the cervix and curettage (scraping) of the interior of the uterus, remained the preferred method to end pregnancies of under 12 weeks' duration.[46] A newer method, widely used in Japan and Europe, is vacuum aspiration or suction. In it, the uterus is emptied by suction through a tube only one-quarter inch in diameter.[47] After the 12th week of pregnancy, the most common abortion method in New York is "salting-out" or saline injection, in which amniotic fluid is withdrawn and replaced by about half a pint of highly saline water which kills the fetus and induces labor in 12 to 36 hours. The method is subject to about

---

[44] "New York Predicts 115,000 Abortions," *Los Angeles Times*, December 18, 1970.

[45] Linda Nessel, "Legal Abortions: A Progress Report," *New York*, 3 (September 28, 1970), p. 64.

[46] Lawrence Lader, "The Scandal of Abortion Laws," *New York Times Magazine*, April 25, 1965, p. 32.

[47] *Newsweek, op. cit.*, n. 29, p. 55.

10 percent failure to produce abortion, and most doctors will not employ it until past the 16th week of pregnancy, when there is adequate amniotic fluid. Thus, between the 12th and 16th week of pregnancy, an abortion was proving difficult to secure in New York.[48]

With the methods in use for legal abortion, the death rate was running at 3.8 per 10,000 abortions, slightly higher than the maternal death rate of 3.2 per 10,000 births. The ratio of abortions to live births was far below the parity level found in some foreign jurisdictions. In New York, it was calculated at 198 abortions for each 1,000 live births.[49]

The most intense controversy with the New York law to date centers about the use of private offices and special clinics for abortions. In October 1970, New York City restricted the practice of abortion to well-equipped hospitals and affiliated clinics. For an affiliate to be licensed, it had to be possible to get a patient to a hospital within ten minutes. Thus, for the moment, legal abortions were being concentrated in hospital settings with the predicted result that there were "endless delays, high costs, complicated procedures, and gratuitous trauma." The last item included the reported practice of one hospital of insisting that an aborted woman look at the fetus before it was destroyed and of another of placing aborted women in maternity wards, forcing them thus to view the excitement and pleasure of new mothers with their infants.[50] As one observer put the matter: "The specter of abortion as an illegal, dirty, immoral practice and the notion that 'those who play must pay' dies hard." [51] Doctors, too, often found that performing abortions downgraded their standing with their colleagues, who tended to regard them as not much better than "back-street butchers."

The difficulties with the new law were underlined by the story of a 17-year-old girl from a small midwestern town whose experiences while attempting to secure an abortion in New York City were detailed by a reporter from the *New York Times*. After going from hospital to hospital in the City, and making some 37 futile out-of-town calls in the effort to locate a cooperative physician, the girl finally was aborted for $375 by a Brooklyn obstetrician recommended by a family planning agency:

[48] Lael Scott, "Legal Abortion, Ready or Not," *New York*, 3 (May 25, 1970), p. 70.

[49] *Los Angeles Times, op. cit.*, n. 44.

[50] Nessel, *op. cit.*, n. 45, p. 58.

[51] Jane E. Brody, "Problems Reduce Effect of Eased Abortion Law," *New York Times*, June 8, 1970.

At 9 a.m. Tuesday, Carol was admitted to the maternity
floor of a small, old hospital in Brooklyn's East New York section. She was already in her nightgown in her hospital bed, two
doors from a nursery full of newborn babies, when the administration decided that Carol's telegram of consent from her father
was insufficient. Carol could stay in the hospital, but the procedure could not be done until they received a letter with her
father's notarized signature.

Another call to her father. "I just want to get it over with
and go home," she said over and over again.

At 10 a.m. Wednesday, the special delivery letter arrived
and a few minutes later the doctor injected the salt solution.
Then there was nothing to do but wait until labor started.
Finally, at 10 p.m. Thursday the cramps began. All night Carol
paced the floor, did situps and jumped up and down with her
labor. At 8 a.m. the next morning she expelled the fetus. Two
and a half hours later, the doctor assisted in removing the
placenta, which she had retained.

When it was over, Carol was exhausted and running a high
fever. In her almost delirious state, she muttered that she never
wanted "anything like it to happen again."

Carol was discharged from the hospital on Saturday morning
with a prescription for antibiotics to control the low-grade fever
she was still running. Seven hours later she was headed home by
plane.

Throughout her experience Carol had said little of how she
felt except for her periodic lament about getting it over with
and going home. But her face spoke what her lips failed to
utter. She left New York 9 days after she had arrived and her
once babyish face seemed to have aged a year for every day
she had been here.[52]

To date, the general story of the experience in New York with
legal abortion does not deviate far from the generalizations that
could be made from Carol's case. It has been summed up in the
judgment that "many women—especially the poor, poorly educated,
timid, embarrassed, frightened, and unaggressive—are finding hospital abortions impossible to obtain." [53]

Nonetheless, it needs to be emphasized that commentators on the
operation of the new New York law tend to concentrate on its fail-
ings—these are the things that make news—and to bypass the idea
that the big story could be that the very existence of the law will
dictate that, given sufficient time, it will be made to work in the
manner that its supporters want it to work. Such a conclusion should

[52] Jane E. Brody, "At 17, the Road to Abortion is Lonely," *New York Times*,
October 18, 1970.

[53] Jane E. Brody, "New Abortion Laws Take Effect," *New York Times*, October 20, 1970.

not, however, be taken as foregone: the changes in educational practices in the United States since 1954, when racial desegregation was
declared the law of the land, indicate no necessary congruity between
legal pronouncement and consequent events, when other strong forces
are at work.

ELSEWHERE IN THE UNITED STATES

The experiences of Colorado, California, and New York, detailed
above, summarize similar kinds of activities taking place in regard
to abortion in other parts of the United States. The New York
legislative enactment of "abortion on demand" has been duplicated
in two other States—Hawaii and Alaska. In Alaska, the measure
became law only after the legislature was able to override the Governor's veto.[54] The Hawaiian law limits eligibility for legal abortion
to persons who have lived in the State at least 90 days. Among its
advocates was the editorial writer for the *Honolulu Star-Bulletin*
who welcomed the measure with the perhaps wishful observation:
"Next year's crop of youngsters in Hawaii will have something
wonderful in common. They will be wanted children." [55]

The State of Washington became the fourth "abortion on demand"
jurisdiction when the electorate approved a new statute in the 1970
general election with a 55.5 percent affirmative vote. Washington,
like Hawaii, required a 90-day period of residence. Legal abortion
is permitted up to the 16th week of pregnancy, and it requires
the consent of parents if the girl is unmarried and under 18, and
the consent of her husband, if she is living with him.[56]

In addition, 11 other States have changed their abortion laws
to follow the same lines as the reforms adopted in Colorado and
California. Early reports indicate that essentially the same objections noted in those States apply to the others. The first year of the
new Georgia law, for instance, saw a legal abortion rate of 1.3 per
1,000 live births, a figure which remained below the national average
of 2.0 per 1,000. There were only 113 abortions in Georgia under
the new law, and, of these, only 10 percent involved blacks, though

---

[54] Alaska Statutes §11.15.060 (1970). See also "Liberalized Abortion Voted in
Alaska," *New York Times*, April 19, 1970 (AP) ; "Abortion Reform Veto Over-
ridden in Alaska," *New York Times*, May 1, 1970 (AP).

[55] Hawaii Revised Statutes §453–16 (1971). Quoted in Herbert A. Probasco,
"Hawaii Abortions, Portend for N.Y.?", *Knickerbocker* (*N.Y.*) *News-Union-Star*,
March 14, 1970.

[56] Washington Revised Code §9.02.060 (1971). Cf., Randy L. St. Mary and
Patrick B. Cerutti, "Washington Abortion Reform," *Gonzaga Law Review*, 5
(Spring 1970), pp. 278–288.

blacks account for one-third of the population of Georgia.[57] It was estimated that were all States to follow the Colorado-California approach, only 15 percent of the abortions now performed illegally could be brought under the new laws. There was the further reservation, expressed by the Committee on Psychiatry and Law of the Group for the Advancement of Psychiatry, that stress on the detrimental mental effect of possible birth would lead pregnant women seeking legal abortion "either . . . to malinger . . . or to emphasize psychiatric symptoms." [58]

In addition to the alterations of State laws, there have been assaults against existing abortion arrangements by various appellate courts, which tended to follow the line of reasoning of the California court described earlier. The District of Columbia, for instance, had been operating under a unique statute which placed the burden of proof upon a physician to show that an abortion he performed was justified, adding unusual legal risk to his position. In November 1969, Judge Gerhard A. Gessell, son of the famed pediatrician, Arnold Gessell, ruled that the District law was so vague and indefinite in regard to its reference to protecting the prospective mother's health as to be unconstitutional. The District of Columbia law was also judged to be an unreasonable infringement on the private right of a woman in the realm of sex and motherhood. In Judge Gessell's words:

> A woman's liberty and right of privacy extends to family, marriage, and sex matters, and may well include the right to remove an unwanted child at least in the early stages of pregnancy.[59]

Judge Gessell's ruling, currently under appeal, left the District of Columbia without a law to regulate abortions.

A similar fate overtook the Wisconsin abortion statute in March 1970. "The state does not have a compelling interest . . . to require a woman to remain pregnant during the early months following her conception," a three-judge Federal panel declared. Wisconsin authorities, located in a State which is 38 percent Catholic, with its largest city, Milwaukee, having a two-to-one Catholic majority, planned to appeal the decision on their abortion statute to the United States Supreme Court.[60]

---

[57] Brody, op. cit., n. 51.
[58] Group for the Advancement of Psychiatry, Committee on Psychiatry and Law, The Right to Abortion: A Psychiatric View (1969), p. 217.
[59] United States v. Vuitch, 305 Fed.Supp. 1032, 1035 (D.C. Dist. 1970).
[60] Babbitz v. McCann, op. cit., n. 10, pp. 301–302.

ABORTION IN FOREIGN COUNTRIES

There has been a long experience with a range of abortion practices in various foreign countries which provides material against which the possible impact of diverse American arrangements might be examined. Such material, of course, must always be looked at with caution, because the practices are occurring in areas with historical traditions and cultural arrangements that are different than those of the United States. To insist categorically, for example, that policemen in the United States ought to abandon carrying guns because such a policy has been associated with diminished violence in Britain, or that the United States ought to move to the controlled clinic method in dealing with narcotics now used in Britain is to ignore a variety of impinging forces that might produce boomerang effects in the wake of the proposed innovations.

On the other hand, to ignore foreign experience is to encourage provincialism. It has been said that a great advantage of allowing States in the United States to implement diverse approaches to social problems is that each jurisdiction then becomes an experimental laboratory, and each can learn from the others. The same observation is clearly in order in regard to foreign countries.

Great Britain

The United States, having taken its law from Britain and sharing a common language with the British, is apt to look first to conditions in the British Isles for possible clues for resolution of social dilemmas. Earlier it was noted, for instance, that the report of the Wolfenden Committee in Britain provided much intellectual underpinning for advocates of legalization of consensual adult homosexuality.

Historically, the traditional approach to abortion in the United States derives from England. In medieval times, abortion on demand was permitted in England until the occasion of fetal "quickening," that is, until late in the fourth or early in the fifth month of pregnancy. In 1803, with the passage of Lord Ellenborough's act, all abortion except that designed to protect the life of the prospective mother was declared criminal. In theory, thereafter the abortion penalties in Britain were among the severest in the world, calling for possible life imprisonment. In fact, however, abortion was rarely prosecuted because authorities did not want to deter women from seeking post-abortion medical assistance.[61]

[61] Miscarriage of Woman Act, 43 Geo. 3, c. 58 (1803). Cf., Glanville Williams, *The Sanctity of Life and the Criminal Law* (New York: Knopf, 1957), pp. 152–156.

In the 1930's, a judicial ruling changed the focus of the British abortion statute dramatically. Alec Bourne, a medical doctor, had performed an abortion on a young girl who had been raped by a group of soldiers, and then submitted himself for criminal prosecution. The jury would not convict Bourne, and the judge went so far as to declare that if a doctor refused to perform an abortion in order to save a woman's life, he would be in "grave peril of a charge of manslaughter by negligence." The same decision by statutory interpretation provided a broad definition of "life." If a medical practitioner were of the opinion, on reasonable grounds, that the probable consequences of continuance of a pregnancy were that the woman would be rendered a physical or mental wreck, the judge noted in the *Bourne* case, "then the jury are quite entitled to take the view that the doctor who, under those circumstances and in that honest belief, operates, is operating for the purpose of preserving the life of the mother." [62]

Immediate impetus for abortion reform in Britain, as in the United States, seemed to be triggered by the thalidomide crisis. At the time, the Lord Chancellor told the House of Lords that possible deformity was not adequate legal ground for abortion.[63] There were then an estimated 100,000 illegal abortions occurring in Britain. Thereafter, the mood of the public on the issue of legalized abortion began to shift significantly. In March 1965, a National Opinion Poll reported a 36 percent favorable response to the question: "Would you favor abortion if a mother has so large a family that another child might cause financial difficulties and financial stress?" Two years later, the affirmative response had grown to 65 percent of the respondents.[64]

The Abortion Act had been introduced into Parliament in mid-1966 and a year and a quarter later it gained approval of both Houses, with a March 1968 effective date. The bill provided for legal termination of pregnancy if two registered doctors concluded that continuance of the pregnancy would involve risk to the life of the pregnant woman, or injury to her physical or mental health or to any existing children in the family, provided that the risk of continued pregnancy was greater than the risk of termination. Abortion was also permissible if there was "substantial risk" that

[62] *Rex v. Bourne*, 3 All Eng. R. 615 (1938).

[63] "British Reaffirm Curb on Abortion," *New York Times*, July 20, 1962.

[64] Gloria Emerson, "Bill Liberalizing 1861 Law on Abortion Advances in Britain," *New York Times*, March 14, 1961.

the child would be "seriously handicapped" by physical or mental abnormalities.[65]

The bill made no mention of rape as a ground for legal abortion because it was believed that medical doctors would not adequately be able to interpret the legal concept of rape, or to decide whether the pregnancy had resulted from rape or from other sexual intercourse. There was also a belief that cases of rape could be included under other categories.[66] The most controversial clause in the act, obviously, was the so-called "social clause," allowing abortion when the birth of an additional child would endanger the well-being of an existing child.

Summarizing the early history of the English law, one commentator noted that "the gateway to legal abortion is now so wide that it may be supposed that some doctors will always be able to convince themselves that the risks of pregnancy are greater than those of abortion where, at any rate, the patient demands abortion insistently enough." [67]

Actually, use of the "social clause" was not as prominent as recourse to the "mental health" clause of the abortion law, though allegation of one or another ground is likely little more than a semantic preference. During 1969, the law saw 54,158 legal abortions, with 75 percent taking place under the National Health Insurance Act in Government centers, where the cost to the patient was $60. The total rose to 83,849 in the second full year of the law's operation and to 126,774 in 1971.[68] Rich patients were tending to use private practitioners, who charged about $500 for an abortion. Makeship quarters had also sprung up to cater to abortion demands, leading to Parliamentary outcries of "financial racketeering" because of overcharges to foreign women, in particular, who accounted for about 20 percent of the total number of legal abortions.[69]

A major complaint against the new law concerned the erratic nature of abortion practices throughout the country. In Newcastle, for instance, the legal abortion rate was 237 per 1 million popula-

[65] The Abortion Act, 1967 (1967, c. 87), Halsbury, 3d ed., Vol. VIII, pp. 682-683.

[66] House of Commons Debates, Vol. 749, col. 1161 (1967).

[67] A. J. C. Hoggett, "The Abortion Act," (1967), *Criminal Law Review*, (May 1968), p. 257.

[68] "126,774 Abortions Reported by British," *Los Angeles Times*, January 25, 1972 (Reuter's).

[69] Gloria Emerson, "British Debate Still Rages Year After Passage of Abortion Law," *New York Times*, May 8, 1969; Philip Evans, "£300,000 For Abortion Doctors," *Daily Telegraph* (London), July 5, 1969.

tion, compared to 84 per 1 million in Sheffield. In Birmingham and Liverpool, abortions were difficult to secure because of the high percentage of Roman Catholic doctors in the two cities. The legislation had included a "conscience clause" which protected from liability any doctor, nurse, or hospital employee who objected to participating in legal abortions.[70]

Despite such problems—the exploitation of clients and the differential implementation of the law—it could be said after the initial year of the British program that "its impact has been greater than its supporters expected and its opponents feared." [71] The 40,000 abortions under the National Health Service compared with 2,580 that had been performed in 1963 and the 7,610 in 1967. It was notable that only 7 percent of all legal abortions following the law reform were performed solely on the fresh grounds permitted. "This suggests," one commentator noted, "that the purely symbolic value of law reform may be very great." [72] Summarizing Britain's early experience, *The Lancet*, the country's leading medical journal, entered the following observation:

> Things were certainly easier for the gynecologists before the public and Parliament made their wishes known in the Act—but they were much harder for women.[73]

Japan

Since the passage in 1948 of the Eugenic Protection Law, abortion can be had on demand in Japan and is permitted up to the 8th month of pregnancy.[74] Exact estimates of the number of abortions in Japan are hard to come by, however. For one thing, if a doctor does not register an abortion with the proper authorities, he can avoid payment of income tax on his fee and the patient can escape payment of the "fetus fee" to the mortician, a fee which is usually higher than the medical charge.[75] Demographic experts think that there are about 1.5 million abortions in Japan each year, contrasting with about 1.8 million live births.

An abortion can be had in Japan for about $40. The death rate tends to be quite low—about seven deaths in 100,000 cases, which compares to the 28 per 100,000 mortality rate for childbirth in the

---

[70] Emerson, *ibid.*

[71] Madeline Simms, "The Abortion Act—One Year Later," *British Journal of Criminology*, 9 (July 1969), p. 282.

[72] *Ibid.*

[73] "The First Year of the Abortion Act," *Lancet*, April 26, 1969, p. 867.

[74] Russell Shaw, *Abortion on Trial* (Dayton, Ohio: Pflaum Press, 1968), p. 125.

[75] Kling, *op. cit.*, n. 2, p. 11.

United States. The unpopularity of birth control in Japan—women are said to be timid about purchasing devices—accounts in large measure for the frustration of government efforts to reduce the abortion rate significantly,[76] though it is believed to be declining gradually. In 1955, for instance, estimates placed the abortion total at 1,170,000 cases; [77] in 1970 at 700,000.[78] Japan today has one of the lowest birth rates in the world—18.4 per 100,000 population.

Critics of the Japanese abortion policy tend to concentrate on what they regard as its impact on economic development. Japan suffers from a labor shortage, and the absence of young workers is said to have reduced the possibility of many persons retiring at age 55, the traditional age for ceasing work in Japan. It is also argued that the lack of surplus labor has created an intense drive toward greater efficiency by the labor that is available, with deleterious consequences for the quality of social life in Japan.[79]

Sweden

Abortions have been permitted since 1938 in Sweden on medical, humanitarian, and eugenic grounds. Medical grounds involve possibilities of endangered health. Humanitarian grounds refer to pregnancies of girls below the age of 15, cases of rape and incest, or the mental deficiency of the prospective parent. Eugenic grounds concern the likelihood of inherited mental disease or deficiency. An abortion must take place prior to the 12th week of pregnancy, except in extraordinary cases. The grounds for abortion were extended in 1946 to include the strain of giving birth to and caring for a new child ("anticipated maternal weakness").[80] In about a quarter of the cases in Sweden, sterilization is combined with legal abortion.

Legal abortions stand in a ratio to live births of 5 to 100 in Sweden, with about 40 percent of the applications for legal abortion being rejected.[81] Studies show that when applications for legal abortion are rejected, the woman is likely to bear the child. Illegal

---

[76] Jane Morse, "Japan's Answer to the Population Explosion," *Parade*, March 15, 1970, pp. 18, 20–21.

[77] Emerson Chapin, "Decline in Births Troubles Japan," *New York Times*, February 2, 1964.

[78] Robert D. McFadden, "In 3 Nations with Legal Abortion, Debate Goes On," *New York Times*, April 5, 1970.

[79] Chapin, *op. cit.*, n. 77.

[80] Lars Huldt, "Outcome of Pregnancy When Legal Abortion is Readily Available," *Lancet*, March 2, 1968, pp. 467–468.

[81] Don Neff, "Illegal Baby Surgery Put at 1.2 Million Yearly," *Los Angeles Times*, August 5, 1962.

abortions were obtained by only 12 percent (1948), 3 percent (1957), and 11 percent (1963) of the women turned down for legal termination of their pregnancy.[82] The highest number of legal abortions in Sweden was in 1957 when the total reached 6,328. By 1962, that figure had declined to 2,600 and it has remained at essentially this level since then.[83]

The length of the Swedish experience with legal abortion and the relative smallness and homogeneity of the country have allowed for a number of studies of the impact of the abortion procedures. Among the more interesting is one which sought to determine the consequences upon the children of women whose abortion applications had been rejected. The study found that 21-year-olds whose mothers had unsuccessfully sought to be aborted were in poorer health than members of a control group, had more psychiatric troubles, used alcohol more, married earlier, and had babies earlier. Among the males, there was a greater number of Army rejects. The difficulty of the experimental design used to obtain these results, however, inheres in the fact that rejection for abortion is not a random procedure and the alleged consequences of the rejection may stem from prior conditions rather than from the abortion committee's decision.[84]

Violations of the Swedish procedures for legal abortion testify to the fact that they do not satisfy all persons who wish to take advantage of them. It is estimated that there are about 10,000 illegal abortions each year in Sweden. In 1965, prosecuting authorities took action attempting to cut off the flow of Swedish women going to Poland for abortions. There have also been complaints about the bureaucratic procedures involved in the abortion screening process. An applicant is often required to make many hospital visits, and the authorities may interview friends and relatives before reaching a decision on eligibility. Recently, two girls whose abortion applications had been rejected testified that they had been subjected to "horror propaganda" by officials of the Swedish Medical Board who were determined, the girls said, to have them reverse their decision.[85] Perhaps the clearest portrait of the impact of the Swedish screening system upon women seeking abortions is that by Agnar Mykle in the novel, *The Red Ruby*, where the female protagonist

---

[82] Huldt, *op. cit.*, n. 80, p. 467.

[83] Shaw, *op. cit.*, n. 74, p. 135.

[84] Hans Forssman and Inga Thuwe, "One Hundred and Twenty Children Born After Application for Therapeutic Abortion Refused," *Acta Psychiatrica Scandinavica*, 42 (1966), pp. 71–88.

[85] "Sweden Reviews Abortion Laws," *New York Times*, April 8, 1965 (Reuter's).

agonizes through a series of experiences with the authorities in an unsuccessful attempt to obtain approval for a legal abortion.[86]

The Soviet bloc

Another major repository of abortion experience exists in the communist countries of Europe, which have tried varying approaches to the situation. In the Soviet Union, abortion was made legal in the 1920's, and then outlawed in 1936, except for narrowly defined reasons. In November 1955,. the Soviet Union returned to its more permissive policy.[87] Statistics are not released regarding the number of abortions, so that the impact of these changing policies, a matter that could be of considerable value for informed decisionmaking elsewhere, remains unknown abroad. It was noted, however, that after the 1936 shift the birth rate rose 83 percent in Leningrad and 93 percent in Moscow. Abortions performed for medical reasons are done without charge in Government clinics; otherwise, the cost is 5 rubles ($5.50). Basic reasons offered for recourse to abortion in the Soviet Union are the housing shortage and the extensive employment of women, who make up half of the Government labor force of 70 million persons, and who hold 86 percent of the jobs in the public health field.[88]

Other European communist countries have abortion policies similar to those in the Soviet Union. A report from Czechoslovakia indicates that in 1968 there were 11,434 births and 11,310 abortions in Prague, and a total of 121,132 abortions throughout the country. These abortions are held to be primarily responsible for the 1 percent decline in the Czechoslovakian birth rate since 1960. Ten percent of the applications for abortion in Czechoslovakia are rejected.[89] Of those approved, 52 percent of the abortions are granted because the family maintains that it has enough children, 14.5 percent on health grounds, and 9 percent because of inadequate housing. In 1963, Czechoslovakian authorities tightened up abortion procedures on the ground that the rate was too high. Evidence indicates that the

[86] Agnar Mykle, *The Red Ruby*, trans. by Maurice Michael (New York: Dutton, 1960).

[87] Paul H. Gebhard, Wardell B. Pomeroy, Clyde E. Martin, and Cornelia V. Christenson, *Pregnancy, Birth and Abortion* (New York: Harper, 1958), pp. 215–218.

[88] Theodore Shabad, "Soviet Births Dip to Postwar Low," *New York Times*, June 6, 1963.

[89] "New Abortion Law Cuts Czech Births," *New York Times*, August 7, 1969 (Reuter's).

stricter enforcement was accompanied by a corresponding rise in illegal abortion.[90]

In Hungary, the rate of abortions to live births is reported to be even higher than in Czechoslovakia—eight abortions for each five live births.[91] The death rate in both Hungary and Czechoslovakia from abortions is officially given as 3 per 100,000. In the United States, as noted earlier, term pregnancies result in a death rate of 23 per 100,000.[92]

MEASURING THE IMPACT

A review of historical developments in the United States and abroad indicates unequivocally the direction in which the issue of abortion is moving. There is no question that abortion on demand will have its day. What occurs, however, bears no necessary relationship to what ought to occur, and our task here is to explore the implications both of restrictive abortion policies and those regarded as more liberal. We will look at these issues from the viewpoint of the major parties to the question: First, the prospective mother; second, the unborn child; third, the medical profession; fourth, the churches; and, finally, the society in general.

Women and Abortion

Abortion patterns in the United States under restrictive laws have been most thoroughly investigated by the Kinsey Institute. Its study was based on interviews with 5,293 white, nonprison women, most of whom were in the upper 20 percent in socioeconomic status. The women had had 4,248 conceptions. These resulted in 2,434 live births, 667 spontaneous abortions, and 1,067 abortions, or about one abortion for every two live births. This was regarded as a low estimate, on the assumption that the interviewed group probably underreported.[93] Surveying the Kinsey results and other literatures, Alice Rossi has concluded that it is "highly probable that one in every two or three married women may undergo an illegal abortion during the years between their thirteenth and fiftieth birthdays." [94]

[90] John L. Hess, "Czech Birth Rate Found Unaffected By Rise in Illegal Abortions," *New York Times*, September 4, 1966.

[91] Edelson, *op. cit.*, n. 5.

[92] Linda Greenhouse, "Constitutional Question: Is There a Right to Abortion?", *New York Times Magazine*, January 25, 1970, p. 90.

[93] Gebhard, *op. cit.*, n. 87, pp. 11, 13, 16, 29, 54.

[94] Alice S. Rossi, "Public Views on Abortion," in Alan F. Guttmacher (editor), *The Case for Legalized Abortion* (Berkeley, Calif.: Diablo Press, 1967), p. 27. Cf., Rossi, "Abortion Laws and Their Victims," in John H. Gagnon and William Simon (editors), *The Sexual Scene* (Chicago: Aldine, 1970), pp. 91–106.

Most of the abortions noted in the Kinsey Institute interviews were performed on married women, and about 85 percent were done by physicians. About 20 percent involved unmarried women.[95] Another study of the unmarried group indicates that a large majority had become pregnant in their first or second sexual experience. As one doctor noted, "They aren't promiscuous. Promiscuous girls know how to take care of themselves." [96] Among the married women, two types of explanations for the abortions were offered to the Kinsey interviewers: Those women married a relatively short time desired to delay having children; those married longer believed that their families were large enough. Blacks showed a lower abortion rate than whites, though they reported higher rates of premarital experience. College-educated blacks, however, had abortion experiences similar to those of the white girls. Religious women had much lower abortion rates than women without religious commitments. In this regard, the Kinsey authors noted:

> There are few instances where the power of religion is more dramatically illustrated than here, where it motivates a woman to retain an unwanted pregnancy, despite economic, social, and even medical contraindications, and not only to endure months of discomfort but also to accept the ensuing years of child care.[97]

That abortions were had primarily to limit the ultimate family size was underlined by examination of the records of a doctor who had performed 363 illegal abortions. One hundred and two of the women were single, 189 married, and 81 previously married. The average age was 29, with a range from 13 to 47. One half of the women, including one quarter of those married, had never had a child, and 18 percent admitted that they had gone through one or more previous abortions.[98]

Psychiatric Consequences of Abortion

A fundamental point of debate concerns the consequences to a woman of bearing an unwanted child as measured against the consequences of undergoing an abortion. Most data on this issue is drawn from followup studies of women who have undergone therapeutic

---

[95] Gebhard, op. cit., n. 87, p. 17. Cf., Christoper Tietze, "A Report on a Series of Illegal Abortions Induced By Physicians," in George F. Mair (editor), Studies in Population (Princeton: Princeton University Press, 1949), p. 21.

[96] James MacGregor, "Clergymen Stir Debate By Helping Women End Unwanted Pregnancies," Wall Street Journal, June 23, 1969.

[97] Gebhard, op. cit., n. 87, p. 118.

[98] Tietze, op. cit., n. 95, pp. 21–23.

abortions or have been refused such abortions. It must be kept in mind, however, that this data need not bear in any way on decisions regarding abortion policies. The earlier noted doctrine of John Stuart Mill, for instance, insists that possible harm to a person is not adequate ground for denying him the right to do as he pleases with his body, that only injury to others justifies restricting his options.

One segment of opinion insists that the aftereffects of abortion are more detrimental than the consequences of the birth of a child believed to be undesired, but the evidence brought to bear on this conclusion is largly suppositional. In England, for instance, the Queen's Physician has maintained that "many women" suffer serious psychological consequences following abortion,[99] while a British gynecologist suggests that "it seems likely that, to an unbalanced woman, the stimulus of normal pregnancy is less deleterious than sudden interruption by operation of the normal physiological changes taking place." [100]

There are, on the other side of the question, equally impressionistic observations, these most often voiced by women. An unmarried 34-year-old woman, who had undergone three abortions between 1960 and 1967 insisted to a legislative committee that to have given birth to an illegitimate child "would have been the end of my life." [101]

More firmly based empirical evidence clearly supports the proposition that women are able to adjust rather readily to the termination of unwanted pregnancies by abortion, at least if the abortion is defined as legally acceptable. A British followup study of 120 women recommended for therapeutic abortions between 1961 and 1967 indicated that "only one was known to be emotionally worse," a conclusion the authors believed was "evidence to refute the fear that psychiatric damage is common." They thought that the emotional definitions surrounding the abortion—particularly the hospital ward atmosphere—were notably important. "The patient's temporary guilt and depression may be deepened by criticisms— spoken or implied—from gynecologist or nurse," the researchers observed.[102]

[99] Emerson, op. cit., n. 44.

[100] James Arkle, "Termination of Pregnancy on Psychiatric Grounds," British Medical Journal, March 9, 1957, p. 560.

[101] "Women Testify in Abortion Law Test," New York Times, January 27, 1970.

[102] M. Clark, D. A. Pond, I. Forstner, and R. F. Tredgold, "Sequels of Unwanted Pregnancy: A Follow-Up of Patients Referred for Psychiatric Opinion," Lancet, August 31, 1938, pp. 501–503.

Similarly, another study found that of 128 women given therapeutic abortions all but two were later satisfied with the course they had chosen. "The most striking general impression," the authors note, "was the lack of serious psychological sequelae from this operation." Of the 120 women whose applications were rejected, one-third went elsewhere, an outcome which has led writers on abortion to conclude that "a determined, desperate woman will somehow abort, whether or not she is given legal permission and resources to do so." Others of the women offered their children for adoption. Of the 49 percent who gave birth and kept the children, slightly more than half reported that they were glad that they had done so. Thirty-four percent of these women said that they felt the burden of the extra child. The researchers concluded that bearing an unwanted child, rather than having it aborted, is what can lead to further psychiatric symptoms. Women who have legal abortions, they said, suffer "remarkably little psychiatric disturbance provided the patient herself wanted the operation." [103]

A similar conclusion was reached in an American study which followed 170 patients who had undergone therapeutic abortions between 1963 and 1965. Nine were not contacted because of various followup contraindications. Twenty-nine questionnaires remained undelivered. One hundred and sixteen women—all of whom had been aborted at least 8 months earlier—responded. Only six women failed to answer affirmatively to the question: "Was therapeutic abortion the best answer for you?" One of the six was an unmarried 16-year-old who felt that she might not have gotten pregnant again if she had not been aborted. A second had had her pregnancy terminated because of rubella—she was now trying without success to have a child—and a third would have preferred, she said, to have risked the prospective anguish of birth rather than to have faced the family disapproval that followed her therapeutic abortion. The authors' conclusion was strongly in support of the psychiatric utility of therapeutic abortion:

> When the decision to abort is made, our findings suggest that the treatment is usually therapeutic in the best sense of the word—the patient feels better and, therefore, functions more effectively. [104]

---

[103] C. M. B. Pare and Hermione Raven, "Follow-Up of Patients Referred for Termination of Pregnancy," *Lancet*, March 28, 1970, pp. 635–638.

[104] Kenneth R. Niswander and Robert J. Patterson, "Psychologic Reaction to Therapeutic Abortion, I: Subjective Patient Response," *Obstetrics and Gynecology*, 29 (May 1967), pp. 702–706.

Physical Consequences of Abortion

Statistics regarding the number of illegal abortions in the United States and the physically injurious consequences of such abortions are highly imprecise. The clandestine nature of illegal abortion insists that its occurrence and any untoward consequences of its occurrence be kept as secret as possible.

Estimates on the number of illegal abortions that took place in the United States prior to the new wave of reform legislation generally span a range from 200,000 to 1.2 million. It is known that private doctors often performed routine D & C's for patients known to them, if there was a complaint of undesired pregnancy, sometimes even without the patient's awareness of what was happening. In contrast to the large number of illegal abortions, there were about 8,000 therapeutic abortions in the United States prior to the new laws. That figure represented a decline from 35,000 therapeutic abortions 25 years earlier, a decline believed to be the result of the inauguration of hospital screening committees, which showed more conservative standards than those of individual physicians exercising their lone judgment.[105] Most of the therapeutic abortions were done under the heading of "psychiatric reasons," with the abortion defined as necessary to prevent suicide. In New York City, 80 percent of the therapeutic abortions were performed for this cause, though, as one doctor noted, "You knew that all these women were not suicidal." "These abortions," he believed, "are done to preserve maternal health, not life." [106]

The number of deaths resulting from illegal abortions is usually estimated as between 5,000 and 10,000 annually.[107] One writer, using unidentified source data, maintained that during 1968, 350,000 women were hospitalized in the United States because of botched illegal abortions and that 8,000 of them died.[108] However, Christopher Tietze of the Population Council has insisted that the death figures associated with illegal abortion are highly inflated, and that the actual total seems to be closer to 500 such deaths each year, with a possible maximum of 1,000 deaths.[109] The most reliable individual study comes from the Medical Examiner's Office in New York City, which reported that, prior to the new State law, about 20 women

---

[105] Harriet F. Pilpel and Kenneth P. Norwick, *When Should Abortion Be Legal?* (Public Affairs Pamphlet No. 429, January 1969), pp. 11–12.

[106] Brody, *op. cit.*, n. 13.

[107] Neff, *op. cit.*, n. 81; Kling, *op. cit.*, n. 2, p. 4.

[108] MacGregor, *op. cit.*, n. 96.

[109] "Doctor Labels Abortion Deaths Estimate 'Nonsense,' " *Indianapolis Star*, September 7, 1967 (UPI).

died each year from the consequences of abortions performed outside hospital settings. This was the largest single cause of maternal death in the City.[110] New York, however, given its economic and ethnic mix and its other metropolitan characteristics, cannot reliably be used as a base for extrapolation to obtain a national estimate of the death rate from illegal abortions. It is notable, however, that in New York abortion deaths struck minority group women much more often than other women. Illegal abortions accounted for nearly half of the pregnancy and childbirth fatalities among black women, 56 percent of those of Puerto Rican women, and only 25 percent of the fatalities of white women.[111]

The evidence seems clear that abortion, performed with the kind of medical care possible under a legally sanctioned system, would reduce injuries and cut the death rate. The statistics available from foreign countries indicate that abortions can be performed with death rates lower than those resulting from childbirth. It is on such grounds that one advocate of more permissive abortion laws has based his argument:

> Since it is obvious the primary goal of the law today is to prevent death or injury to the mother, is society indeed protecting the mother's welfare by maintaining harsh and unyielding laws that drive her to the unskilled criminal abortionist?
> Is there not a lesson to be learned from the prohibition era when the indirect evils of the law far exceeded the evil at which the law was directed?[112]

Doctors and Abortion

The medical profession is generally regarded as among the more conservative forces in the society. For one thing, doctors enjoy high incomes, and persons with high incomes are wont to see things remain much as they are. For another, doctors are committed to the preservation of life and well-being and, in subtle ways, such a commitment often tends to involve arrogation to oneself of decision-making powers about what is right for other people, with the employment of such powers being defined as a matter of paternal benevolence, done for someone else's own good.

In 1871, the American Medical Association made its first pronouncement on abortion: "That it be the duty of every physician in the United States to resort to every honorable and legal means in

---

[110] "Mayor Endorses Abortion Appeal," *New York Times*, November 4, 1970.
[111] *Newsweek, op. cit.*, n. 29, p. 54.
[112] Jerome M. Kummer, quoted in Robert Goldenstein, "Easing of Therapeutic Abortion Laws Urged," *Los Angeles Times*, January 9, 1966 (AP).

his power to rid society of this practice." [113] Over the years, this
attitude has been reinforced by the sanctions of the criminal codes.
In recent times its essence was reflected in the practices of hospital
medical review committees which tended to oppose vigorously the
relaxation of rules under which therapeutic abortions were granted.
An examination of the data on abortions done where the approval
of a hospital committee was required concluded: "There seems to be
good reason to believe that the use of the committee device has had
a tendency to reduce the ratio of therapeutic abortions to live births
in hospitals where it has been adopted." [114]

A major explanation for the reluctance of doctors to give ground
on therapeutic abortion is found in the observation of a British
gynecologist:

> Of all gynecological operations, that of therapeutic abortion
> is the one that causes me the most discomfort. Not only is there
> the destruction of the fetus—one can feel the shudder of the
> operating room staff—but also the constant vision of the coro-
> ner's court—deaths do occur.[115]

Nonetheless, a survey of 388 obstetricians undertaken prior to the
amendment of many State laws on abortion found 10 percent admit-
ting that they referred patients to abortionists, and guessing that
14 percent of their colleagues also did so. For the majority of those
making such referrals, there were four or five cases each year, though
a few said that they referred from 30 to 40 cases annually.[116]

In many ways, the response to this survey pinpoints the focal
point at which public pressure for relaxed abortion laws was exerted.
Frantic women imploring their doctors to provide surcease from a
condition which they found intolerable had either to be turned away
or else referred to criminal abortionists. Both alternatives were in
many respects offensive to the medical calling, and both of course
created tension in the doctor-patient relationship. Thus, the inexorable press on doctors to support relaxation of abortion laws gained
momentum.

A 1969 inquiry into the opinions of 2,257 general practitioners,
obstetricians and gynecologists found a sliding scale of approval as
the presumed degree of abortion necessity decreased. Thus, 91 per-

[113] Richard Lyons, "AMA Eases Abortion Rules," *New York Times*, June 26,
1970.
[114] Herbert L. Packer and Ralph J. Gampell, "Therapeutic Abortion: A Problem in Law and Medicine," *Stanford Law Review*, 11 (May 1959), p. 422.
[115] William C. W. Nixon, quoted in "The Ethics of Abortion," *Time*, July 15,
1957, p. 93.
[116] Lader, *op. cit.*, n. 46, p. 59.

cent would allow abortion to save a life; 86 percent when the pregnancy was the result of rape or incest, or when the physical or mental health of the prospective mother was likely to be permanently impaired; and 81 percent if the pregnancy was likely to produce a deformed child. Less than half of the sample favored abortion on demand, with only 35 percent of the younger doctors (those with less than 10 years of practice) supporting abortion as a "personal right" of a pregnant woman, compared to 45 percent of the older doctors. In fact, the more permissive attitudes of the older doctors prevailed in all areas related to abortion about which inquiries were made, leading the surveyers, the American Public Health Association, to suspect that the older doctors had developed more empathy with the viewpoints of their female patients because they had seen more.[117]

A few years later, a national survey found 51 percent of a physician sample of 27,741 providing an unqualified "yes" answer to the question: "Should abortion be available to any woman capable of giving legal consent upon her own request to a competent physician?" Only 4.4 percent of the sample gave an unqualified "no" response, indicating their belief that abortion should never be legally permissible. Despite sample differences, it is not unlikely that the two surveys document growing favor of "abortion on demand" in the medical profession.[118]

Surveys also found a considerable differentiation between obstetricians and gynecologists when their attitudes about abortion were compared to those of psychiatrists. A 1968 questionnaire inquiry by *Modern Medicine* of 40,089 doctors found 87 percent in favor of some liberalization of the old abortion laws, with obstetricians and gynecologists the lowest of all the specialties (83.7 percent) taking such a view and psychiatrists the group providing the greatest support (94.6 percent).[119] One doctor, less than totally sympathetic to the stand of the obstetricians, thought that it could be interpreted in terms of the personalities of the practitioners:

> Ob-Gyn's are mama's boys. They go into obstetrics because they identify with women and the whole reproductive process. Now ask them to do an abortion and it's against what they're psychologically attuned to. They're trained to deliver babies and put them at the mothers' breasts. The woman who doesn't want

---

[117] Harry Nelson, "Older Doctors Tend to Favor Abortion Reform, Study Finds," *Los Angeles Times,* August 24, 1969.

[118] Brian Sullivan, "Abortion Should Be Available If Wanted, Doctors' Poll Says," *Schenectady* (*N.Y.*) *Gazette,* November 3, 1969 (AP).

[119] Cited in Brody, *op. cit.,* n. 13.

to go through the natural birth bit and the nursing—why she's a tramp to them.[120]

Today, the medical profession clearly seems to have swung into line with the surge of public opinion in regard to "abortion on demand." In 1967, the American Medical Association liberalized its official policy to conform with the Colorado statute, endorsing abortion under specified conditions of protection of life and health, crime (rape or incest), and potential birth deformity. A move favoring further liberalization was overwhelmingly defeated, however.[121] But by 1970, the tide had turned dramatically, and at its annual meeting the Association heard fiery debate on the proposal that had been put down so forcefully only 3 years before. To go further on abortion, members of the National Federation of Catholic Physician Guilds told AMA delegates "may place the profession of medicine at the disposal of the government . . . as was the case in Nazi Germany." Abortion on demand, insisted a female doctor, the mother of five children, was a "manic simplistic solution of the New Left." The debate was not without its lighter moments. One of them came in the speech of a delegate opposing abortion for unmarried women who wished to save their children from illegitimacy. "There are a lot of bastards in the United States who have made significant contributions to American society," he pointed out.[122] Nonetheless, opposing views prevailed, and the Association voted in favor of allowing physicians to perform abortions for social and economic reasons provided they were done in consultation with two other doctors and in accredited hospitals.[123] This stand was not as permissive as that taken by the Committee on Psychiatry and Law of the Group for the Advancement of Psychiatry, which advocated that "abortion performed by a licensed physician should be entirely removed from the domain of criminal law," [124] but it was strikingly different from the position the AMA usually took on controversial social issues.

In all, then, it seems reasonable to maintain that the medical profession, exercising its collective training and wisdom, is overwhelmingly in favor of statutes such as that operating in Colorado and is

---

[120] Quoted in Scott, *op. cit.*, n. 48, p. 68.

[121] Richard Lyons, "Abortion Reform Debated By AMA," *New York Times*, June 23, 1970. Cf., American Medical Association, Committee on Human Reproduction, "AMA Policy on Therapeutic Abortion," *Journal of the American Medical Association*, 201 (August 14, 1967), p. 544.

[122] Lyons, *ibid.*

[123] Lyons, *op. cit.*, n. 113.

[124] Group for the Advancement of Psychiatry, *op. cit.*, n. 58, p. 219.

supporting—with some procedural reservations—the abortion on demand laws enacted in New York, Hawaii, and Alaska. There remain a number of difficulties in implementation of abortion statutes, most of them inherent in the nature of the delivery of medical services and the training practices of the medical profession. Hospital procedures, for instance, are dictated in large measure by the perceived needs of the residents who do the largest part of the work, and who are expecting to learn about the rarer cases and the more challenging aspects of their field. Abortion, however, is an assembly-line procedure, rather monotonous and routine, and inevitable resistance develops among medical residents to allowing abortion cases to crowd hospital facilities.

Problems such as these, however, are logistic matters, hardly insurmountable, given an interest in seeing them overcome. In terms of our basic concerns in this paper, it seems fair to conclude that the medical profession does not represent either in ideological terms or as a matter of practicality a force that ought to be regarded as dictating the continued criminalization of abortion.

Abortion and the Unborn Child

Several highly emotional issues center about the nature and the future of the fetus which is destroyed in abortion. The destruction of the fetus ends its earthly prospects and, depending upon the religious doctrine accepted, this may or may not be a defensible outcome.

On ethical grounds, the controversy is rather more intricate, since it lacks the categoric elements of the religious debate. It is often argued that forcing women to bear "unwanted" children severely undermines the quality of life in store for these children. Other persons, though they may grant this as a statistical conclusion, insist that the most unpredictable kinds of achievements may eventuate in the lottery of life from even the most unwanted children. There are also those who insist that the use of any outcome criteria is a presumptuous mortal enterprise. Relatively few persons, they point out, no matter how objectively wretched their lives may appear, choose to end them themselves, though they have this option. Persons taking this view are wont to point out that "what gives peculiar poignancy to the moral question is the fact that the person—or object—whose existence hinges on the decision has no way of registering his—or its—view of the matter." [125]

It may be presumed that all of the children illegally aborted in

---

[125] Louis Cassels, "Liberalized Abortions Moral Questions," *Knickerbocker* (*N.Y.*) *Union-Star*, May 29, 1970 (UPI).

the United States were in some sense unwanted. Interviews conducted with a nationwide sample of 5,600 married women also found that about 35 to 45 percent of the population growth in the United States between 1960 and 1968 involved births which were not desired by the parents. This figure is regarded as minimal, since some of the women interviewed were undoubtedly unwilling to grant that children since born had not been wanted.[126]

Materials on the consequences for the child of being born to parents who did not want it indicate quite clearly that to an extent greater than that for wanted children their lives will be blighted. Earlier, it was noted that a Swedish study of children born to parents whose applications for therapeutic abortions were rejected tended to fare more poorly than members of a control group in terms of a range of measures of social adequacy and adjustment.[127] In the United States, a 28 percent increase in the infanticide rate between 1963 and 1967 is regarded as evidence of either a rise in the number of undesired births or an increase in an unwillingness to tolerate such births.[128] It has also been pointed out that 15 percent of the adoptions in the United States involve intact families in which the parents have decided that they have enough children.[129] From such data, some authorities conclude that "compulsory" continuation of pregnancies are related to "child abandonment, child abuse, infanticide, gross neglect, and forms of rejection such as overprotectiveness." "Is it defensible," one woman holding such a view asks, "to place an utterly helpless child in the custody of rejecting parents who happen to be biological parents only?"[130] Thus, it is said that the number of "battered children" would be reduced if abortion were available to women who do not care to bear the children they have conceived.

So, too, a reduction in the number of deformed children could reasonably be achieved by more ready access to abortion, coupled with more adequate diagnostic techniques for the prediction of deformity. Here, too, however, the ethical issue is complex. Why abort a child on the speculative possibility that he might be born

[126] Larry Bumpass and Charles F. Westoff, "The 'Perfect Contraceptive' Population," *Science*, 169 (September 18, 1970), pp. 1177–1182. Cf., Sandra Blakeslee, "Unwanted Births Found High in U.S.," *New York Times*, October 29, 1969.

[127] Forssman and Thuwe, *op. cit.*, n. 84.

[128] Lynn Lilliston, "Wanted 'Humane' Laws on Abortion," *Los Angeles Times*, April 10, 1969.

[129] *Ibid.*

[130] Mildred Beck, quoted in "Conference on Abortion is Told of Harm to Unwanted Children," *New York Times*, May 12, 1969.

with a deformity? one writer asks. "It would indeed be fa
reasonable," he suggests with venomous mock sincerity, "t
until the child was born and then dispatch it if it was found deformed." [131] It is in such terms that the debate proceeds, with one
side finding the arguments of the other nothing more than rationalizations for self-indulgence and with the other side defining its opponents as fanatics expressing vindictiveness and self-righteousness in
the form of bittersweet reasonableness.

It is sometimes said that abortion would largely become unnecessary if adequate birth control practices were used, and it is the
custom of many facilities providing therapeutic abortions to com-
bine the operation with a lecture on birth control. Australian evidence suggests, however, that birth control practices need not have
any clear relationship to the degree of illegitimacy in a society.
Public health statistics indicate that the illegitimacy rate in Australia is one of the highest in the world, despite the fact that the
country is reported to have the world's highest per capita consumption of birth control pills, with 750,000 women, constituting one-third
of those of childbearing age, using oral contraceptives. Nonetheless,
8 percent of the births in Australia are out of wedlock, and the
authorities estimate that there are 90,000 illegal abortions each
year.[132]

Given such findings, predictions regarding the possible implications of widespread use of so-called "morning after" pills must
remain uncertain. Such pills, now under development and testing in
Sweden, initiate the menstrual flow when taken once a month at
the end of the menstrual cycle, whether or not the woman has conceived. If the pills prove reliable and safe, it is estimated that they
will be available for marketing in about 5 years.[133]

Religion and Abortion

The most intense debates about abortion tend to be framed with
reference to religious doctrine, and most notably that of the Roman
Catholic Church. Debate centers about the idea of "ensoulment," a
concept seeking to define the exact moment when a fetus becomes
an individual with a God-given right to life.[134] "After all the constitutional arguments have been heard," one writer notes, "the abortion

---

[131] Norman St. John-Stevas, "Abortion Law," *Commonweal*, 85 (November 11,
1966), p. 165.
[132] Robert Trumbull, "South Australia Acts on Abortion," *New York Times*,
December 9, 1969.
[133] Brody, *op. cit.*, n. 13.
[134] *Los Angeles Times, op. cit.*, n. 21.

issue comes back to what it has really always been—a question of
how one views the fetus." [135]

The historical record shows that in early times Catholic church
authorities held that abortion during the early months of pregnancy
did not constitute an ecclesiastic offense. This view was enunciated
by Gratian in *Decretum* (c. 1140), a systematic private treatise
which was to become the kernel of the *Corpus Juris Canonici*, and
in the proclamations of Innocent III, pope from 1198 to 1216, and
those of his successors. The dividing line between "early" and "late"
pregnancy was 40 days after conception for a male fetus and 80
days for a female fetus. In practice, since it was impossible to determine the sex of the fetus, 80 days became the latest time for sanctioned abortions. This early church position was abandoned in 1869,
however, when Pope Pius IX put forward the doctrine of "immediate animation" of the fetus and declared that both early and late
nonspontaneous abortions were acts of homicide.[136]

The official Catholic position today derives from the 1869 pontifi-
cal pronouncement, a view dictated by church interpretation of
divine will and possibly also by secular considerations of the importance for church vitality of propagation of the faithful. Contemporary declarations by prominent persons in the Roman Catholic
hierarchy in support of the church stand are plentiful. On an issue
regarded by many Catholic scholars as unreasonably hypothetical—
that concerning whether the fetus or the pregnant woman is to be
saved from death if such a choice is necessary, Pope Pius XI has
said: "The life of each [mother and fetus] is equally sacred and no
one has the power, not even the public authority, to destroy
either." [137] Pope Pius XII spelled out the details of this position in
a 1951 encyclical:

> Any direct abortion whatsoever, even if it is performed in the
> presence of a manifest therapeutic indication to save the mother
> by its means, when otherwise she together with the child would
> perish, is immoral and forbidden by divine law. Innocent human
> life, in whatsoever condition it is found, is immune, from the
> very first moment of its existence, to any direct, deliberate
> attack.[138]

---

[135] Greenhouse, *op. cit.*, n. 92, p. 90.

[136] Cyril C. Means, "Eugenic Abortion," Letter to the Editor, *New York Times*,
April 16, 1965.

[137] Pope Pius XI, quoted in Monroe, *op. cit.*, n. 19, p. 11.

[138] Quoted in Duncan Chappell and Paul R. Wilson, "Public Attitudes Toward
Reform of the Law Relating to Abortion and Homosexuality. Part II: Abortion," *Australian Law Journal*, 42 (August 30, 1968), p. 124.

Polemicists of other religious persuasions often dispute the fore-going doctrine vigorously. To them, the unborn child seems the lesser sacrifice, and the spared mother, they would argue, may at a later date bear another child. But to most leaders in the Catholic hierarchy, such views appear to be no more than expediency, the taking into one's own hands of divine prerogatives. In addition, of course, traditional Catholic writers begin from a theological posi-tion which defines the pregnant woman's death as something other than tragedy, given the possibility of eternal salvation in the here-after. To theologians such as Patrick Cardinal O'Boyle of Washing-ton, D.C., abortion is "exterminative medicine" and "exactly the same kind of solution that Hitler found to the 'Jewish problem.' " For Cardinal Cooke of New York that State's abortion bill repre-sented a "direct attack on the sanctity of human life and the welfare of our society." [139] A bishop in San Diego put the matter in meta-phorical terms. "Abortion," he said, was "a kind of lynching in the womb." [140] Finally, a Roman Catholic pastor in New York indicated clearly the irreconcilable nature of the theological issue if categoric positions are adopted: "Even though the State of New York has changed its law," he noted after passage of the new abortion meas-ure, "it does not mean that God has changed His law." [141] Another Roman Catholic Church leader thought that legalized abortion would open "a tremendous roadway for the legalization of sterilization, compulsory abortion and euthenasia." [142] A similar kind of incre-mental erosion of principles supporting the preciousness of human life was predicted as a consequence of legalized abortion by another Catholic writer:

> Every human life is infinitely precious. Abortion cheapens life. Our times have seen human life devalued too often already. It must not happen again in the name of abortion.[143]

Proponents of the Roman Catholic stand against abortion also, on occasion, have insisted that most, if not all, of the alleged reasons for liberalization of the existing laws are based on erroneous data. Thus, during a panel discussion, a Roman Catholic spokesman main-tained that illegal abortions are far fewer than statistics indicate, that conception from rape is extremely rare, that emotionally dis-

---

[139] Harry F. Rosenthal, "Cardinal O'Boyle Blasts Plan for D.C. Abortions on Request," *Schenectady (N.Y.) Gazette*, December 10, 1969 (AP).

[140] William Kenneally, quoted in Monroe, *op. cit.*, n. 19, p. 11.

[141] Deidre Carmody, "Catholic Bishops Assail Abortion Bill," *New York Times*, April 11, 1970.

[142] *Ibid*.

[143] Shaw, *op. cit.*, n. 83, p. 191.

turbed pregnant women do not commit suicide, and that there is neither a population explosion nor lack of food for coming generations. In addition, the panelist argued, legal abortion denies to prospective fathers their right to parenthood and leads to "biological control by the State." [144]

In general, the Roman Catholic stand does not find favor among leaders of other religious denominations in the United States. Typical of a contrary position is that of the Cleveland Consultation Service on Abortion, a group of more than 20 Protestant ministers and rabbis, founded in 1969, to direct abortion-seeking women away from quacks and extortionists to more reputable sources. The Cleveland ministerial alliance maintains a 24-hour telephone answering service and reports that it had inquiries from more than 700 women during its first 6 months of operation.[145] Similarly, many religious bodies have taken official stands favoring liberal abortion laws. In 1968, for instance, the American Baptist Convention advocated that termination of pregnancy prior to the end of the 12th week be allowed "at the request of the individuals concerned" and subject "only to the laws regulating medical practice and licensure." [146]

Nor has there been consensus within the ranks of the Roman Catholic clergy regarding abortion. Representing the more liberal segment of the church, Father Robert F. Drinan, dean of the Boston College School of Law prior to his election to the U.S. Congress in 1970, strongly opposed all State regulation of abortion on the ground that it put the State in the position of "deciding who shall live and who shall die." Drinan's reasoning took the following line:

> If you say a problem exists, and that women will get an abortion and the law can't prevent this, all right then, withdraw the law. If we're going to have a change, I say the nonlaw has greater potential for solving the problem than the law.[147]

In a similar vein, Richard Cardinal Cushing, before his death, had maintained publicly that "Catholics do not need the support of civil law to be faithful to their religious convictions, and they do not seek to impose by law their moral views on other members of society." [148]

In essence, these final two positions would seem to constitute those views most congruent with the principles of an open society. Theo-

---

[144] Mary Barber, "Panelists' Views Differ on Abortion," *Los Angeles Times*, December 29, 1970.

[145] MacGregor, *op. cit.*, n. 96.

[146] Pilpel and Norwick, *op. cit.*, n. 105, p. 9.

[147] Quoted in Brody, *op. cit.*, n. 13.

[148] Quoted in Lader, *op. cit.*, n. 46, p. 60.

logical forces may exert pressure—short of legal coercion—upon communicants and others to follow their tenets. They may warn, scold, and excommunicate in an effort to gain conformity to their views. But they should not be able to interfere with the right of those who do not accept such views to behave in a contrary manner, if by so behaving those persons do not interfere with the rights of other members of the society.

This position does not, of course, respond adequately to the view that insists that the unborn child is a human being and that abortion represents his murder. "Abortion on Demand is Murder by Request" a full-page advertisement in the *New York Times* insisted during the height of the State's debate over alteration of its abortion law.[149] It is tempting to say that those who believe this to be true should under no conditions permit themselves to be aborted, but that they should not interfere with the right of others to engage in such activity. Such an answer begs the question, however, for we do not permit individuals who commit murder out of conviction to do so with impunity (at least, unless we have defined the situation as one of war). The one proper resolution of this question, it seems, is a personal one, shakily buttressed by a few external facts. Fetuses do not appear to be humans, certainly in their earliest periods of growth, and various biological insufficiencies may be alleged in the attempt to support this view. It may be argued that a similar observation could be made for blacks, mental defectives, Jews, or other outgroups in certain societies at certain times. But we are not taken by that analogy. A standard of "reasonableness" may represent a shelter for viciousness and self-righteousness, but we risk that possibility with the observation that we believe that reasonable people should be able to differentiate the unborn, who are voluntarily aborted by the person who conceived them, from the outcast, so labeled by the illogical tyranny of state rulers or powerful segments of their followers. If that distinction is real—and we think it is—it should be sufficient for decisionmaking, for it will not do to suggest that one inroad inevitably produces in its wake terrifying excesses. The "burn rubbish first and you'll burn martyrs next" kind of argument is often as silly as the foregoing representation of it indicates. It is much too inexact and speculative a position.

Public Opinion on Abortion

Public opinion polls indicate that Americans are now about evenly divided on the issue of legal abortion on demand. It also seems evi-

---

[149] *New York Times*, January 10, 1970.

dent from examination of longitudinal inventories that the pendulum is swinging toward endorsement of liberal positions. These taps into public opinion do not, of course, provide irrefutable underpinning for any declaration of public policy; they only indicate the receptivity likely to be accorded proposed statutory alterations.

The best measure of public attitudes in the United States toward abortion appears in referendum results in the State of Washington on the issue, since the act of casting a ballot represents a considerably more formal commitment to a position than a response to a public opinion poll. Washington, of course, has a particular demographic structure, and an off-year election is apt to be contested in terms of many local issues and personalities, and to attract a selective sample of voters. Nonetheless, the 55 percent endorsement of abortion on demand in Washington in 1970 appears to be an excellent measure of citizen attitudes in the western region of the country, in a State with a. relatively low Catholic population.

Earlier polls indicate that Americans were rather satisfied with the restrictive laws which allowed abortion to protect health, but refused it for what were regarded as more "selfish" reasons. A survey of 1,484 adult Americans by the National Opinion Research Corporation in 1966 found more than 5 to 1 opposing abortion as a form of birth control. Eighty-three percent of the respondents would not permit abortion if the woman simply said that she did not desire more children, 77 percent would not allow it for economic reasons among the poor, and 80 percent would not approve of abortion for a single woman who did not want to marry the man who had impregnated her.

Like most surveys on attitudes toward abortion, this one indicated that men tend to be slightly more liberal than women. It showed only a slight variation between Catholics and Protestants, with Jews registering the most permissive views on abortion. Interestingly, 58 percent of the Catholic female respondents and 64 percent of the Catholic male respondents said that they would permit abortion to protect the pregnant woman's health.[150]

Three years later, the Gallup Poll was asking primarily about attitudes toward abortion on demand and finding that 40 percent of the American population favored such a program if the abortion was performed 3 months or less after conception. College-trained persons were much more favorable toward such a position than the noncollege trained, with 58 percent endorsing it, and younger per-

---

[150] Austin C. Wehrwein, "Abortion Reform Supported in Poll," *New York Times,* April 24, 1966.

sons indicated their approval of abortion on demand to a greater extent than older persons. Three out of ten Roman Catholics and eight out of ten Jews supported demand abortions.[151]

More interesting was the fact that the Gallup results showed an increase in attitudes favoring abortion on demand from 27 percent of the population in 1966 to 40 percent in 1969.[152] This result would appear to square with that noted earlier in Great Britain, where in March 1965 only 36 percent of the respondents on a National Opinion Poll responded affirmatively to the inquiry: "Would you favor abortion if a mother has so large a family that another child might cause financial difficulties and psychological stress?" Two years later, however, approval of abortion under such conditions had risen to 65 percent.[153]

The explanation for such a dramatic alteration in views seems to be in large measure a rearrangement of attitudes so that they square with legislative changes. Also, abortion is a more personal matter than, say, addiction and homosexuality which may be regarded by most members of the society as the vices over which an individual ought to be able to exercise control. Pregnancy, on the other hand, is a routine topic of social conversation and unwanted pregnancies are matters of considerable interest and discussion. Thus, the lottery of personal involvement—birth control pills notwithstanding—may select out any of the respondents in the appropriate age bracket. Also, when a matter becomes more controllable—such as when pregnancy may almost always be scheduled—then the remaining erratic elements become particularly irritating and aggravating. If there is little prospect of avoiding unwanted pregnancy, then there may be less pressure to take measures to avoid its consequences. But when the possibility of avoiding unwanted pregnancy is considerable, then the outcome is apt to be defined as more appalling than it otherwise would have been.

Whatever the explanation, the record itself is clear. A reading of the public mood indicates that a slight majority of the citizens in the United States favors abortion on demand. If statutes allowing abortion are enacted and no dramatically untoward consequences attend them, it is likely that additional persons will embrace their advocacy. Absent other considerations of overriding importance— and we have not found such considerations—there would seem to be no reason why the majority should not be allowed to have its way.

[151] George Gallup, "40% of Adults Favor Legal Abortion Laws," *Los Angeles Times*, November 30, 1969.

[152] *Newsweek, op. cit.,* n. 29, p. 54.

[153] Emerson, *op. cit.,* n. 64.

Society and Abortion

Legal abortion, in one sense, runs contrary to the burgeoning public concern about ecological matters. The ecology movement has at its heart a premise that "natural" phenomena are good and that the effluvia of "civilization" are what downgrade the environment. Under such conditions, the assumption might be that tinkering with natural processes produces untoward consequences. In this regard, abortion might be defined as an interruption of a natural process, and one which might bring about results detrimental to the society. This is rarely the logic pursued, however; the major thrust of the ecology argument concerning abortion is that environmental degradation is itself a direct consequence of overpopulation, with excess people imposing destructive demands on their surroundings, and that legal abortion, to the extent that it would reduce population pressure, represents an ecologically attractive program.

There seems to be no dispute that access to legal abortion will cut into population growth. All countries which have inaugurated permissive abortion policies have clearly evidenced a downward trend in live births. The consequences of this are, however, difficult to assess. An "excessive" population growth in India appears in considerable measure responsible for the Malthusian dilemmas of that country. In Japan, on the other hand, we have noted earlier that the absence of what is regarded as an adequate labor force has led to certain economic conditions which, by some standards, might appear undesirable, things such as more demanding working routines and the postponement of retirement. Nonetheless, all told, in those countries with abortion on demand, the consequences in terms of population disturbance seem minimal, hardly of such overwhelming proportion that they would override other considerations pointing toward abortion on demand policies.

In the United States, at the moment, the average family size is 3.2 children. For the population to be stabilized that figure would have to drop to a 2.2 average.[154] The consequences of a stable population are debatable: Some say that it allows for systematic planning and avoids cycles of expansion and contraction associated with fluctuating birth rates. Others maintain that it creates a certain flatness in a society, and that growth and advance go hand in hand, just as stability and stagnation are synonymous. Neither view, however, has very substantial factual undergirding.

A notable social argument favoring freer access to abortion centers about the discrimination against poorer persons inherent in

---

[154] Blakeslee, op. cit., n. 126.

restrictive abortion policies. Until recently, with the appearance of the newer statutes, abortion had largely been the prerogative of the rich. Sherri Finkbine's trip to Sweden to obtain legal assistance in the abortion of her fetus indicates the avenues that were open to persons able to afford the price. On the East Coast, affluent women often traveled to Cuba prior to the Revolution there, and to Puerto Rico subsequently, for abortions performed by licensed physicians under sterile conditions.

More widespread access to abortion on demand would then become, as a Federal health official has put the matter, "back-up birth control for the poor." [155] In this regard, it could be argued that legal abortion would tend to reduce the birth rate among persons least able to afford the financial and often the psychological drain of additional children. This outcome, however, need not necessarily take place, since it is debatable whether free abortion would arrange birth rates so that those persons "best" able to afford children had the greatest number of children. For one thing, the ability of certain persons to support offspring well is often in part a function of the same traits that keep them from having a larger number of children. Further, there is no evidence that the country would be better off for the production of a larger number of children from middle-class homes than it would be by the production of a disproportionate number of lower-class children. It is easy to point to welfare statistics and crime figures as these correlate with socioeconomic condition and to reach such a conclusion by this means. But social life is an extraordinary blend of experiences, and in many ways the diminution of the membership of one social class may produce quite unexpected consequences in the behavior and attitudes of persons in other classes.

The argument is sometimes advanced that advocates of abortion on demand are fundamentally racists, persons intent upon using this circuitous means to reduce the percentage of black persons in the society, and thereby to make blacks even more numerically vulnerable than they are today.[156] The premise underlying this argument is probably accurate: Abortion on demand statutes are apt to cut down the birth rate among blacks, who tend, like other generally poor persons in our society, to be relatively unable to afford birth control techniques and to be relatively ineffective in their employment. It seems unreasonable, however, to maintain that black women

---

[155] Roger O. Egeberg, quoted in "Egeberg Would Aid Indigent in Obtaining Abortions," *New York Times*, April 13, 1970.

[156] MacGregor, *op. cit.*, n. 96.

who elect to abort unwanted pregnancies ought to be kept from so doing because of supposititious suggestions about the implication of such behavior for racial advancement. It is quite possible that a reduction in the relative birth rate of blacks might produce kinds of power desired both by members of the group and their supporters, that it might lead to increased strength as a product of more concentrated resources being devoted to fewer people. The issue here seems clearcut: Blacks and others ought to exercise whatever persuasive tactics appear necessary to obtain ends they desire to achieve, and if it seems reasonable to discourage abortion then tactics should be mounted to convince the target population of the desirability of such a policy.

Fierce resistance ought to be made, of course, to any effort whatsoever to insist upon abortion—or sterilization—for any member of the society as a precondition to eligibility for welfare benefits. Welfare mothers should be allowed to have as many children as they desire. If the society does not care to support them adequately—as it does not care to do now—that becomes another problem, one to be debated on its own terms. Ultimately, the society might be made to conclude that it is to its own benefit to provide care and training of such a sufficiency that in the future it will not again be called upon to support the offspring of those it had earlier neglected.

The benefits to social existence of an official abortion policy permitting persons to do what they want to do, so long as they do not injure others, should not be underestimated as a national asset. The Reverend Joseph P. Fitzpatrick of Fordham University seems correct in his premise, though his conclusion is a good deal less persuasive, when he summarizes the consequences of abortion on demand in the following terms:

> The social effects of legalized abortion will be judged to be good or bad largely in terms of the way one judges social developments in a framework of one's moral values. In the framework of my own values, the legalization of abortion is another indication of a loss of sensitivity around the basic issues of human life about which I cannot be optimistic.[157]

To meet the Reverend Fitzpatrick on his own moral field, it does not seem unreasonable to suggest that in many respects concern for human life today, however short it may be of some ideal goal, is more deep rooted than it has been at any time in human history. A reading of historical archives indicates that the idea of responsi-

---

[157] Israel Shenker, "Sociologists Offer Varying Predictions on the Moral and Political Effects of Liberalized Abortion Laws," *New York Times*, April 12, 1970.

bility for another's well-being was a late arrival on the ideological scene. Abortion on demand, though it may disregard the rights of the fetus—whatever these may be—can be seen essentially as a response to women insisting upon greater control of their own lives and fate. In this respect, liberal abortion policies could represent further extension of a concern for human welfare and for the idealistic principle that a person ought to have as great an amount of freedom as a society can reasonably tolerate. Morris Janowitz, a sociologist, has noted that abortion may also contain elements which add vitality to social life. Contraception is a first chance, Janowitz notes, "abortion makes possible a second chance, and a second chance is essential for any form of social change." [158]

At any rate, if nothing else, permitting abortion on demand puts down that element of vicious self-righteousness which at times underlies attempts to resist changes in the laws. Former United States Senator Maurine Neuberger has illustrated the attitudes that sometimes lie behind support of restrictive abortion policies with the following story:

> I'll never forget a woman who came up to me and shook her finger in my face. She cried, "A girl who has her fun has to pay." [159]

History provides little evidence with which to determine the impact, if there has been any, of diverse kinds of abortion policies on the vitality of a nation over a reasonably long period of time. The Early Greeks and Romans condoned abortion,[160] but lest the decline of these civilizations be tied in some manner to their abortion practices, it need only be noted that Middle Assyrian culture, no more long lasting and much less glorious than Greek or Roman culture, impaled women on stakes if they were found guilty of aborting.[161] Among preliterate societies, policies appear to run the gamut and to show no particular relationship to tribal vitality or senescence. Some people impose no penalties for abortion, others, such as the Truk Islanders, resort to mild scoldings, while still others, such as the Jakuns, exact the penalty of death for abortion.[162]

In all, the conclusion to be reached on the relationship between

---

[158] *Ibid.*

[159] Lilliston, *op. cit.*, n. 20.

[160] Joyce O. Hertzler, *The Crisis in World Population* (Lincoln: University of Nebraska Press, 1956), p. 242.

[161] James B. Pritchard (editor), *Ancient Near Eastern Texts Relating to the Old Testament,* 2d ed. (Princeton: Princeton University Press, 1955), p. 185.

[162] George Devereux, *A Study of Abortion in Primitive Societies* (London: Yoseloff, 1960), p. 62.

abortion and social well-being seems unavoidable. There exists no persuasive evidence that the consequences of abortion on demand are of such an overpowering nature that they will inevitably or even likely contribute to a decline in the society.

IV. Narcotic and Drug Use

No other crimes appear to be involved in greater controversy today than those concerned with voluntary ingestion of agents defined as illegal—drugs such as heroin and marihuana—and with the employment of drugs such as amphetamines and barbiturates for purposes other than those prescribed by physicians. These "victimless" offenses differ in significant ways from homosexuality and abortion, which we have discussed earlier. Unlike abortion, drug offenses tend toward continuing patterns of involvement. Unlike homosexuality, the parties to the drug exchange play very different roles; the seller supplies the pharmacological agent, which he may or may not use himself, to the buyer, often for a profit. The buyer obtains the drug for a wide variety of reasons, and the results of his use may manifest themselves in a number of different forms, some of which appear patently "harmful" (such as erratic automobile driving behavior), others of which may be regarded as beneficial (such as relaxation and pleasurable feelings).

The drugs themselves are very different entities, and grouping them together for review represents a certain distortion, since it implies that considerations bearing upon one might reasonably be applicable without further consideration to another. In regard to heroin, for instance, the addictive quality of the drug adds a range of considerations unique to crimes without victims. Once "hooked," the heroin addict is unlikely to cease usage voluntarily. In addition, his habit will require ever increasing dosages for its satisfaction. The illegality of the drug tends to keep its price well beyond the earning capacity of the user, so that he will be required to commit criminal offenses to purchase a drug supply. These items are not present in regard to marihuana, where users may obtain at low prices sufficient quantities of the drug to engage in a heavy use pattern. For LSD, the quality of tolerance inherent in the drug dictates against its use more than once or twice in any week—the desired effect will not occur if it is employed more often—so that purchase of the commodity poses no particular problem for the user, presuming he is able to locate a source of supply.

For marihuana, there are other social factors that make analysis of the law bearing upon use of the drug particularly noteworthy.

Among other things, the fact that there exists rather general consensus among authorities that marihuana is not likely to produce any untoward effects of a nature more serious than those now brought about by legal items such as alcohol and cigarettes makes its continuing ban subject to attack on the ground of social hypocrisy. Such hypocrisy seems particularly intense when efforts to legalize marihuana emerge only in the wake of spread of use of the drug to middle-class segments of the society. When marihuana usage was almost exclusively located among persons in the lower economic strata of the social system little attention was paid to "shortcomings" of the statutes which now are so strenuously attacked.

Drug use, then, is an activity in which the offender introjects into his body, almost invariably by choice, a pharmacological product that demonstrably affects only himself, though it can be said that he may also indirectly harm those who are dependent upon him. There is medical agreement that persons could use drugs such as the opiates throughout their lives with no serious consequences to their general health attributable to the drugs. (See "Consequences of Opiate Use," p. 131, this chapter.) Ultimately, because of the tolerance syndrome, they would be ingesting amounts sufficient to kill numerous nonaddicted persons, but the dosage-tolerant user would suffer no untoward consequences. In fact, it may be recalled that bygone monarchs often consumed ever-increasing daily dosages of potentially lethal substances such as arsenic to render themselves immune to assassination by poisoning.

The possibility of social harm from use of opiates today lies, therefore, not in the drugs themselves but in various outlying aspects of their use. Among addicts, insensitivity to hygienic considerations produces diseases such as hepatitis, transmitted from nonsterile needles utilized serially by diverse persons, some of them infected.[1] Failure to eat and rest properly accounts for a strikingly high morbidity rate among narcotic users. There is, in addition, always the possibility of overdosing, sometimes because of the deliberate failure of the seller of narcotics to "cut" or dilute the drug to its usual concentration. Such destructive consequences of narcotics use ultimately deprive the society of manpower and talent and may impose additional costs upon citizens making regular contributions to the maintenance of the community.

---

[1] See, e.g., Veronica I. Batonbacal and Alvin Slipyan, "Transmission of Serum Hepatitis in Heroin Addicts," *New York State Journal of Medicine*, 59 (January 15, 1959), pp. 320–323.

It is the incessant commission of crimes to secure funds with which to purchase opiates that stands as the social consequence most condemned in regard to the narcotics traffic. Much debate concerns whether narcotic addicts are originally juvenile delinquents or adult criminals who only happen to use drugs, or whether it is the establishment of a pattern of drug use which inexorably demands illegal activity for its sustenance from persons who otherwise would have remained law-abiding. In either event, it is clear that opiate users, whether criminal or noncriminal to begin with, are unable to abandon criminal careers as long as they are unable to stop using the drugs. Under such circumstances, the social cost may be regarded as heavy. In a recent statement, for instance, the executive director of the Har-You Project in New York City indicated that unless the narcotics problem could be solved all other ameliorative efforts in the slum would prove fruitless. "If we save one person, heroin will take three," the Har-You leader said. "Every time a youngster in Harlem is stuck with a needle, it's like turning a werewolf back into the community to plunder." [2]

Because dependence upon opiates almost invariably demands criminal activity, there has been some call for experimental programs under which addicts have legitimate access to drugs under close medical supervision. It is questioned whether the failure of the 44 clinics operated during the period between 1919 and 1923, a failure widely publicized by the Federal Bureau of Narcotics,[3] necessarily forebodes the doom of more sophisticated and better planned contemporary experiments.[4] The major thrust of such experimental programs, in the words of Judge Morris Ploscowe, their leading advocate, would be "to aid in the determination of whether it is possible to rehabilitate addicts, in a noninstitutional setting, so that they can live and function without drugs." [5] The logic of such an approach was expressed by a New York judge in 1970, when he introduced a bill which would have made it possible for registered addicts to receive doles of heroin and other hard drugs in State clinics:

[2] Livingston Wingate, quoted in "Narcotics Are Root of Harlem Ills, Wingate Declares," *New York Times*, January 4, 1965.

[3] U.S. Treasury Department, Bureau of Narcotics, *Narcotic Clinics in the United States* (Washington, D.C.: Government Printing Office, 1953).

[4] Alfred R. Lindesmith, "The Narcotic Clinics," in *The Addict and the Law* (Bloomington: Indiana University Press, 1965), pp. 135–161.

[5] Morris Ploscowe, "Some Basic Problems in Drug Addiction and Suggestions for Research," in *Drug Addiction: Crime or Disease?* (Bloomington: Indiana University Press, 1961), p. 103.

If an addict wants to destroy himself, there is nothing we can
do about it. But at least we can keep him from destroying other
people.[6]

Providing prescriptions for clinic-administered drugs, it was
argued, would enable addicts to lead nearly normal lives and would
make it possible to eliminate organized crime from drug trafficking.
Other programs dealing with addicts now in operation, a New York
Assemblyman maintained, were "absurd and self-defeating" since
they forced the addict to support his habit through criminal
activity.[7]

Intense controversy regarding proposals such as the foregoing,
regarding distinctions between users and sellers of drugs, regarding
the value of outpatient programs, regarding the potentialities of
substitutive drugs, such as methadone for heroin, all compound the
difficulty of analysis of the consequences of varying approaches to
what is defined as the "drug problem." The dilemmas are highlighted in a report by the California Interim Committee on Criminal
Procedure which noted, not without exasperation, the highly con-
fused nature of debate regarding the best means for dealing with
drug use:

> The battle wages . . . . If one argues for stricter penalties
> one is immediately branded "procop" and "antipeople." If one
> argues for more lenient penalties and more flexible laws one is
> branded "anticop" and "soft-on-narcotics." The truth of the
> matter is that both sides are concerned with finding a solution
> to a problem of human misery. There is a difference of opinion
> on how the law helps or hinders the effort to find a solution.
> But the nature of the debate has become so hysterical and emo-
> tion charged that there has been little rational discussion about
> how the law can be changed to achieve that end . . . .[8]

Not only is the philosophical battleground something of a sham-
bles, but the approaches being made to control of narcotic use present a conflicting array of often-contradictory items. "It's getting
to be a major industry," Jerome Jaffe, head of the Federal program
to deal with drug use, has noted sardonically. "Either you sell dope
or you cure addicts." [9] A newspaper reporter summed up conditions
as he saw them in New York City, where more than half of the

---

[6] Amos Basel, quoted in "State Drug Doses for Addicts Urged By Assembly
Bill," *New York Times*, February 13, 1970.

[7] Franz S. Leichter, quoted in *ibid.*

[8] California Assembly Interim Committee on Criminal Procedure, *Report on
Narcotics Control*, Vol. X22I (January 1967), p. 17.

[9] Jerome Jaffe, quoted in Tom Buckley, "The Fight Against Drugs Is In a
Mess," *New York Times*, March 22, 1970.

Nation's estimated 200,000 heroin addicts are believed to reside, in the following terms:

> There is general agreement that the fight against drugs here has become a chaos of competing programs, theories, and personalities locked in an exhausting and expensive fight for limited funds and personnel, in which the major arenas have become the press and legislative hearings rather than the laboratory and clinic.[10]

Nonetheless, behind the confusion, there does lie information which can be brought to bear upon recommendations concerning public policy in regard to the various drugs now outlawed. We will review this material as it relates to two types of drugs: the opiates and marihuana.

OPIATE DRUGS

Addiction to opiates has a record in the United States going back more than 100 years. By an accident of history, the United States was the first nation to use morphine on a widespread basis. This took place during the Civil War, when morphine was employed to treat the wounded. The result was what was called the "Army Disease," the addiction of some 45,000 soldiers. After the war, the importation of Orientals—many of whom smoked opium—to work on the transcontinental railroad, added another chapter in the Nation's narcotic record. So did the widespread use of paregoric, an opium derivative—in the South.[11]

It is widely believed that before the passage of the Harrison Act in 1914—the initial statute outlawing opiates—addiction was more widespread than at present. The inclusion of opiates in patent medicines sold at the time created addicts located at all levels of the social structure, though there apparently was a preponderance of women over men because of the use of palliatives containing drugs for "female troubles." Narcotics could be purchased over the counter in drug stores and general stores or ordered through the mails. For some of the pre-1914 addicts life apparently went on in much the same manner as it always had; for others, the drugs represented tragedy. Few persons who have seen the vivid portrayal of the morphine addiction of the mother in Eugene O'Neill's *A Long Day's Journey into the Night* will forget the torment that could be associated with drug use in the pre-1914 period.

After 1914, addicts increasingly came to be concentrated in the

---

[10] *Ibid.*

[11] Martin Tolchin, "Involvement of the Middle Class in the Narcotics Problem Arouses Demands for Action," *New York Times*, March 9, 1970.

lower socioeconomic classes.[12] The ratio of male to female addicts changed significantly with the disappearance of opiate-saturated patent medicines. In 1935, the Federal narcotics hospital at Lexington, Kentucky, was established and 3 years later, the Federal hospital at Fort Worth, Texas, began operation. The opening of these facilities encapsulates many of the contradictions that mark the erratic course of social responses to addiction. During dedication ceremonies at the Fort Worth hospital, for instance, the surgeon general— Thomas Parran—observed that the United States had finally begun a humane and forward-looking policy in regard to drug addiction:

> Errors were at first made in the treatment meted out to addicts. From doing nothing about the narcotic problem, we started in a sudden burst of enthusiasm to clean up the situation without proper regard for human values and without considering the suffering and distress entailed in a rigid enforcement of the law as it then stood.
>
> The law, in effect, made criminals out of persons who were guilty only of suffering from the effects of weakness they could not control . . . .
>
> It soon became evident that we were in danger of losing by too harsh application of repressive measures what we were gaining by more intelligent attention to some phases of the addiction problem. We often completed the ruin of individuals whom it was our duty to save.[13]

Parran's remarks notwithstanding, however, the opening of the Federal hospitals brought toleration of addicts by the community to an end, now that there were special sites to which they might be dispatched.[14] There was, in addition, at this time a significant shift in the public definition of addiction, a shift which is described by O'Donnell in the following manner:

> Public attitudes, which before had regarded addiction as a mildly deviant behavior, harmful to the individual and his family, now regarded it as one of the worst of evils, and as a threat to the community. Achieving abstinence was regarded as requiring only an act of will, so that when addicts relapsed after treatment they were perceived as hopeless weaklings, or as having chosen evil in place of good.[15]

---

[12] John C. Ball, "Two Patterns of Narcotic Drug Addiction in the United States," *Journal of Criminal Law, Criminology, and Police Science*, 56 (June 1965), pp. 203–211.

[13] Quoted in *ibid.*, p. 209.

[14] Harris Isbell, "Historical Development of Attitudes Toward Opiate Addiction in the United States," in Seymour M. Farber and Roger H. W. Wilson (editors), *Conflict and Creativity* (New York: McGraw-Hill, 1962), pp. 166–167.

[15] John A. O'Donnell, "The Rise and Decline of a Subculture," *Social Problems*, 15 (Summer 1967), p. 80.

The Second World War interrupted traffic in narcotics to the United States and military considerations led to a deemphasis of the narcotics issue. Following the war, however, narcotic use clearly began to be defined as the formidable public problem that it is seen as today. The medical profession deserted the field of treatment, partly as a response to implicit threats by the Federal Bureau of Narcotics, based upon the Bureau's idiosyncratic reading of several Supreme Court decisions.[16] In addition, doctors found narcotics addicts to be unrewarding patients, with a high degree of intransigency and a low rate of payment.

Law enforcement efforts, dominating the field, drove narcotics usage into slum areas. The trend is clearly evidenced by an examination of the 84,625 admissions to the Federal hospitals during the past three decades. The change in the portrait of the hospital populations is outlined by John Ball:

> The major changes have been that addict patients are younger, a great percentage of those admitted are Negro and Puerto Rican, the use of heroin has increased, and both the number and percentage of addicts admitted from the largest metropolitan areas have markedly increased.[17]

The same writer notes that there was a rise in the number of voluntary patients coming to the hospitals in the years after the Second World War, a trend which reflects in part the stepped-up pace of enforcement efforts and the increased penalties for narcotics offenses. Addicts on the verge of being apprehended or those whose drug habit had reached substantial proportions so that they felt hard-pressed to acquire adequate funds for its support would see striking advantages in leaving States such as New York for the comparatively benign detoxification program at Lexington. Afterwards, when they had been withdrawn from the drug, they could return home and resume use, requiring diminished dosages for equivalent "kicks."

It is moot whether the program of escalated penalties would ultimately have made a significant dent in the narcotics problem, though the removal of addicts from the streets for long periods would inevitably have altered in some manner the nature of the drug trade. In any event, before any definitive evaluation of the impact of harsh retaliatory methods could be made, court decisions and legislative enactments altered the nature of the official approach to addiction.

[16] Lindesmith, *op. cit.*, n. 4, p. 7.

[17] John C. Ball and Emily S. Cottrell, "Admissions of Narcotic Drug Addicts to Public Health Service Hospitals, 1935–1963," *Public Health Reports*, 80 (June 1965), p. 475.

Chiefly, the new approach was marked by the inauguration of civil commitment programs, which defined the addict as a sick person in need of treatment rather than punishment. Facilities for the involuntary retention of addicts were renamed "hospitals" and parole relabeled as "outpatient treatment." The judgment of Alfred Lindesmith on such events, as we shall later attempt to document, seems squarely on target: "Programs of compulsory civil commitment represent ways of punishing addicts under the guise of treatment; what is new in these programs is the vocabulary rather than the practices." [18]

The Robinson Case

Civil commitment received forceful impetus when the United States Supreme Court in late June 1962 declared that statutes making addiction to narcotics a criminal offense violated constitutional principles. In a 6–2 decision, the Court relied upon the eighth amendment, outlawing "cruel and unusual punishment," to overrule the conviction of Lawrence Robinson, who had been sentenced to 90 days in jail in Los Angeles 2 years earlier after a jury had found him guilty of the misdemeanor of drug addiction. The majority of the Supreme Court concluded that drug addiction is an illness "comparable to leprosy, insanity, and the common cold" and that criminal punishment could not be inflicted for such an illness.[19] Two dissenters from the majority view insisted that addiction itself cannot be separated from use or possession of drugs and that the States should have the right to penalize addicts.[20]

At issue in the case was the question of whether Robinson could be convicted solely on evidence that he was an addict and not because he had been caught in possession of drugs.

The evidence was based upon a series of discolorations and punctures on Robinson's arm, which police said were the result of narcotic injections. Robinson testified (though the jury did not believe him) that the marks were due to an allergic condition contracted when he was in military service. Justice Stewart, in writing the Supreme Court's majority opinion, noted that he was not unmindful of the vicious evils of the narcotics traffic, but that he believed that there were "countless fronts on which these evils may be legitimately attacked." [21]

---

[18] Alfred R. Lindesmith, *Addiction and Opiates* (Chicago: Aldine, 1968), p. 240.

[19] *Robinson v. California*, 370 U.S. 660, 666–667 (1962).

[20] *Ibid.*, pp. 679–689.

[21] *Ibid.*, pp. 667–668.

The *Robinson* case was not without a strong element of irony, and in fact it may have been moot when the Supreme Court rendered its decision, for Robinson had died in a Los Angeles alley nearly a year before the decision. According to police reports, the cause of death was an overdose of narcotics.[22]

Ad Hoc Panel on Drug Abuse

It was largely to explore frontiers suggested by the *Robinson* case that the White House Conference on Narcotic and Drug Abuse was convened in September 1962. Prior to gathering, conferees were asked to study a preconference report prepared by an eight-man Ad Hoc Panel appointed by President Kennedy. The Panel stressed that "treatment and rehabilitation of narcotics addicts is best achieved through a strictly supervised and highly controlled parole system," and it declared its belief that drug abuse was "not a disease" but rather that it was "a manifestation of an inadequate personality unable to cope with the stresses of normal life." The Panel deplored, equally forcefully, both long prison terms and programs of drug maintenance, believing that "the compulsive drug abuser can be rehabilitated to a legal end and, in many cases, a productive place in society." [23]

The Ad Hoc Panel recommended that as a general rule a person withdrawn from drugs should remain in a drug-free environment about 5 months. Such an environment, the Panel said, should be "an institutional setting which allows freedom of movement within it, but which has perimeter security adequate to prevent introduction of drugs." Vocational training, physical fitness programs, and psychiatric help were seen as valuable approaches for the rehabilitation of drug addicts.[24]

At the same time, the Panel came out against periods of confinement extending beyond 5 months. After this length of institutionalization, it said, levels of recidivism approach those associated with premature release. The explanation for the Panel seemed to involve the building up of inordinate dependence upon institutional routine, a disabling consequence for the addict-prone personality. It was pointed out by the Panel that parole supervision would cost approximately $350 a year in the Federal system while incarceration in a

[22] "Drug Case Victory Won After Death of Addict," *Los Angeles Times*, June 26, 1962.

[23] White House Conference on Narcotic and Drug Abuse, *Proceedings* (Washington, D.C.: Government Printing Office, 1962), Appendix I, pp. 295–301.

[24] *Ibid.*, p. 297.

penitentiary would run to approximately $2,000 per person per year.[25]

White House Conference

Addressing the White House Conference on Narcotic and Drug Abuse during its opening ceremonies, Robert Kennedy, then Attorney General, gave voice to its keynote theme—that "we can relegate the anguish of drug addiction to the medical histories, along with Black Death, yellow fever and other onetime scourges of mankind." [26] Toward this end, the most noteworthy emphasis of the Conference was its strong support for programs of civil commitment.

Opposition had clearly crystallized by the time of the White House Conference against the harsh mandatory Federal sentences for narcotics offenses. A survey showed that 92 percent of the wardens of Federal prisons opposed mandatory sentences and 97 percent opposed the ban on parole for narcotics offenders. Judges were opposed to the same items in 73 percent and 86 percent of the cases; probation officers 83 and 86 percent; and United States attorneys 50 and 53 percent. The mandatory sentence, with no possibility of parole, it was said, "thwarts all efforts to deal sensibly and rationally with addicts and completely sweeps under the rug the tragic problem which they represent." [27]

Particular attention was paid at the White House Conference to a New York experiment which had concluded that it was essential that the family relationships of the addict be altered in some significant manner if the man was to become drug abstinent. As Meyer Diskind put the matter:

> It was recognized that in most instances the family was at the root of the addict's problem—either the family took no interest in him, permitting him to do as he pleased; or it dominated and directed his every move, leaving him with little or no freedom of action. Since the addict is part of the familial milieu, returning him to the same forces that caused his downfall in the past would inevitably lead to the same disastrous consequences. While treating the addict, some changes must also be effected in the family to bring out the constructive values of family living.[28]

A strong word of caution was entered into the Conference record by Harris Isbell, who had spent a lifetime conducting research on

---

[25] *Ibid.*, pp. 297–298.

[26] Leslie H. Whitten, "Executive Unit to Map Wide Narcotics Act," September 29, 1962.

[27] Thomas J. Dodd, in White House Conference, *op. cit.*, n. 22, pp. 230–232.

[28] Meyer H. Diskind, in *ibid.*, p. 78.

narcotic addiction. Isbell noted the failure of rehabilitative work at the Federal hospitals, and the emerging emphasis on newer kinds of programs. The treatment approaches being urged, Isbell stressed, were based on intuition only. Such innovations in the field of addiction, Isbell said, had to be approached experimentally and should be "broadly framed and sufficiently flexible to permit a testing of a variety of approaches, and to permit changes based on ongoing experience. The new programs should not," Isbell maintained, "be regarded as universal or final answers; but should be set up in part as rigidly controlled, but limited clinical trials." [29]

Current Treatment Methods

Methods of dealing with narcotic addicts cover a wide range and cater to highly discrepant populations, so that it is difficult to declare that one method is superior to another without specifying clearly the kinds of populations being served, the goals being sought, and the accuracy of reported results. Some programs, for example, report outcome in terms only of persons who remain affiliated with the treatment regimen for more than 3 months; for these, program dropouts are not failures. Obviously, such measurement tactics make comparative statements highly misleading.

Extramural approaches may be categorized in terms of their stress upon the following rehabilitative themes: (1) the community approach; (2) communal treatment programs; (3) treatments with a religious stress; and (4) chemotherapy regimens. Each type will be considered in some detail below.

The Community Approach. The community treatment approach to narcotic addiction is founded on the assumptions that (a) the addict developed his dependence on drugs in his own environment; (b) he will almost invariably remain in or return to that environment; and (c) treatment must therefore concentrate not upon removal of the addict from the cues of his drug condition but upon providing him with the ability either to ignore or to revise his previous responses to such cues. It is to be noted that such an approach has inherent hazards because it normally operates in neighborhoods with heavy drug traffic, and that its subjects are apt to have longstanding reciprocal obligations with persons involved in drug traffic.[30]

---

[29] Harris Isbell, "Need for Research on Methods of Treatment of Narcotic Addiction," *ibid.*, p. 93.

[30] Leon Brill, "Community Approaches to the Addiction Problem," in *Perspectives on Narcotic Addiction* (Boston: Massachusetts Health Research Institute, 1964), pp. 45–58.

The community approach may also concentrate energies upon changing the community itself, by mobilizing its leaders and its citizens to clean up some of its more patent elements of social malaise. As Donald B. Louria has noted: "Unless we stop just treating the disease after it has occurred and do something about prevention by eliminating urban decay and deterioration we will not succeed in minimizing the heroin problem." [31]

Citizen groups may also be mobilized to provide assistance to narcotic addicts, to secure jobs for them if they are able to work, and to provide detoxification resources, if they are desired. It is, of course, often difficult to get the addict and community members together, and there is always the risk of further alienating the addict by community disapproval.

Communal Treatment Approaches. Perhaps the greatest publicity ever accorded a correctional rehabilitative program has been that given to Synanon, a self-help treatment program for onetime addicts operated by abstinent addicts. With vast real estate holdings, a comprehensive program, and a large coterie of drug-free members, Synanon has forever dispelled the myth that "once an addict always an addict." [32] Typical of the Synanon attitude is its resistance to allowing a resident to be tested by any method of drug detection. It is claimed at Synanon that testing by urinalysis or by Nalline indicates a distrust of the addict that may deflate his already shaky ego.

One problem associated with communal approaches to addicts, such as that at Synanon, concerns the tendency of persons involved in them to segregate themselves from what may be regarded as more desirable ways of life. [33] It has been said, for instance, that Synanon is "unlikely to be helpful as a general rehabilitative program because it is a secretive cult. It has returned fewer than 100 persons to the community in 7 years." [34] On the other side, it can be maintained, of course, that freedom from drug addiction is itself an inherently desirable goal, and that lifelong association with a communal treatment facility is a perfectly adequate raison d'etre.

[31] Donald B. Louria, "Cool Talk About Hot Drugs," *New York Times Magazine*, August 6, 1967, p. 47.

[32] Barbara L. Austin, *Sad Nun at Synanon* (New York: Holt, Rinehart, and Winston, 1970) ; Daniel Casriel, *So Fair A House* (Englewood Cliffs, N.J.: Prentice-Hall, 1963) ; S. Guy Endore, *Synanon* (Garden City, N.Y.: Doubleday, 1968) ; Lewis Yablonsky, *The Tunnel Back: Synanon* (New York: Macmillan, 1965).

[33] David Sternberg, "Synanon House—A Consideration of Its Implications for American Correction," *Journal of Criminal Law, Criminology, and Police Science*, 54 (December 1963), pp. 447–455.

[34] Louria, *op. cit.*, n. 30, p. 44.

Treatments with a Religious Stress. Some of the most effective work with drug addicts has been accomplished by programs operating with a strong religious motif. It may be that the emotional approach of a religiously toned program has more to offer drug addicts than any other kind of offender. Both drugs and religion have elements of self-transcendence, and it was not wholly by chance that Karl Marx, inveighing against organized religion, labeled it the "opiate of the masses." Few persons working regularly in the field of narcotic addiction have remained unimpressed with the power of religious conversion to compete with the attraction of narcotics. On the other hand, of course, there are many addicts to whom a program with religious overtones is unacceptable, and in whom such an approach would create more antagonism than well-being. Missionary work for churches, particularly those of an evangelical bent may, however, offer an outlet for some addicts and supply a self-identity that they may be lacking.

A newspaper report of a Teen-Challenge Center in Brooklyn, New York, provides some of the flavor of the rehabilitative emphasis and potential of religiously oriented programs for addicts:

> Patients normally remain at the Teen-Challenge Center about 3 weeks and live under a strict daily schedule. This includes minor chores around the building, praying and attending chapel for several hours, individual counseling and Bible study. Smoking is prohibited.
>
> The reward for a youth who responds well is a trip to the Teen-Challenge farm in Pennsylvania. The farm, nestled in the rolling hills of the Pennsylvania Dutch country, "sure beats the Harlem streets," according to one young man who has been there 3 months.
>
> "This is the best place for us," said Phil, a 28-year-old Harlem resident. "We're serving the Lord here." Phil, like many of the young men in Teen-Challenge, hopes eventually to attend Bible school and work full-time for the program. Several others admitted they were not yet secure enough to face the city. But one seemed to speak for many when he said, "I'm in with the Lord now, so I know I'll make it." [35]

Chemotherapy Regimens. Continuous efforts are underway by chemists to synthesize a drug which will have the same effect as the opiate derivatives but will not produce the addiction syndrome and not throw the user into withdrawal when he is deprived of the drug. If such a compound is ultimately developed, it is apt to have a tremendous impact upon social and legal attitudes toward drug addiction.

---

[35] "Youth Program Aids Narcotic Addicts," *New York Times*, February 16, 1964.

Meanwhile, intensive efforts are currently in progress which use other drugs to wean addicts away from the opiates. The most promising results to date have been obtained through use of methadone, a synthetic narcotic which was developed by the Germans during World War II, and has now been employed for more than 5 years in an experimental program under the direction of Vincent P. Dole and his wife, Marie Nyswander, in New York City. Addicts' intake of methadone, a water-clear, slightly bitter tasting liquid, can be stabilized at about 100 milligrams daily, and a week's supply of the drug costs about $2. Promising early results have led to the initiation of methadone programs for 9,000 addicts in seven different States. In New York City, the methadone program involves 12 participating hospitals and several street clinics. Of the 2,500 persons enrolled in the program, according to Dole, 83 percent have remained free of illicit drug use, and the great majority are working, keeping house, or going to school.[36] "They are," Dole observes, "successfully holding jobs in banks, hospitals, as couriers for jewelry concerns, as guards and engineers in major industries." [37] Weekly urinalysis tests for all methadone patients are required by Federal regulations which govern experimental use of the drug, so that readdiction rates can be rather readily determined. Methadone is a pain-killing drug, and it counteracts heroin by blocking its narcotic action. Patients taking methadone build up a tolerance to opiates so that they no longer can get "high" from them.[38]

Major objection to methadone maintenance concentrates on the belief that methadone itself is similar to heroin and that no significant progress has been made therefore toward freeing the addict from his condition of drug dependence. As one critic has put the matter, using methadone is "like giving the alcoholic in the Bowery bourbon instead of whiskey in an attempt to treat his alcoholism." It is also said that methadone, being a painkiller, masks disease entities so that the user may never become aware of suffering from things such as appendicitis. It is said as well that methadone users constitute a public danger as automobile drivers and in situations requiring control and skill.[39]

---

[36] Buckley, op. cit., n. 9.

[37] Gerd Wilcke, "Growing Use of Narcotics Saps Industry," New York Times, March 22, 1970.

[38] John Langrod, "A Bibliography of the Methadone Maintenance Treatment of Heroin Addiction," International Journal of Addictions, 5 (September 1970), pp. 581-591.

[39] Gertrude Samuels, "Methadone, Fighting Fire with Fire," New York Times Magazine, October 15, 1967, pp. 44-45.

Leakage of methadone drugs also has been raised as an objection to maintenance programs which, once the number of persons involved in them becomes large enough, usually allow the exaddict to take some of the drug with him for self-administration, rather than have him report daily for his supply. Under such circumstances, there have been cases of young children obtaining methadone in quantities which for them were lethal, and instances of diversion of methadone to the black market.[40] Proponents of methadone maintenance, however, counter these allegations by noting significant drops in crime among their clientele and the establishment of patterns of productivity that meet social criteria of adequacy, and they contrast these outcomes with those for other programs and with the life styles of the addicts with whom they are working prior to their involvement with methadone maintenance.

Two other drugs have also been employed for experimental purposes in attempts to deal with opiate addiction. Cyclazocine is used much the same as methadone, but it is reported to have less addictive potency and to be more effective in blocking the impact of heroin.[41] Naloxone is regarded as having similar qualities as cyclazocine.[42] Neither drug, however, has been subjected to extensive testing as yet.

Civil Commitment. Civil commitment procedures, as we noted earlier, are used for narcotic addicts who, since *Robinson*, may no longer be punished under criminal law for their condition. Examination of the results of the work of narcotic civil commitment programs provides material regarding possible consequences of the substitution of civil procedures for criminal law for offenses with which this review is concerned.

In New York, for example, verdicts on the addict civil commitment program are summarized in a caustic lead sentence of a newspaper story: "The State Narcotic Addiction Control Commission, set up 2 years ago, is in need of rehabilitation itself, a growing number of critics say." At the time—April 1969—four Commission employees

---

[40] Cf., "Yonkers Addict is Indicted in a Death by Methadone," *New York Times*, February 26, 1972 (AP); Jay Levin, "Ex-Addict's Methadone Kills Boy," *New York Post*, July 10, 1969; James Markham, "Study Finds Black Market Developing in Methadone," *New York Times*, January 2, 1972.

[41] Jerome H. Jaffe and Leon Brill, "Cyclazocine, A Long Acting Narcotic Antagonist," *International Journal of Addictions*, 1 (January 1966), pp. 99–123.

[42] S. Archer and R. M. Rees, "Narcotic Antagonists and the Problems of Drug Dependence," in Robert T. Harris, William M. McIsaac, and Charles R. Schuster, Jr., (editors), *Drug Dependence* (Austin: University of Texas Press, 1970), p. 5.

were awaiting trial on charges of beating up addicts with "booted feet, a blackjack, and handcuffs." Most of the addicts committed to the program maintained that it was no different than those run by correctional authorities and that the results obtained showed no improvement over the criminal approach.[43]

Confirmation of the failure of civil commitment of narcotic addicts to achieve success rates different from those of prison programs is supplied by a comprehensive study of the work of the California civil commitment program for addicts, which has been operating since 1961. By statutory provision, the purpose of the program is to treat, rehabilitate, and control, not to punish. Commitment to the program is based not only on determination that an individual is an addict, but also on the ground that he may be in danger of becoming an addict. The median length of stay in the program has been about 14 months. Subsequently, the detoxified addict is placed on "outpatient" status for a statutory limit of 7 years. Outpatients report regularly to supervising agents, must be tested for drug use, and may be required to attend group counseling sessions. It is said that the restrictions on outpatients are "slightly more encompassing than parole restrictions on nonaddict felons and are usually administered more strictly."

Statistics show that only 35 percent of the 1,209 outpatients released from the program between June 1962 and June 1964 remained in good standing for one year and only 16 percent for 3 years. Most of the failure to remain in good standing came as a consequence of a return to drug use. The rate of failure for the civil commitment program was found to be essentially similar to that of other regimens for addicts operated under correctional auspices. Under such conditions, arguments for civil commitment become attenuated, since there are no compensating gains to accommodate for losses in due-process protections. John Kramer summarized these legal objections by noting that they maintain "that commitment for a treatment which is not proven effective is cruel and unusual punishment and that it is a subterfuge around the stringent protection afforded to a person accused of a crime but not to one 'accused' of an illness." The same writer, summarizing empirical and legal strictures bearing on civil commitment, observes: "The trouble with the California civil commitment program, and perhaps the New York and Federal civil addict programs too, is not merely that

---

[43] Richard Severo, "Addicts and the State: An Unfulfilled Aim," *New York Times*, August 21, 1969.

it violates the spirit, if not the letter, of the Supreme Court decision in *Robinson v. California*, but also that it does not work." [44]

Similar kinds of reservations have been voiced regarding the premises underlying therapeutic approaches such as that involved in civil commitment. Francis D. Wormuth, for instance, has maintained that such programs run contrary to the fundamental tenets of democracy. "It is doubtful that democracy could survive in a society organized on the principle of therapy rather than judgment, error rather than sin. If men are free and equal, they must be judged rather than hospitalized." [45] In more strident tones, Thomas S. Szasz, a psychiatrist, maintains that "most of the legal and social applications of psychiatry, undertaken in the name of psychiatric liberalism, are actually instances of despotism" and that there is a danger abroad in the society of "tyranny by therapy." Szasz, referring to civil commitment programs, insists that:

> [T]he psychiatric disposition of offenders seems to me a colossal subterfuge. It provides the "offender-patient" neither absolution from criminal guilt *nor* treatment. It is nothing more than an expedient method for "disposing" of persons displaying certain kinds of antisocial conduct. Every form of social oppression . . . has, at some time during its history, been justified on the ground of helpfulness toward the oppressed. [46]

Narcotics Control in Britain

The British experience with narcotics is often used to buttress advocacy of alteration in American procedures, though it is difficult to extract from the British records a fair reading of the likely consequences in the United States of use of similar approaches. It is difficult to say, for instance, whether the increase in recent years in addiction in Britain represents a failure of its treatment approach to drug prescribing, or whether the relatively low overall national rate of addiction in Britain represents a triumph of that approach. Or, indeed, whether factors having little to do with the treatment approach underlie the drug situation in Britain, just as the low British crime rate is said to be a function of "national character" rather than enforcement strategies.

[44] John C. Kramer, Richard A. Bass, and John Berecochea, "Civil Commitment for Addicts: The California Program," *American Journal of Psychiatry*, 125 (December 1968), pp. 816–824.

[45] Francis D. Wormuth, *Origins of Modern Constitutionalism* (New York: Harper and Row, 1949), p. 212.

[46] Thomas S. Szasz, *Law, Liberty and Psychiatry: An Inquiry into the Social Uses of Mental Health Practices* (New York: Macmillan, 1963), pp. vii, 114, 185.

Britain, as it often has been noted, does not have a system for handling drugs, but has operated in terms of a series of administrative responses under medical auspices since passage of the Dangerous Drug Act of 1920, which placed stringent restrictions on the import, export, manufacture, sale, and possession of narcotics. Until 1968, all British physicians were allowed to prescribe drugs to any patient, with the understanding that their expertise would dictate their treatment technique. They could sustain an addict on heroin if his removal from that drug was contraindicated, but they were expected (though not required) to attempt to withdraw a patient for whom the prognosis appeared favorable.[47]

During the period following the Second World War the average addict in Britain was a woman over 50 years of age. In 1954, there were but 57 addicts known to the Government (reporting was mandatory), with most of them using morphine. That figure had risen to 489 by 1960, made up of 94 persons who were using heroin and 177 addicted to morphine. Another 218 regularly used cocaine, methadone, or pethidine.[48] Thereafter, the number of heroin addicts nearly doubled every 16 months, and by 1970 it was estimated that there were about 3,000 heroin addicts in London.[49] English authorities were inclined to blame this rapid rise on the practices of a few doctors who, it was said, either out of a desire for money or because of feelings of humanity, had lavished more heroin on addict patients than these persons required for their own use, giving them the wherewithal to feed a black market trade in opiates. Nonetheless, to keep the matter in perspective, it was pointed out that London is about the size of New York City, and that the 3,000 addicts in the British capital represent but 3 percent of the total number of addicts found in New York.

The 1968 regulations required physicians to be licensed by the Government if they were to treat addicts. To date, about 500 doctors, all attached to Government clinics, have been licensed. About half of them are using methadone to treat their patients, and official statistics now indicate that there are 1,417 heroin addicts and 1,687 methadone addicts in Britain. English reports indicate, however, that addicts are reluctant to take methadone orally. "The reason," a British physician notes, "apparently lies in a peculiar syndrome that

[47] See, generally, Edwin M. Schur, *Narcotic Addiction in Britain and America: The Impact of Public Policy* (Bloomington: Indiana University Press, 1962).

[48] Richard Severo, "The British Drug 'System,'" *New York Times Magazine*, September 13, 1970, p. 47.

[49] Richard Severo, "Britain Curbing Legal-Heroin System," *New York Times*, March 30, 1970.

develops with heroin addiction—the enjoyment of sticking a needle into the body." Taken by needle, methadone offers a high—a "kick"— and a subsequent euphoria that, according to some addicts, is almost as effective as that provided by heroin.[50]

Policy Considerations in the United States

Analysis of the impact of opiate addiction upon the individual, other persons, and the society has to specify the conditions under which various consequences occur. The health of the addict, for instance, may differ in situations where he can obtain opiates under sterile, medical conditions in contrast to conditions apt to prevail when drugs are outlawed. The crime rate associated with drug use would also likely vary significantly under different types of control systems. In addition, there are outcomes, some of them of basic importance, which are not readily predictable. We are not certain, for example, whether duplication of the British approach would reduce the number of addicts or increase that number in the United States, or whether it would change the character of the addict population in an essential regard from that found today.

While present policies regarding opiates are a matter of intense public concern, there appears to be little agreement on the proper procedures to follow. There are those who favor tougher penalties against both users and sellers of opiates, and particularly against the latter, and there are those who insist that the only acceptable national policy is to permit a free trade in opiates, with the user choosing whether or not to use the drug. Various alternative suggestions, taking positions nearer to the middle of the road, have also been put forward. Samples of such positions will be presented below, so that they may be kept in mind when we review the known and anticipated consequences of proposed policies.

Three possible approaches—with a fourth, that of favoring legalization of heroin, notably absent—appear in a statement by Alan M. Dershowitz of the Harvard Law School which reviews the contemporary drug scene. Particularly significant is Dershowitz' conclusion that none of the likely methods for dealing with narcotics offers a particularly attractive resolution. The same pessimism will be found in most reasoned reviews of present conditions. What is striking in these statements is how different their tone is from that taken in regard to abortion and homosexuality, which we have considered earlier. In those debates, partisans were likely to take strong posi-

---

[50] Richard Severo, "Legal Heroin Rare in Britain as Doctors Turn to Methadone," *New York Times*, January 24, 1971.

tions and to argue that failure to follow their programs would produce unconscionable results, while changes such as those they propose
would bring about something resembling the best of all possible
worlds, at least in regard to the behavior under question.

But Dershowitz finds none of the likely options in regard to
opiates particularly satisfactory:

> Various amelioratives, such as methadone, are being tried:
> But large numbers of addicts will not accept substitutes; they
> will continue to want heroin regardless of what else is offered.
> Moreover, the likelihood of real cure is still statistically small.
> Accordingly, three options would seem to be available for those
> hard-core addicts who do not respond to currently available
> programs: (1) they can be confined for longer periods of time
> (on the theory that at least while in prison they will commit no
> acquisitive crimes); (2) they can be treated as they are today
> (confined for short periods, and then released to commit more
> crimes); or (3) they can be given free heroin at state-run clinics.
> None of these options is satisfactory; each has considerable
> drawbacks. But . . . we must select the least bad from among
> a number of unsatisfactory alternatives.[51]

Taken in context with the rest of what he writes, there is little
doubt that Dershowitz' inclination is toward the clinic approach to
dispensation of opiates, though he would require a good deal more
evidence, both empirical and logical, before he would clearly endorse
such a stand. Quite different is the position of the Hudson Institute,
which undertook the preparation of a position paper, *Policy Concerning Drug Abuse in New York State*, for New York State's
Bureau of the Budget. The Institute clearly opts for more stringent
control measures, though it too grants that its program is no panacea.

"Medical treatment is not the answer (at least not yet)," one of
the subheadings of the Hudson Institute report notes. "The basic
reason is that medicine does not yet know enough about how to cure
or treat narcotics addiction."[52] The report stresses the necessity for
"quick improvement in the enforcement program," a policy statement almost universally put forward by persons who believe that
the Government should remain in the business of attempting to control narcotics traffic. "We believe that good police performance,
combined with appropriate supports from courts, corrections, and
prosecutors, could deal a very damaging blow to the heroin distribu-

[51] Alan M. Dershowitz, "Law and Order: Crimes of Degree," *New York Times
Book Review*, February 21, 1971, Part II, p. 4.
[52] Max Singer and Jane Newitt, *Policy Concerning Drug Abuse in New York
State* (Vol. I: *The Basic Study*) (Croton-on-Hudson: Hudson Institute, May 31,
1970), p. 128.

tion system and substantially reduce the amount of heroin that flows through the distribution system to users." [53]

The Hudson Institute recommends allowing an addict the option of joining a methadone maintenance program, with institutionalization if he fails to remain with the program. It would have areas of high opiate use, such as New York City, establish special schools, or at least, designate special sections of regular schools into which students found using drugs would be assigned. These schools, it is argued, "would make it more difficult to infect nondrug users, and perhaps provide some useful treatment or extra education for youthful drug users." It is noted that such an approach would not involve use of the criminal law, but "merely" an extension of the powers of the Board of Education and its administration of truancy laws. The Institute writers argue against educational programs in schools as a method for attempting to deal with recruitment of new addicts. "Anecdotal evidence," it is said, "suggests that many popular types of education programs for children tend to increase rather than to decrease drug use." [54]

The Institute reporters felt that their proposals, while they would reduce the size of the heroin problem, would nonetheless leave "substantial" numbers of opiate addicts untouched. Only a "quarantine concept," which they supposed "may well be too strong medicine for the State to use" would radically cut into the size of the addict population. But the approaches offered, it was believed, would be "a good-sized bite at the problem," and then "after 3 or 4 years it would be time to see whether more stringent or different efforts need to be tried." [55]

Perhaps as much as anything else, the recommendations for New York State by the Hudson Institute, after the Institute's long and penetrating survey, underline the complexity of the narcotics situation and the tendency to single out one or another emphasis for concentrated remedial attention. The Institute, its fancy caught by the idea of "quarantine" for addicts, because of its apparent conviction that the use of opiates is "contagious" and can only be attacked by isolating carriers, backs away at the last moment from this as a somewhat unpalatable resolution. Instead, there is talk of stepped-up and tougher law enforcement as a secondary method for achieving withdrawal of the addict from the free society, though there are few very definite suggestions on how a method that has been tried in

[53] *Ibid.*, p. 127.
[54] *Ibid.*, pp. 129–131.
[55] *Ibid.*, p. 130.

varying degrees for almost 60 years can suddenly be turned into an effective weapon.

Rather more simple and direct is the proposal endorsed at the 1970 biennial conference of leaders of the American Civil Liberties Union (though not as yet approved by the group's Board of Directors, to which it was forwarded).[56] Here, by a stroke of the pen, the legal problem of addiction is eliminated, simply by redefining the traffic in and the use of drugs as something other than a matter of concern of the criminal law system. The ACLU group felt no need to speculate on the implications of such an action either for individuals or for the society at large, presumably since it was its conviction that the loss in individual liberty involved in the continuation of criminalization of opiate addiction was more important than the consequences of the approach that they endorsed. This is, of course, not unlikely, though it is also possible that other losses of liberty, some of them rather subtle, might ensue in the wake of implementation of the ACLU suggestion. It may perhaps be fanciful to suggest that for some their liberty has been increased when the consequences of a suggested social policy is their immutable dependence upon a depressant drug, involving a binding timetable of need to secure the drug in order to avoid intense physical pain. This is, of course, a unique trait of heroin. One is free to choose to use it or not, but one is not free thereafter—or at least not nearly as free as he originally was—to cease heroin use with equanimity. But perhaps this is not a significant issue. The same, and more, may be said about suicide. If an individual is to be free to end his life on his own terms, without state interference even upon rather convincing demonstration that this is indeed his almost certain intent, then, after the suicidal act, his earthly freedom has most assuredly come to an end. And, both with suicide and with the use of heroin, it most often may be presumed, perhaps, that the person making the choice was aware of the later implications of his chosen behavior.

Somewhat more complex, though further removed from the original focus of argument, are the implications for other members of a society of the free choice of some members to select dependence upon a drug that, at least to some extent, may undercut their social effectiveness in terms of the more usual definitions of this concept. This, however, is a consideration equally applicable to a wide range of commitments by individuals made with as free a choice as they can exercise without suasion by the criminal law, a commitment, say, to beach lounging rather than to factory work. We will assume that

---

[56] "Drug Use Held No Crime 'Per Se,' " *New York Times*, January 15, 1970.

such choice and its consequences must be tolerated by others in a free society as part of the defense of their own choices, at least until there can be such a compelling demonstration of substantial interference with ordinary life as to dictate interference with the person choosing opiates. We shall return to this item later, after we have an inventory of the apparent implications of opiate use for a range of personal and social conditions. First, though, we can record the ACLU proposal, issued under the heading of "Control Over One's Body."

1. An individual has a right to use his own body as he wishes and this right includes the use and possession of narcotics.

2. The use and possession of drugs is not per se a crime and should involve no criminal penalties; however, conduct resulting from the use or possession of drugs may invoke civil or criminal penalties.

3. The government may regulate, including by means of government monopoly, the sale of drugs.

4. Compulsory treatment or incarceration of drug users is a violation of civil liberties.

5. Resolutions one through four apply only to adults and no position is taken as to the right of juveniles to use or possess drugs other than to recommend that a comprehensive study of the rights of juveniles in this and other areas be instituted.[57]

Causes of Opiate Addiction

Etiological speculation often seems to be a vainglorious enterprise in regard to drug addiction because, as with so many social behaviors, the causal explanations seem to reduce themselves to tautological statements and to be of little predictive, curative, or policy utility. It is said, for instance, that addicts tend to be passive persons, easily prone to dependence upon a pharmacological agent that will allow them to avoid confrontation with the imperatives of "reality." [58] But not all passive persons, by any means, are attracted to or remain with opiate use. And, in many ways, the demands of an addict's existence are a good deal more "real" and inexorable than the demands of life lived in most any other manner. "Scores" must be made, dangers must be avoided, and this must be done very regularly; otherwise, physical pain, often of considerable severity, will strike.[59]

[57] *Ibid.*

[58] David P. Ausubel, *Drug Addiction: Physiological, Psychological, and Sociological Aspects* (New York: Random House, 1958), p. 42.

[59] Cf., Gilbert Geis, "Hypes, Hippies, and Hypocrites," *Youth and Society*, 1 (June 1970), p. 374.

So, too, other "explanations" seem either superficial or, at best, after-the-fact descriptions. "Drugs are the instant mother, the instant mother they never had, the nurturing mother they never had," Bruno Bettelheim, a psychiatrist, has insisted,[60] but how far one may proceed with such an observation is not clear. It is based, of course, on the supposition that there is a necessary quantity of "mothering" required to produce "normal" behavior, and that drug use is "abnormal" and that it has certain qualities which allow it, in its "deviant" and "sick" way, to compensate for the original absence of healthy upbringing. The intricate web of arguable value premises threaded through such a series of postulates makes accepting them at face value foolhardy. One may argue, for instance, that if the opiate drugs adequately substitute for lack of love then they ought to be permitted to do so, absent any "better" method of providing "necessary" maternal nutriment.

It is said that heroin use is a function of the misery of slum existence and poverty, since this is where such use tends to be concentrated, and that the most effective means to reduce addiction is to reduce the manifestations of social malaise in our midst. This may, of course, be true, but certain societies, such as Sweden, which have been reasonably successful in making life less hazardous and threatening, nonetheless report high rates of drug use.[61]

It is said, with truth, that drug use is a necessary function of the availability of the drug, and that many persons "prone" to heroin use avoid addiction simply because they do not move in circles where the drugs are available and where examples and definitions regarding their use encourage such behavior. On such a ground, programs to dry up the heroin supply are obvious attacks—perhaps the only clear kinds of obvious attacks—on the drug problem. But such attacks do not contain within themselves the elements of their own justification, unless the case can be made for elimination of drugs on other grounds. After all, women (and rape), and art exhibits (and the theft of art objects) are all a function of the availability of people and things for legitimate and for illegal ends.

It seems necessary, nonetheless, to gain some insight into the wellsprings of opiate use before attempting to assess the impact of such use on individuals and on the society. Perhaps the simplest and most

---

[60] Quoted in Murray Schumach, "Psychiatrist Discounts School Help to Addicts," *New York Times*, February 7, 1970.

[61] Richard Severo, "Drug Problem in Sweden is Similar to That in U.S.," *New York Times*, April 10, 1970; "The Swedish Experience," in U.S. House of Representatives, Select Committee on Crime, *Amphetamines* (House Report No. 91–1807, 91st Cong., 2d Sess., 1971), pp. 19–21.

efficient way of doing so is to indicate that, like most, if not all, behaviors—legal or illegal—heroin use provides for the person involved in it a satisfying outcome. For drug use that outcome is clearly one of physical pleasure from the response to injection of a euphoria-creating drug into the body. Opiates are often said by addicts to be more pleasurable than orgasm. "It's like, the best way I can think of, sweet death," a lifelong addict has said. "Because it is sweet, overpoweringly so in a lot of ways, but with an edge of real terrible danger, I guess that's why everyone has to play with it." [62] The physical pleasure of drug use is, of course, a common theme. Less often noted is the pleasure of involvement in the drug scene. That satisfaction has been enthusiastically portrayed by an addict in the following terms:

> . . . if narcotics was easy to come by, there wouldn't be half as many addicts. To take narcotics right now, it is cloak-and-dagger, it's spy work, it's something out of television, believe me. You have to walk the street, you have to secure a pusher, you have to locate the money to buy this narcotics, you have to check in dark hallways, on roofs, go through cellars, all this running about, all the time, keeping one eye out for the police.
> All this. This is an adventure for a young man. And when you finally get your narcotics back to your pad where you can use it, you say to yourself: Man, I did it, I beat the fuzz. I made the scene. And you feel relieved.[63]

Of notable importance in regard to drug addiction is the fact that the user has not developed adequate inhibitions against use of the drug, that is, that the society does not have an ethos of sufficient conviction to persuade him that what he is doing is so wrong that he must cease from doing it. Perhaps such an ethos cannot be developed except at the sacrifice of other values and the intolerable closing of avenues to "acceptable" kinds of pleasure. Here, too, of course, such ideas are tautological: it is obvious that anybody who does anything voluntarily does so because he is not adequately convinced that he ought not to do so. But the point is worth emphasis because it insists that either adequate means ought to be found to persuade persons against opiates—if such persuasive points can be found and conveyed—or the effort to criminalize heroin use ought to be abandoned. Illustrative of the reasoning process of an addict regarding drugs are observations contained in a letter to the present writer,

---

[62] Helen MacGill Hughes (editor), *The Fantastic Lodge* (Boston: Houghton Mifflin, 1961), p. 124.

[63] Jeremy Larner (editor), *The Addict in the Street* (New York: Grove, 1964), p. 100.

after the addict who is writing had returned to drugs following a long abstinent period:

> But one thing I'm certain of . . . was that the addiction that followed was predictable. Not only predictable, but axiomatic. And what is perhaps most ironic is that I knew this; I was absolutely convinced that drugs equaled death; moreover I was convinced that drugs were the one thing I couldn't handle—that they rendered me powerless over my acts . . . . I can only marvel at this, and wonder. A strong death-wish? An inability to assimilate success? The uncontrolled anger and rebellion of my earlier years? Christ! Who knows? Least of all I.
>
> It's very difficult for me to assume a moral stance. My morality rests on other values than those society calls illegal. The best I can say for illegality is that it will cause one to go to jail—a not particularly appetizing prospect. Consequently, I feel no remorse for the countless felonies I committed during my readdiction. But I am deeply shamed by using [my co-worker's] checking account in one of my activities. It goes against *my* morality. The truth of the matter was that I didn't have to. Even though I knew he personally wouldn't be financially harmed, still I had other options. There were already many other ways of securing checks. I remember when I got them I told myself, "You're going to be sorry for this." When I answered myself in the affirmative and went ahead anyway, I told myself, "You're doing something else then." When I again answered in the affirmative I asked, "What, then?" I can only describe my response in terms of a well-recognized feeling: the welling of a seething anger which shouted to all the unhearing. . . . Again it was a final, irrevocable act of defiance, shouted into a void, reverberating against walls of indifference. The act had meaning for me . . . .

If the foregoing may serve as a basis for generalization (though it is difficult to say how applicable its ideas are to heroin addicts as a group), it certainly emphasizes the selective morality of the addict, choosing one set of laws for his allegiance (you should not betray a friend) and rejecting another set (you should not be concerned about personal habits which do not affect others). It might be noted, however, that in this particular case his personal morality was not sufficiently strong to prevent his violating his own code, so that it can hardly be said that the articulated acceptance of beliefs necessarily protects against their violation. For the therapeutically inclined, of course, the letter writer's expressed anger at his social "invisibility" would undoubtedly provide fuel for interpretation, such interpretation taking the form, perhaps, of a conclusion that an inability to accept the fact that the world attends to its own business, and not to ours or to us, is one of the "reality" principles that must be accepted before a state of nondrug-dependent "maturity" can be achieved.

Consequences of Opiate Use

For the individual, we have already indicated that steady use of opiates over a long period of time likely would not produce untoward physical sequelae, presuming that no unusual events accompanied the drug use [64]—that is, provided the drug was uncontaminated and administered under sterile conditions and that its use was not attended by neglect of other aspects of self-care. It might be said that there is no reason why these circumstances cannot rather readily be achieved, if the society is so inclined; that is, drug use certainly need not be related to things such as nutritional neglect.

The drugs themselves mask and may in fact treat certain problems. "With amazing consistency," Marie Nyswander has written, addicts "insist that when on drugs they never have colds, whereas they are dogged by all sorts of minor ailments when they are off drugs." [65] The involvement of an 85-year-old addict, who had used drugs all his adult existence, in the Portland, Oregon, methadone maintenance program may be taken as indicative of the fact that under regular opiate use an individual may live as long as others, with the drug creating certain liabilities (less concern for one's well-being, for instance) and certain assets (less tension, for instance) that probably balance out on an overall health inventory.[66]

Nor do the drugs appear to effect either intelligence or physical performance. Intelligence tests of addicts while on and off drugs show no appreciable difference, nor do tests of their capacity for physical performance, no matter how many years they have been on drugs—a rather astonishing fact in view of their generally unproductive lives.[67]

The matter of consequences of drug use to individual well-being is not nearly so benign under present conditions, with the opiate drugs outlawed. In such circumstances, there is a good deal of physical disability and a not-inconsequential death rate resulting from opiate addiction.

[64] See, e.g., Marie Nyswander, *The Drug Addict as a Patient* (New York: Grune and Stratton, 1965), p. 60.

[65] *Ibid.*, p. 110.

[66] Robert Reinhold, "Methadone for Drug Addicts is Gaining in Popularity," *New York Times*, July 26, 1970.

[67] Ralph R. Brown and J. Edward Partington, "The Intelligence of the Narcotic Drug Addict," *Journal of General Psychology*, 26 (January 1942), pp. 175–179.

The lethal character of heroin use today can be read from the fact that narcotic overdosing, involving heroin primarily, is the leading cause of death in New York City in the 15-to-35 year age group. In 1969, there were 1,031 such deaths in New York City. About half of the persons dying were under age 23, another 215 were under 19, and one person was only 12 years old. This compares to an average age of 35 years for persons overdosing fatally in 1950 in New York City. The increasing number of such overdose deaths—in 1968 there were 654; in 1965, 306, and in 1960, 199—has been attributed to the growing number of addicts, to the growing carelessness of the sellers, and to the increasing adulteration of the drugs for sale, which may lead users who occasionally encounter an uncut dosage of heroin to be particularly susceptible, because of their low tolerance level, to its lethal impact.[68]

Heroin usage with unsterile needles and contaminated drugs is also believed to be related to high rates of hepatitis and tetanus, both debilitating and dangerous diseases. The association between tetanus and drug addiction has been known for more than 90 years. The majority of patients treated in Chicago and New York City today for tetanus are drug addicts, and in a study of the New York cases, 90 percent of the patients died. All told, approximately 8 percent of the total number of addict fatalities are due to tetanus.[69]

Serum hepatitis, a painfully debilitating and sometimes fatal liver disease, is the most frequently observed infectious complication hospitalizing the heroin addict. The high incidence of hepatitis among addicts is said to result from sharing of hypodermic needles and from "naive ideas about sterilization." [70] From the addict population hepatitis may be spread to the nondrug using population, particularly through blood transfusions, since addicts, often hard-pressed for money, constitute a disproportionately high percentage of persons who sell their blood to blood banks in metropolitan areas. Since the beginning of 1971 in New York, Massachusetts, and a number of other States, all donated blood must be tested serologically for the recently uncovered Australia antigen, an indicator of the presence of hepatitis in the blood sample. The accuracy of the test, however, is believed to be no better than 50 percent.[71]

---

[68] Martin Arnold, "Narcotic Deaths Put at Over 1,050," *New York Times*, December 30, 1970.

[69] Charles E. Cherubin, "The Medical Sequelae of Narcotic Addiction," *Annals of Internal Medicine*, 67 (July 1967), pp. 23–33.

[70] Batonbacal and Slipyan, *op. cit.*, n. 1, p. 321.

[71] Martin Arnold, "Risk to Public Seen as Hepatitis Rises Among Drug Users," *New York Times*, February 7, 1971.

Opiate use has further possible implications for the health of the addict because of his traditional neglect of his personal well-being, which is often a consequence of the necessity to employ all of his available financial resources to pay for his drug supply. Among women, heroin use is associated with a high rate of death and trauma in newborn babies. Children of addicted mothers go through withdrawal following their birth, a procedure rife with danger for the infant. In New York City, an estimated 1,000 children are born to addicted mothers each year.[72]

Such personal difficulties are in large measure a function of the illegal character of heroin use and the fact that heroin is available only from black market sources and under conditions of great danger from law enforcement intervention. This situation is undoubtedly responsible for the high price of drugs in the United States and the extremely high profit, which keeps importers active in the narcotics trade. The price of drugs is also directly related to the rate of acquisitive crime in a jurisdiction. "New York City, which was renowned for its night life," one writer has observed, "has become a city with a veritable medieval fear of the dark and of the addicts who must support drug habits." Addicts may account for as much as 50 percent of all property offenses in large cities.[73]

The crimes committed by addicts and the criminal nature of the drug traffic also impose a great burden on the criminal justice system in the United States. Police time is heavily committed to work against narcotics offenses, court calendars are jammed with narcotics cases, and the prisons are saturated with offenders convicted of offenses related to the use of narcotics. In all these parts of the criminal justice system corruption in regard to narcotics is rampant. Smuggling of narcotics into prisons is commonplace. Informers are endemic to the enforcement of the narcotics statutes and, at times, their imagination stretches to achieve the rewards used to keep their revelations flowing. Appellate court decisions concerning search and seizure cases almost invariably are related to narcotics arrests. In New York, narcotic violations lead to a variety of enforcement subterfuges. Thus, in one instance a judge complained that he had never had before him so many defendants allegedly suffering from "dropsy," a malady involving—according to police testimony—an inability among addicts to hold on to narcotics in

---

[72] Samuel O. Krause, Peter M. Murray, James B. Holmes, and Reynold E. Burch, "Heroin Addiction Among Pregnant Women and their Newborn Babies," *American Journal of Obstetrics and Gynecology*, 75 (April 1958), pp. 754–758. Cf., "Pre-Natal Drug Addiction Rising," *New York Post*, April 10, 1970.

[73] Richard Severo, "Rx for Addiction," *New York Times*, May 30, 1970.

their possession and a tendency to drop such items right at the feet of the arresting officer. The judge said that he had heard the same tale "hundreds, perhaps thousands" of times, and that he was rather inclined to believe that in a considerable number of instances "dropsy" was a fictional reconstruction of what had happened, created to camouflage violations of constitutional principles that had preceded the discovery of the narcotics.[74]

Drug cases, cluttering court calendars, are also largely responsible for the delays in delivering justice that now mark the courts in most metropolitan areas of the United States. "Congestion is strangling the courts in big cities throughout the country and is turning justice into a commodity that Americans regularly find elusive, capricious and uncertain," a reporter noted after a nationwide survey. He quotes an angry and frustrated judge, after a particularly questionable case, shouting at some policemen in the courtroom: "There are wolves out there, and you keep sending me chipmunks and squirrels!" Summarizing conditions in Philadelphia as a prototype, the reporter notes:

> When officials talk about the basic quality of cases coming into the system and the various elements that contribute to overloading the courts, sooner or later most of them cite enforcement of the drug laws.
> More people in Philadelphia came before the Court of Common Pleas for drug offenses than for any other cause last year. The judges handled 2,848 of these cases but only 2,613 burglaries, 1,330 robberies and 452 murders.
> Nearly half (1,419) of those accused of drug violation were acquitted. Only 1,120 were ruled guilty of the particular crime with which they had been charged, while 209 others were convicted of some lesser offense.[75]

Attempts to cope with long delays in court processes include suggestions, as this survey notes, "that cases designed to uphold the community's moral standards have no business in court, no matter how carefully prepared and ironclad the evidence seems." The argument suggests that such cases could be better handled by social agencies, if necessary:

> The idea is discussed fairly widely and openly, but the suggested pruning is far too rigorous for many. No one wants to think of promoting, say, legalized smut in his state legislature.

[74] Lesley Oelsner, "Judge Says Police Frequently Lie in Drug Cases," *New York Times*, September 19, 1970.

[75] Walter Rugaber, "Justice is Slow and Unsure in Nation's Busy Courts," *New York Times*, March 8, 1971.

And the "social agencies" already are admittedly inadequate to the task.

A number of judges seem to be asking instead for law enforcement that is a little more discreet. The police could concentrate informally, for example, on cases most important to the community—more wolves, fewer chipmunks and squirrels.[76]

Addiction is also reported to be a problem of "great gravity" to the business community. It is said to rob employees of the motivation to do their job properly, to make thieves of them because their salaries tend to be inadequate for the support of a burgeoning drug habit, and to turn them into security risks. A 1971 nationwide survey by the Conference Board, covering 222 companies, indicated that the drug problem in business may be "more extensive than earlier believed." The survey discovered that 53 percent of the concerns responding had discovered "drug abuse" among employees, including a few instances of selling and use of heroin on the facilities. Many business firms now insist on urine chromatographic examinations during preemployment interviews, and a few demand such urinalysis periodically from their employees.[77]

These, in short, constitute some of the dangers of widespread opiate addiction: Under conditions of illegality, use of the drug is apt to be a rather severe health hazard. The illegal nature of the drug is also apt to attract underworld elements who are enabled to make vast profits from black-market dealings. Enforcement of the narcotics statutes places a considerable strain on the criminal justice system and seems to lead to a greater amount of corruption than appears in regard to the enforcement of other laws. Stories of narcotics agents retaining a portion of the drugs they have confiscated and reselling them are commonplace, and aberrant practices in the courts appear to have become routine in the prosecution of narcotics violations. For the average resident of a metropolitan area, rampant addiction is apt to make him a crime victim and to circumscribe his freedom to move about his neighborhood or other parts of his larger environment freely and without fear. The business world is bothered by the lack of motivation of the addict—the drug is, fundamentally, a depressant which sends its user "on the nod"—and by his unreliability, especially as a likely predator stealing to obtain funds with which to purchase drugs.

The same considerations, with a good deal more emotional overtone, apply in the conflict over opiates found today in ghetto areas.

---

[76] *Ibid.*

[77] Wilcke, *op. cit.*, n. 36; Alfred L. Malabre, Jr., "Heroin, Marihuana Use By Workers, Applicants Climbs at Some Firms," *Wall Street Journal*, May 4, 1970.

Claude Brown has indicated in *Manchild in the Promised Land* that addiction to opiates protects the ghetto resident from the demands of aggression, from gang fighting and the possibility of severe injury attendant upon such fighting. Addiction in this paradoxical sense becomes a means of survival.[78] On the other hand, of course, the addict, withdrawn from political and racial concerns, represents a manpower liability in the ghetto. Thus, the rules of the Black Panther party ("Every member of the Party must know these verbatim by heart. And apply them daily. Each member must report any violation to the leadership or they are counterrevolutionary and are also subjected to suspension . . . .") include at the head of the list— as the first and second rules—the following:

> 1. No party member can have narcotics or weed [marihuana] in his possession while doing party work.
> 2. Any party member found shooting narcotics will be expelled from this party.[79]

Ghetto dwellers are apt to regard the public attention presently devoted to heroin addiction as indicative of social hypocrisy and class discrimination, noting that little attention was devoted to the condition—except in terms of shrill outcries for harsher penalties— until it was observed that middle-class youngsters were joining ghetto residents in the use of heroin.

An indication of public attitudes and concerns regarding heroin is found in an analysis of the contents of television dramas which included narcotic themes. The analysis concluded:

> Although heroin in the United States is actually consumed by poor blacks and Puerto Ricans, half of whom reside in a few sections of New York City, white middle-class America on TV is seething with heroin addicts. Fully 11 out of 24 plays analyzed deal with this subject.
>
> Five plays portray the hazards of pep pills and barbiturates— three of them featuring hooked middle-class *parents*.
>
> By contrast, the major "youth" drugs are soft-pedaled. Although marihuana is peripherally mentioned or suggested in nine plays, only one play actually dramatizes the hazards of this drug. Similarly, only one play dramatizes the hazards of LSD. And no play dramatizes the hazards of hashish, mescaline, peyote or the host of synthetics being brewed today in college laboratories and upper middle-class kitchen sinks.

---

[78] Claude Brown, *Manchild in the Promised Land* (New York: Macmillan, 1965), p. 113.

[79] Melvin L. DeFleur, William V. D'Antonio, and Lois B. DeFleur, *Sociology: Man in Society* (Glenview, Ill.: Scott, Foresman, 1971), p. 93.

On network TV, the *primary* drugs of the chic white middle-class "drug culture" are played down.[80]

"When does a problem become a problem for politicians?" ghetto spokesmen ask rhetorically. And answer: "When it afflicts the white middle class." Richard Cloward, professor of social work at Columbia University, has maintained that longstanding social outrages, such as the narcotics traffic, are tolerated by government when they aid the status quo. As long as slum dwellers remain on drugs, Cloward theorizes, they cannot mobilize against landlords, or fight to dump political leaders.[81]

The possibility of successful interruption of addiction might perhaps be considered an important element in determining whether interventions of the present types ought to continue to be undertaken. To date, experimental evidence seems to indicate that under regimens which withdraw the addict from society for periods from 6 to 9 months and then keep him under supervision in the community thereafter, about one-third of the persons so treated will abstain from drug use and avoid involvement with the legal system for major crimes during the first year after their release from an institution, be it a prison, a public health facility, or a civil commitment setting. The remaining two-thirds will return to drugs and/or criminal activity.[82] Under methadone regimens, the rule-of-thumb at the moment is that about half of an area's opiate-using population is likely to enroll in methadone maintenance programs if offered the opportunity, and about half of these persons are likely to remain drug-free under the programs.

Thus, the present potentialities of success in handling addicts are not overly attractive numerically. It is likely that more recruits are coming to addiction than are being siphoned off from addiction by rehabilitation programs. The process of aging seems to be the most effective "treatment," causing the onetime addict to "burn out," that is, to lose his incentive for hustling drugs, in part, perhaps, because of lesser energy, in part, perhaps, because of a diminishing satisfaction with the pleasures provided by the opiate.[83] Some theorists,

[80] Edith Efron, "TV Drama and the Drug Peril," *TV Guide*, 19 (March 13, 1971), p. 10.

[81] Quoted in Tolchin, *op. cit.*, n. 11.

[82] Kramer, Bass, and Berecochea, *op. cit.*, n. 43; Gilbert Geis, *The East Los Angeles Halfway House for Narcotic Addicts* (Sacramento: Institute for the Study of Crime and Delinquency, 1966).

[83] Charles Winick, "Maturing Out of Narcotic Addiction," *Bulletin on Narcotics*, 14 (January–March 1962), pp. 1–7. But see John C. Ball and Richard W. Snarr, "A Test of the Maturation Hypothesis with Respect to Opiate Addiction," *Bulletin on Narcotics*, 21 (October–December 1969), pp. 9–13.

Freudian-oriented, maintain that the movement away from drugs by aging addicts represents their decreased necessity to avoid engaging in sexual performance. Opiates, of course, decrease sex drive dramatically; men are apt to lose the ability to ejaculate and women cease menstruation. For some, the psychiatrists would argue, these drug-induced conditions relieve them of the necessity to compete and perform sexually. In their later years, the physiological processes have performed the same function performed by the drug, making the drug expendable. Whether true or not, the view underlines the consideration that opiate addiction, to be eliminated, will probably have to be replaced by some combination of fear and satisfaction, fear of consequences of such a magnitude and satisfaction with other methods for achieving similar results as provided by drugs of such a magnitude that heroin use no longer offers superordinately attractive opportunities.

These are the implications of illegal heroin use. Legal heroin, either freely available by prescription or available from doctors working in medical clinics, is another matter, and the consequences of such approaches are a good deal more speculative. Among the issues are those noted in an assessment of the meaning of the British approach for possible American policy:

> What effect will tens of thousands of addicts, euphoric on government drugs and existing on public welfare (most would not work—the recent British experience shows this), have on the rest of society? Should society subsidize an individual in his own destruction? [84]

Judgments on present conditions are ubiquitous, however, though they have a tendency to straddle the policy questions, hoping to achieve the best of all possible worlds—to eliminate drug use, which is regarded as a horror, and yet in the process to safeguard other values which are seen as at least as important or more important than control of drug addiction. In a recent Supreme Court decision, Justice Hugo Black noted that the defined terrors of drug use, which he stipulates, tend to produce civil liberties violations, which he deplores. His summary of drug addiction takes the following form:

> It cripples intellects, dwarfs bodies, paralyzes the progress of a substantial segment of our society and frequently makes hopeless and sometimes violent criminals of persons of all ages who become its victims. [85]

---

[84] Severo, *op. cit.*, n. 72.
[85] Black, J., dissenting, in *Turner v. United States*, 396 U.S. 398, 425, 426–427 (1970).

In a similar vein is a description of mob rule and violence that has erupted at times in New York City in the face of frustration with regular efforts to control opiate addiction:

> Meanwhile, the victimized public has become impatient toward drug addiction, which has caused social upheaval, decimated families and entire neighborhoods, diverted thousands of law enforcement officials and cost hundreds of millions of dollars. As a result, residents in some New York neighborhoods have resorted to vigilante violence aimed at pushers and addicts in the belief that nothing else will work.[86]

Is it possible, under such conditions, actually to achieve both control of addiction and the preservation of fundamental social values? If not, what things must be given priority, and how can this be done? These are the issues that we will examine below, after first taking a reading on the state of public opinion regarding opiates since it is with regard to such opinion that policy decisions will probably be made.

A 1970 Gallup Poll indicates that the public makes sharp distinctions between pushers of heroin and users of the drug. The Gallup interviewers sampled in 300 geographic areas, putting the following questions to respondents:

> There has been a lot of discussion as to what jail terms, if any, should be given persons 18 years of age and older who are convicted of certain offenses. Would you please tell me in the case of each of the following offenses what, in general, you feel should be the jail term:
> A. For a person caught taking heroin or having it in his possession?
> B. For a person who sells or "pushes" heroin?

The large majority of the persons polled thought that pushers should be given stiff sentences. The survey results, detailed below, showed that 24 percent of the persons interviewed favored life imprisonment, 4 percent advocated the death penalty, and 43 percent were for jail terms of 10 years or more. Attitudes toward users of drugs were more lenient, with 6 percent of the respondents asking no penalty at all, and 12 percent suggesting medical help. Another 13 percent felt that a year or less imprisonment was a fair response to heroin use. All told, then, excluding the Don't Know responses (12 percent), and the Other responses (2 percent), 31 percent of the sample felt that a penalty of a year imprisonment or something

---

[86] Severo, *op. cit.*, n. 48.

more benign would be an appropriate response to heroin use, while 55 percent of the sample opted for penalties of imprisonment for 2 years or more.[87]

Table IV–1

Proposed penalties for use and sale of heroin

	Pushers (%)	Users (%)
No penalty	—	6
1 year or less	—	13
2–5 years	10	27
6–9 years	3	2
10 years or more	43	23
Life imprisonment	24	3
Death	4	—
Medical help	1	12
Other	8	2
Don't know	7	12
Total	100%	100%

The Gallup results underline the tendency of the public to distinguish between the user of the drug, who tends to be defined as a victim of exploitation by an organized crime syndicate, and the pusher, who is regarded as a low-echelon cog in the organized crime machinery. This distinction between seller and user, which is also prominent in the laws, often tends to be a superficial one, since the seller of drugs much more often than not is himself addicted to his product and is merchandising it in order to sustain his own habit. Thus, the pusher-user and the user tend to be interchangeable units in the drug world and, under present conditions, distinctions that bear down heavily on one and show indulgence toward the other usually do little more than illustrate the capricious nature of control tactics.

New Directions

The public obviously regards the sale of heroin and, to a lesser but still considerable extent, the use of heroin, as behavior that ought to be proscribed and penalized. The reasons for this public attitude are not, however, readily apparent, except as they represent

---

[87] "Stiff Drug Terms Backed in Poll," *New York Times*, April 26, 1970.

the end product of a self-fulfilling prophecy. That is, persons may defend the view that heroin should be outlawed on the ground that addiction to heroin causes users to commit crimes to support their addiction. It is self-evident, however, that crimes undertaken to gain funds to purchase heroin are directly related to the unavailability of the drug from legal sources and the marketing monopoly thereby enjoyed by the underworld.

There would be little disagreement, probably, with the proposition that heroin use offends many basic values deeply rooted in American life. Such values insist upon the virtue of hard work, upon the importance of involvement in social affairs, and upon the living of one's life—the facing of "reality"—without the aid of "artificial" assistance, or at least without use of the more blatant kinds of things which tend to blunt the impact of the slings and arrows of human existence. Heroin, as a potent physiological depressant, tends to restrict the free choices which are allegedly the precious birthright of the human being, and to make the election of good or evil the product of pharmacological coercion rather than the product of conscious selection.

There are, of course, those who insist that reasoning such as the foregoing is quite specious, and that heroin is but one of an infinite variety of impinging items which restrict human choice and which dictate how human beings behave. Life expectancy in the United States, for instance, is sixteenth among the nations of the world. Obviously, some persons would argue, there are social arrangements of a perfectly legal nature which are dooming to premature death a sizable number of persons who could remain alive if the resources of the country were dedicated to seeing to it that they do so. To say that heroin addiction is a more serious problem than untimely death, such persons continue, is to confuse priorities. Yet few social emotions are concentrated on such things as infant mortality, while intense social concern is displayed about the heroin addict and his presumed self-indulgence and self-destructiveness.

There are other persons who tend to take a cross-cultural view by pointing out that opium has been around for eons, and that ways of cultivating and preparing it are described on tablets written by the Sumerians in 7,000 B.C. Historical records, according to D. S. Bell, an Australian psychiatrist, show that patterns of addiction such as the world is now experiencing have repeated themselves throughout time. "Epidemics of drug addiction," Bell believes, "usually erupt when a population is exposed to a new drug, the use and control of which is not incorporated in its culture." Bell, studying historical evidence, concluded that addiction "may be the aberrant fringe of social processes necessary for a productive and effective nation." [88]

In such terms, there are those who maintain that unless some convincing grounds be found—and they insist that such grounds do not now exist—to demonstrate that heroin use is so intolerably detrimental to the quality of social life, its use should not be outlawed. To determine proper social policy, they suggest, there must be a weighing of the dangers involved in a variety of approaches: methadone maintenance, clinic programs, programs operated by individual medical practitioners, and free trade in heroin.

Among the alternatives, it seems to the present writer that the most attractive involves the implementation of a large number of different approaches, allowing the individual to select whichever he chooses, with full knowledge of the likely consequences of his choice. In regard to heroin, American society has an unusual opportunity to maximize those virtues that it claims for itself, the virtues of free choice based on adequate information. Accurate data regarding the decidedly limiting aspects of drug addiction can be widely disseminated. If human beings seek their own self-interest and if their self-interest truly lies in opiate-free behavior, then the effect of such education ought to be profound. Inevitably there will be those who, for a variety of reasons, prefer the heroin. For them, a free society ought to offer several options: they may continue use of the drug under benign (sanitary, underworld-removed) circumstances as long as they do not injure others by theft or violence. If they choose methadone, they should have the opportunity to enroll in a maintenance program. If they choose to spend their days in a heroin-induced nirvana, then they ought to be treated in the same manner that the society deals with other persons who do not care to make the kind of contributions the society requires (not demands, but requires) for its continued well-being.

It needs to be stressed that, regardless of the social policy on heroin which is adopted, use of the drug is undoubtedly self-limiting. There is a considerable tendency among moralists of suppression to presume that "vice" is so attractive that only the strongest kinds of legal barriers will keep untold numbers of persons from diligently pursuing it. Were homosexuality to be legalized, they seem to believe, there would be an astronomical increase in the number of homosexuals. Were heroin to be made available, then most of us would become addicted. But it is not really the law that fundamentally keeps persons from rampant hedonism. More importantly,

[88] "Psychiatrist Says Drug Use Patterns Have Not Changed," *New York Times*, November 1, 1970.

it is their regard for the esteem of others, their adherence to moral systems, their calculation of what they want for themselves and how best to achieve such goals—these are the things that make heterosexuals, drug-free existences, and nongamblers. It seems difficult for suppressors to understand that conforming behavior may be a much more attractive, self-indulgent mode than "vice" behavior.

There has to date been rather little debate regarding proper public policy concerning heroin, except among a rather limited group of specialists. For one thing, heroin has not yet been defined as a social problem requiring novel solutions, but rather as a problem of an encapsulated minority, a truculent, nonconforming group which ought to be brought into line by social sanctions.

What is probably the major statement insisting upon basic changes in public policy concerning drugs is that issued by Isidor Chein and his associates at the conclusion of a meticulous investigation of heroin use among youngsters in New York City. Chein presents his data in strict conformity to the demands of elegant statistical analysis, and his colleagues write carefully about the Freudian-interpreted inadequacies among the heroin users they studied. The Chein research group obviously regards addicts as something less than "adequate" personalities, and something other than self-fulfilled and actively functioning citizens, something other than the kind of people they feel ought to make up the population of a democracy.

In their concluding chapter, however, Chein and his associates—having carefully presented their study data—enter a strong polemic for altering public policy on heroin. It reads as if their compassion for the depressed, powerless subjects they had studied demanded from them this articulate advocacy of the rights of heroin users to a more enlightened approach to their problems.

These are some of the elements of the Chein position, reported here because they represent to the present writer a fair reading of the current situation and a decent blueprint for the future.

Attempts to control the traffic in drugs under present conditions, Chein argues, is a futile policy. Opiates are not exempt from the law of supply and demand and the very effectiveness of efforts to suppress the traffic creates a situation in which prices rise if there is no corresponding decrease in demand. "The effectiveness of police activity," it is suggested, "may simply have the consequence of increasing the efforts to outsmart or to corrupt the police, the volume of business fluctuating around some stabilization point." [89] For

---

[89] Isidor Chein, Donald L. Gerard, Robert S. Lee, and Eva Rosenfeld, *The Road to H: Narcotics, Delinquency, and Social Policy* (New York: Basic Books, 1964), p. 369.

Chein, it is not enough that police activity be moderately successful in catching and convicting violators of the narcotics laws; it must offer the promise of being almost perfectly successful for a long period of time before it can be taken seriously as a measure of control.

It seems a rare month, indeed, when newspaper readers are not treated to accounts of the smashing of a major narcotics ring. We cannot but admire the persistence, the ingenuity, and the devotion to duty of the narcotics officers who score these triumphs. Nor can we persuade ourselves to believe that these victories make much difference in control of the traffic. The more successful the police, the greater the inducement to new rings. In fact, we find it quite easy to believe that, if the police were to desist entirely, the narcotics traffickers themselves would carry on for them. The illegal narcotics traffic cannot afford free competition, and, considering the unprincipled characters involved, it seems likely that, if there were signs of competition's developing, they would start assassinating one another—as even now they seem to do from time to time. The police, of course, carry on the job of reducing competition in the business in a socially more acceptable way.[90]

To reduce the demand for heroin on the illegal market, Chein advocates making available to addicts a cheaper, better quality drug. "No one, of course, advocates putting narcotics on the open shelves of supermarkets," he observes. "The basic idea is to make it completely discretionary with the medical profession whether to prescribe opiate drugs to addicts for reasons having to do only with the patient's addiction." Chein does not believe that under his suggested approach large numbers of addicts would continue to buy their supplies in the illegal market, that they would not keep medical appointments, that they would become unhappy about the quantities of drug allotted to them, or that they would avoid medical programs out of a desire to avoid the risk of becoming identified.[91] But, even if all the undesirable outcomes did indeed result, he still feels that his ideas have surpassing merit compared to present policies:

Suppose all this were so. Still, no one contends that *no* addicts would take advantage of the availability of narcotics via medical treatment. Or, to put the issue differently: if addicts were to take only trivial advantage of the opportunity to receive drugs legally, the present situation would not be materially altered by giving physicians total discretion as to whether to

[90] *Ibid.*, pp. 370–37.
[91] *Ibid.*, pp. 371–373.

prescribe narcotics. If, on the other hand and as is far more likely, many addicts were to take advantage of the opportunity, then, even though many of the same individuals were to continue to purchase some of their supplies on the illegal market, the demand on the latter would markedly diminish—provided, of course, that there were no compensatory increase in the number of addicts making some use of the illegal market.[92]

Meeting the expressed reservation that the foregoing would apply only if the number of addicts were not to increase significantly, Chein argues that the turning of many addicts to medical sources would tend to remove the profitability from the narcotics traffic, to put prices out of reach of the nonmedical addict, and to allow law enforcement officers to concentrate more effectively on the lesser number of traffickers. Also the new addict, unfamiliar with the addict subculture, would be a likely recruit to medical programs once his drug habit was established. The combination of these items, Chein believes, would serve to keep the number of nonmedical addicts at a relatively low level.[93]

Such arguments are primarily economic, touching on an area rarely analyzed in depth in regard to heroin. Having put them in place, Chein moves on to philosophical territory:

> Let us now assert that the premise that *human beings in distress are morally entitled to the best help that can be offered them is valid regardless of the effect on the illegal narcotics traffic.* The only condition that can ever justify any action contrary to this premise is a due-process judgment, reluctantly arrived at in the light of overwhelming evidence, that the welfare of the individual must be sacrificed for the general welfare. This is basic to the democratic way of life, and it is basic to those religions which take it as given that every human being was created in the image of God. We can think of no valid reason to suspend the premise in the treatment of addiction.[94]

Chein finds no general welfare considerations necessitating sacrifice of the addict's rights. Instead, he offers the view that addiction represents a resolution of difficulties that define inadequacies of the social system:

> Suppose, however, if only for the sake of argument, that there were, in fact, many people who would pursue [addiction]. Note that we are positing that they would be doing this in order to escape from their miseries. In other words, these would be individuals who had already failed to find alternative solutions

[92] *Ibid.,* p. 373.
[93] *Ibid.,* p. 374.
[94] *Ibid.,* p. 380.

to their problems and who had not received any effective help in doing so. It follows that the posited line of action would, for them, be adaptive; they would be seeking what seemed the best available treatment for their distress. It may be that, in thus calling attention to themselves and to their problems, they could be helped to find more adequate solutions. But what if not? By the very premise we have just been discussing, what moral right would we then have to interfere? If the best that our society has to offer them is narcosis, what moral right would we have to withhold it from them? Dare we, in our arrogance, take the position that it is proper to keep these people from finding relief merely because their method of finding relief is offensive to us? Is a society which cannot or will not do anything to alleviate the miseries which are, at least subjectively, alleviated by narcotics, better off if it simply prevents the victims of these miseries from finding any relief? [95]

And, finally, there is the insistence by Chein that recourse to criminal penalties for heroin users represents a failure of the society that becomes redefined—and thus explained away—by calling it a personal failure of the addict:

If the ideas presented (here) seem visionary, then those who fall by the wayside are, by that very token, entitled to their drug-induced nirvanas. Obversely, if that seems intolerable, then we cannot afford to regard these ideas as visionary. The price of moral indignation is civil responsibility.[96]

MARIHUANA

A major difficulty with much writing about marihuana is its inability to separate fact from ideology. Such writing often possesses a set of hidden premises which confound the examination of issues. Much argument, for instance, surrounds the question of the long-range physical effects of chronic marihuana usage. Some writers suggest that there is tentative evidence supporting the conclusion that use of marihuana several times a day for a period of, say, a decade, is apt to produce deleterious organic results. Others maintain that extrapolation from the experience with marihuana in foreign countries, particularly with regard to the fact that the marihuana typically smoked in the United States is of low potency compared to foreign samples, indicates that the drug has no serious harmful consequences. Then there are those who say only that the evidence presently available is not adequate to support any definite opinion.

---

[95] *Ibid.*, pp. 380–381.
[96] *Ibid.*, p. 386.

For most of such commentators, however, there is no indication what they would regard as a reasonable conclusion on public policy in regard to marihuana which could be drawn from whatever facts might emerge. Suppose, for example, it becomes rather evident that marihuana does, indeed, produce organic damage if used heavily over a 10 or 15 year period. The writers suggesting this possibility seem to be saying that obviously under such conditions the drug should continue to be illegal. Thus, for example, a University of California psychiatrist indicated recently that he had altered his previously favorable view toward legalization of use of marihuana. This change of opinion had come about, he said, as a result of his treatment of more than 500 students during the past 5 years. From such experience, he had decided that marihuana may have harmful long-term effects, and that it could produce personality changes "similar to those seen in organic brain disease—islands of lucidity intermixed with areas of loss of function." [97]

The accuracy of the psychiatrist's hypothesis is, for the moment, uncertain, but what needs stress is that the policy conclusion bears no necessary relationship to the factual belief, even if the belief is accurate, and that substantiation of the policy position requires considerably more detailed support than a rote recital of possible organic damage inferred from clinical experience. Intervening premises need to be made clear. Such premises might indicate a belief that any harmful pharmacological agent producing certain kinds of results ought to be proscribed, or, perhaps, that any pharmacological agent now illegal ought not be permitted if it is found—or if it might be found—to have certain kinds of consequences. Otherwise, there is a tendency to debate the accuracy of the clinical observation as if the resolution of the policy discussion hinged upon it instead of upon latent and unarticulated premises.

Similarly, persons suggesting that facts of sufficient quantity and quality are not yet known about marihuana to allow for a reasonable judgment on public policy rarely make clear what kinds of facts they will require for what kinds of judgments. In this regard, the debate on marihuana really is an ideological debate, camouflaged by an overlay of factual disputation, with the factual controversy of quite secondary importance. This matter has been well summarized by Erich Goode:

> The public believes that with the gradual accumulation of "scientific" information the mysteries surrounding marihuana

---

[97] Doug Shuit, "UC Doctor Changes Mind on Marihuana," *Los Angeles Times*, March 28, 1971.

will be resolved. Instead, the mounting number of studies and reports is merely sharpening disagreement, with each side continuing to claim truth on its behalf, citing scientific findings in support of its position. If we realize that this is essentially an ideological struggle, which no amount of fact gathering will resolve, and that the invocation of science is a tactical and strategic device, then we will face up to the political and social realities of the marihuana controversy. It will be resolved in the political arena and not in the laboratory.[98]

With this observation clearly in mind, we will first look at some of the facts as the background against which the political debate regarding marihuana will be played, and then we will incorporate these facts into an ideological conclusion, one which should not distort the facts, but which must basically stand on its own for what it is, a value judgment. We will, in turn, first examine the law on marihuana, and then the extent of marihuana use. After that, we will look at the evidence indicating the physical and psychological consequences of marihuana use for the individual and the evidence bearing upon its social consequences. Then we will attempt to summarize these matters in terms of prior considerations bearing upon the legal status of the series of criminal offenses here under review.

The Law on Marihuana

The most comprehensive discussion of marihuana legislation now available appears in a 333-page article in the October 1970 issue of the *Virginia Law Review*. With meticulous care, the authors—Richard J. Bonnie and Charles H. Whitebread, II—combed newspapers from several States to determine public response to early marihuana legislation, and reviewed medical sources, legislative hearings, and appellate court decisions. Their conclusions suggest that little respect ought to be paid to such legislation as precedent of weight or wisdom. Marihuana laws did, however, serve to form present public attitudes and they do represent a codified public position. Repudiation of that position now is apt to be regarded as endorsement of the behavior that would no longer be proscribed.

The *Virginia Law Review* survey indicates that in contrast to the liquor prohibition, "early narcotics legislation was promulgated largely in a vacuum." The process went like this:

Public and even professional ignorance of the effects of the narcotic drugs contributed both to the dimensions of the prob-

---

[98] Tom Wicker, "Another Report on Pot," *New York Times*, February 9, 1971. The original article, discussed by Wicker, is Erich Goode, "Marihuana: The Pseudo Scientific Debate," *University Review*, 3 (Autumn 1970), pp. 24–28.

lem and the nature of the legislated cure. The initial legislation was attended by no operation of the public opinion process, and instead generated a new public image of narcotics use. Only after this creation of a public perception occurred did the legislative approach comport with what we shall call latent public opinion.[99]

Prior to the 1930's, there had been no national policy regarding marihuana. The drug was said to be as commonly used in medical practice as aspirin is today and was known to have various relaxant and euphoric effects. Among State and municipal jurisdictions, New York City in 1914 was the first to list marihuana as a prohibited drug. In 1915, Utah enacted the pioneering state statute prohibiting the sale or possession of marihuana, and by 1931, 22 States had enacted such legislation. This legislative action and its subsequent judicial approval, Bonnie and Whitebread maintain, "were knee-jerk responses uninformed by scientific study or public debate and colored instead by racial bias and sensationalistic myths." [100] The racial and ethnic slurs underlying legislation against marihuana are painfully apparent in discussions which took place at the time the initial laws were passed. The *Montana Standard*, for instance, printed the following item on January 27, 1929, while a proposed antimarihuana bill was being debated:

> There was fun in the House Health Committee during the week when the Marihuana bill came up for consideration. Marihuana is Mexican opium, a plant used by Mexicans and cultivated for sale by Indians. "When some beet field peon takes a few rares of this stuff," explained Dr. Fred Fulsher of Mineral County, "he thinks he has just been elected president of Mexico so he starts out to execute all his political enemies. I understand that over in Butte where the Mexicans often go for the winter they stage imaginary bullfights in the 'Bower of Roses' or put on tournaments for the favor of 'Spanish Rose' after a couple of whiffs of Marihuana. The Silver Bow and Yellowstone delegations both deplore these international complications." Everybody laughed and the bill was recommended for passage.[101]

Similar kinds of ethnocentrism were later to appear in the medical literature, masquerading as scientific investigation of the impact of marihuana. Several studies published during the Second World War, for instance, make note of a disproportionate number of blacks

[99] Richard J. Bonnie and Charles H. Whitebread, II, "The Forbidden Fruit and the Tree of Knowledge: An Inquiry into the Legal History of Marihuana Prohibition," *Virginia Law Review*, 56 (October 1970), p. 981.

[100] *Ibid.*, p. 1010.

[101] *Ibid.*, p. 1014.

among marihuana users referred to neuropsychiatric services. In a study of patients at Fort McClellan, Alabama, for instance, 55 were black and one white; [102] all but one of 35 marihuana cases at March Air Field in California were Negroes,[103] and 95 percent of 150 marihuana cases among servicemen in India were also Negroes.[104] The Fort McClellan study shows the often self-defeating process involved in generalizing from a sample whose characteristics are not measured by adequate sampling or control techniques. The researchers concluded that "the preponderance of Negroes is due, we believe, to the peculiar need marihuana serves for them"; marihuana, they maintained, "enables the Negro addict to feel a sense of mastery denied him by his color," [105] a conclusion that has been rendered somewhat less than prescient by the spread of marihuana use today to persons who possess an obvious sense of mastery of both themselves and the world around them. One contemporary report notes, for instance: "Fifteen percent of the students at Princeton admit smoking pot—two-thirds of them in the upper academic 20 percent, a third of them members of varsity athletic teams." [106] In addition, the Fort McClellan study went on to detail a panorama of personal and background characteristics found among marihuana users, which, three decades later, sound like nothing more than a description of life and its consequences for a large part of the population of the black ghetto.

Nor were the appellate court judges any more sophisticated. "The nonchalance with which Utah and Louisiana courts cited sensationalistic, nonscientific sources to support the proposition that marihuana produced crime and insanity," Bonnie and Whitebread observe, "suggests how widely accepted this hypothesis was among decisionmakers, both judicial and legislative, in the early period." By 1937, the time of the passage of the Federal Marihuana Tax Act, every State had enacted some form of legislation related to marihuana. Use of the drug, however, was still slight and still confined to the underprivileged or fringe groups who had no access either to public opinion or to the legislatures. "The middle class," it

---

[102] Sol Charen and Luis Perelman, "Personality Studies of Marihuana Addicts," *American Journal of Psychiatry*, 102 (March 1946), pp. 674–682.

[103] Eli Marcovitz and Henry J. Myers, "The Marihuana Addict in the Army," *War Medicine*, 6 (December 1944), pp. 382–391.

[104] Herbert S. Gaskill, "Marihuana, An Intoxicant," *American Journal of Psychiatry*, 102 (September 1945), pp. 202–204.

[105] Charen and Perelman, *op. cit.*, n. 101, p. 674.

[106] Anthony Gollan, "The Great Marihuana Problem," *National Review*, 20 (January 30, 1968), p. 78.

is noted, "had little knowledge and even less interest in the drug and the legislation." [107] These early laws, providing medium-severe penalties, were escalated during the immediate postwar World War II period, particularly as marihuana came to be grouped with heroin in the narcotic control statutes, with similar penalties levied for possession and sale of either drug. Then:

> . . . sometime after 1965 the wisdom of the marihuana laws suddenly became dinner-table conversation in most American middle-class homes along with the Indochina war and campus dissent. Many sons and daughters, and even mothers and fathers, of the middle class had tried the drug, and those who had not were certainly familiar with "pot" and the law. The medical profession finally commenced a research effort to determine who was right—the user who said the drug was a harmless and pleasant euphoriant or the lawmakers, who by their actions had condemned it as a noxious cause of crime, addiction, and insanity.[108]

Today, the nationwide pattern of laws relating to marihuana is something of a "crazy quilt," with maximum sentences ranging from 7 days in jail in Nebraska to life imprisonment in Texas for the possession of marihuana.[109] Typical of the newer laws is that in Arizona which allows the judge to decide whether the first-time defendant charged with possession should be convicted of a felony or a misdemeanor.[110] Equally typical of the kinds of situations which can occur under present laws was the conviction in Minnesota of a man for possession of 1/2800th of an ounce of marihuana, which was recovered when the lining of his jacket was vacuumed and the sample was identified under a microscope. The defendant was sentenced to an indeterminate term with a 20-year maximum, though the sentence was stayed and he was placed on probation.[111] In February 1971, despite a minority opinion which insisted that the legislature could not have intended to proscribe acts such as this, the Minnesota appellate court upheld the conviction.[112] In Minnesota, as elsewhere, some attorneys are insisting that marihuana statutes are increasingly being employed against persons who are

---

[107] Bonnie and Whitebread, *op. cit.*, n. 56, p. 1034.

[108] *Ibid.*, p. 1096.

[109] Nebraska Revised Statutes §28–4.125(4) (1971 Supplement) ; Texas Penal Code, Vol. II, §725b (Vernon 1971). Cf., Linda Charlton, "Marihuana Terms Range from Seven Days to Life," *New York Times*, March 24, 1971.

[110] Arizona Revised Statutes §36–1062 (1971).

[111] Charlton, *op. cit.*, n. 108.

[112] *State v. Siirila*, 193 N.W. 2d 467 (Minn. 1971) ; "A Marihuana Ruling Shifts in Minnesota," *New York Times*, February 7, 1971.

outcaste on other grounds, perhaps because of their attitudes, their background, or their political activities or persuasion.

The trend, however, is clearly toward relaxation of State penalties concerned with the possession of marihuana, though this move is energetically challenged at each step. In New York, the Governor submitted a bill to the State legislature in March 1971, which had made first offenders accused of possessing up to a quarter-ounce of marihuana (enough for about 25 cigarettes) guilty of only a non-criminal violation punishable by 15 days in jail. No criminal record would be involved in such an offense. In New York, at the moment, persons can receive a year in jail on a criminal misdemeanor charge for possession of marihuana. The proposed New York statute would have reduced the maximum penalty for possession of more than 16 ounces of marihuana from 15 to 7 years, and would have permitted the courts to dismiss a charge, adjourn the case, or prescribe appropriate supervision for a first offender caught with up to 8 ounces of marihuana in his possession. The bill, however, though it passed the State Senate, was defeated 79 to 64 in a bipartisan vote in the Assembly.[113]

In California, also during March 1971, a bill was approved by the Assembly Criminal Justice Committee which sought to reduce the maximum penalty for marihuana possession from 10 years to 90 days. Opposition to the measure came not only from opponents of leniency for marihuana offenders but also from proponents of more liberal approaches. "This is an attempt to deescalate the war on marihuana," John Kaplan, a Stanford Law professor, told the Assembly committee. "What's needed is withdrawal." Kaplan called the bill "silly" and argued that marihuana should be placed only under the same legal controls as liquor. On the other side, the present law in California—defining marihuana possession as a felony but allowing judges at their discretion to reduce it to a misdemeanor for first offenders—was regarded by a representative of the Peace Officers and District Attorneys Association as "fair and realistic." The law enforcement representative argued against "any change" in the present laws and insisted that there was "mounting evidence" that marihuana could not be equated with alcohol.[114]

---

[113] Francis X. Clines, "Bill Easing Marihuana Penalties is Turned Down by Assembly," *New York Times*, May 19, 1971; Bruce B. Detletsen, "Assembly Rejects Softening Marihuana Penalties," *Poughkeepsie (N.Y.) Journal*, May 19, 1971 (AP).

[114] "Assembly Unit OKs New Marihuana Bill," *Los Angeles Herald-Examiner*, March 31, 1971 (UPI).

Extent of Marihuana Use

The most comprehensive survey in the United States of marihuana use is that annually conducted in San Mateo, California among junior high school and high school students in the county by the Department of Public Health and Welfare. The study has now been done for three consecutive years. In 1970, it indicated that 50.9 percent of the senior high school students had used marihuana at least once during the previous year, an increase of 0.8 percent from 1969, and an increase of 5.3 percent from 1968. For the other high school classes, the figures were 34.1 percent (freshmen), 45.5 percent (sophomores), and 48.2 percent (juniors).[115] The surveyors, who put some space on their questionnaires for respondent observations, report the following:

> There were many comments regarding marihuana. Repeated over and over was the sentiment "legalize marihuana." One comment indicated that if marihuana was legalized and sold in the supermarkets that there would be less possibility of contact with persons selling other and more dangerous substances. There were also a great many comments that the person had experimented with marihuana, but had not continued use, or that they had discontinued use during the 12 months.[116]

The San Mateo results are interpreted in the following way: They are, first of all, regarded as somewhat higher than use figures which would be found elsewhere in the United States, in the belief that drug use patterns tend first to be established in the San Francisco area and then diffuse—sometimes with lesser intensity—to other parts of the United States. It is also believed that the latest San Mateo results may indicate that marihuana use is reaching something of a plateau, that future years will find about the same amount of use as is now reported among the high school seniors.

Other surveys also indicate relatively heavy use of marihuana among young persons and on college campuses. A January 1971, Gallup survey reported that "The number of college students who have tried marihuana . . . has grown at a remarkable rate over the period of less than 4 years." The national survey, conducted among 1,063 full-time students on 63 college campuses, found 42 percent of the students saying that they had tried marihuana—almost double the 1968 figure of 22 percent and 8 times the 1967 result of 5 percent. More than a fourth of the respondents—28 percent—said that they

---

[115] San Mateo County, Department of Public Health, Research and Statistics Section, *Five Mind-Altering Drugs (Plus One)*, (1970), p. 5.

[116] *Ibid.*, p. 31.

had used marihuana during the 30 days prior to the Gallup survey. About one in six—17 percent—used the drug an average of 4 times a week during that 30-day period. Detailed analysis indicated that the most frequent user was a male senior or graduate student in the social sciences or humanities at an eastern college, whose father had a college background. More than half—51 percent—of senior or graduate students in the social sciences had used marihuana within the 30 days prior to the poll. Eighty-nine percent of the marihuana users told the Gallup representatives that they did not believe that the drug was harmful to their health.[117]

An earlier Gallup Poll—taken in October 1969—had sought to determine marihuana usage in all strata of the society, not only among college students. It estimated that if all age groups, including teenagers, are taken into account, some 10 million Americans have tried marihuana, and that another 5 million would try a marihuana cigarette if it were offered to them. All told, as Table IV–2 indicates, 4 percent of the total population of the United States has tried marihuana at least once.[118] Both Table IV–2 and Table IV–3, which concerns receptivity to marihuana use, indicate sharp differences based on age, education, and region in which the respondents live.

Table IV–2

Responses to Question: Have you, yourself, ever happened to try marihuana?

Category	Percent "Yes"
National Sample	4
21–29 Years	12
30–49 Years	3
50 and Over	1
Men	6
Women	2
College Background	9
High School	3
Grade School	1
East	5
Midwest	2
South	2
West	9

[117] "Student Use of Drugs Rising, Gallup Finds," *Los Angeles Times*, January 17, 1971. Cf., William H. McGlothlin, David O. Arnold, and Paul K. Rowan, "Marihuana Use Among Adults," *Psychiatry*, 33 (November 1970), pp. 433–443.
[118] "Marihuana Tried by 4% in Survey," *New York Times*, October 26, 1969.

Table IV-3

Responses to Question: If a friend or acquaintance offered you a marihuana cigarette, would you try it, or not?

Category	Percent "Yes"
National Sample	4
21–29 Years	10
30–49 Years	4
50 and Over	2
Men	6
Women	3
College Background	8
High School	4
Grade School	2
East	7
Midwest	3
South	4
West	4

The Gallup survey also found that 84 percent of Americans oppose the legalization of marihuana, with, as might be expected, sharp differences on the basis of age, educational background and region of the country.

Physical Consequences of Marihuana Use

The most sophisticated review of the physical consequences of marihuana use appears in the March 1971 report, *Marihuana and Health*, sent to the Congress by the secretary of the Department of Health, Education, and Welfare in accord with the requirements of the Marihuana and Health Report Act, requiring an annual statement concerning the health consequences of marihuana usage.

The 1971 HEW report notes that most of the American experience has been limited to the widespread and relatively infrequent use of a rather weak form of marihuana. The physiological changes accompanying marihuana use at typical American levels of social use, it is noted, are relatively few. One of the most consistent is an increase in pulse rate. Another is a reddening of the eyes at the time of use; also, dryness of the mouth and throat are uniformly reported. The HEW survey also notes that although enlargement of the pupils was earlier reported as a consequence of marihuana smoking, more careful study had indicated that this does not occur. From the standpoint of lethality, cannabis products, it is noted, are among the safer of drugs in widespread use.[119] The margin of safety for marihuana is far greater than that for ethyl alcohol. The only physical effect firmly linked to long-term cannabis use at present, according to the report, is permanent congestion of the transverse ciliary vessels of the eye and an accompanying yellow discoloration.[120]

Perhaps the most serious allegation so far regarding marihuana is that it produces what has been called an "amotivational syndrome," a condition defined by psychiatrist David Smith, the founder of the Haight-Ashbury Clinic in San Francisco, as follows:

> . . . a loss of desire to work, to compete, to face challenges. Interests and major concerns of the individual become centered around marihuana and drug use becomes compulsive. The individual may drop out of school, leave work, ignore personal hygiene, experience loss of sex drive and avoid social interaction.[121]

The HEW report observes, reasonably enough, that "it is not certain to what degree this 'amotivational syndrome' is the result of marihuana use per se or of a tendency for those who lack conventional motivation to find drugs unusually attractive." Nonetheless, the report takes seriously foreign speculations that marihuana use detracts from social concern. "There is," the HEW document observes, "increasing evidence that frequent, heavy marihuana use is correlated with a loss of interest in conventional goals and the development of a kind of lethargy. Research in humans is being conducted in an attempt to determine to what extent this observed correlation is due to an alteration in brain function." All told, though, the report writers are not hopeful that there will shortly be clearcut answers to the questions concerning the physical and psychological consequences of marihuana use:

> The issue of long-term mental deficit is an exceedingly complex one. The lack of sufficiently sophisticated methodology may be crucial. The problem of determining harmful effects of chronic drug use and especially psychological harm is very difficult. Unless the type of deficit is distinctive or dramatic, it is likely that the same symptoms will be exhibited by many non-drug users. Furthermore, if the harm done to the user is not so gross as to be noticeable in a higher percentage of users, it may

---

[119] U.S. Senate, Committee on Labor and Public Welfare, Subcommittee on Alcoholism and Narcotics, *Marihuana and Health: A Report to the Congress from the Secretary, Department of Health, Education, and Welfare,* 92nd Cong., 1st Sess., March 1971, p. 5.

[120] *Ibid.,* p. 71.

[121] *Ibid.,* p. 74.

readily be attributed to such other factors as poverty or poor nutrition. Tobacco furnishes an apt example of the difficulties encountered in determining even the physical hazards of use. It was only after many years of use by a substantial segment of the population that the role of smoking in the development of various types of diseases was recognized.[122]

The findings and cautious interpretation appearing in the NIMH report on marihuana contrast sharply with the gossip and propaganda that tends to be associated with writing on marihuana. "There is more disagreement surrounding the use of marihuana and its effects than of the other drugs on the illegal market," a medical report has noted.[123] Typical of the class of reports which masquerade as impartial observations is that of the New York Temporary Commission to Evaluate Drug Laws. The Commission presentation grants the inaccuracy of the more wild-eyed views about marihuana. In its turn, however, the Commission presents a variety of consequences of marihuana use which seem rather awful, but which have never been proven to represent direct consequences of ingestion of the drug:

> Although we reject the old notions that marihuana is physically addictive, that it leads to violent or aggressive behavior or that it is a direct cause of graduation to heroin and other narcotic drugs, we have found substantial evidence that marihuana is a dangerous drug. Sufficiently high doses of marihuana can cause unpredictable, acute—although temporary—psychotic episodes manifesting themselves in the form of illusions, hallucinations, paranoia, depression, and panic. In addition, preliminary research indicates that continued regular use of marihuana or extremely high dosages may cause liver damage, genetic effects, brain damage, and upper respiratory ailment.[124]

Considerably more blatant, though perhaps less important because of its obviously fanciful nature, is the 1971 press conference observation of a newly elected president of the American Medical Association that use of marihuana contributed to birth defects and to sexual impotency.[125] The doctor's remarks were widely quoted on the front pages of American newspapers, though less prominence was given to a later statement in which the official maintained that he had been "misinterpreted" and that he wanted to "clear the air" on "this

---

[122] *Ibid.*, p. 8.
[123] Olive E. Byrd, *Medical Readings on Drug Abuse* (Reading, Mass.: Addison-Wesley, 1970), p. 94.
[124] Frank Lynn, "State Study Asks Eased Drug Laws," *New York Times*, January 9, 1971.
[125] Wesley Hall, quoted in *Narcotics Control Digest*, March 1971, p. 4.

important subject." [126] "It is likely to take some time before long-term effects of marihuana use in this country can be fully assessed," the statement said, summarizing thusly the more accurate picture of the consequences of marihuana use as they are understood today.

Social Implications of Marihuana Use

Public opinion polls indicate that the average person in the United States regards traffic in marihuana with something less than benign approval, though his feelings are less severe than with respect to heroin. A 1970 Gallup Poll found that 63 percent of the American population favored sentences of less than 10 years in prison for marihuana users, including 15 percent who thought that there should not be any penalty for use. Fourteen percent of the respondents thought sentences should be 10 years or more, including 1 percent who favored life imprisonment for marihuana use. In regard to the sale of marihuana, 16 percent of the population favored life imprisonment, 2 percent the death penalty, and 47 percent prison terms of 10 years or more. The remaining 29 percent of the respondents favor penalties of fewer than 10 years imprisonment, including 3 percent who would invoke no penalty for the sale of marihuana.[127]

Hidden within the overall poll figures are respondent variations by age that are notably striking. Persons in their twenties are much less likely than are older persons to favor harsh penalties for either "pushers" or "users" of marihuana.[128] In this regard, views on marihuana pinpoint a considerable attitudinal splintering within American society. As one writer has put the matter: "The middle-class parent looks behind and realizes that his children are not following." [129]

It has also been noted that "for the first time, pot is entrenched in our society, with untold millions using the drug. We have passed the point of no return." [130] Perhaps so. But it is also clear that public opinion remains interested in seeing that penal sanctions—generally of a harsh nature—are brought to bear upon persons involved in marihuana transactions, presumably in the hope that such tactics will have a significant effect in reversing present trends.

---

[126] "Stand on Marihuana Clarified by A.M.A.," *New York Times*, April 4, 1971 (UPI).

[127] "Marihuana traffic in the United States is . . . largely unorganized. There are a multitude of independent operators, large and small, almost all of them young. There is no evidence to support a belief that traditional, organized criminal elements are involved." Wayne King, "Marihuana Selling in the U.S.: Efficiency Despite Some Chaos," *New York Times*, February 17, 1971.

[128] *New York Times, op. cit.*, n. 86.

[129] "Pop Drugs: The High as a Way of Life," *Time*, September 26, 1969, p. 68.

[130] Leo Hollister, quoted in *ibid.*, p. 68.

In regard to the generational gap on the subject of marihuana, it is arguable whether the drug use illustrates standardly varying views of cross-generational behavior, or whether use of marihuana by the young has served to promote a chasm between younger and older generations. It is also arguable whether such variation in views is socially healthy or socially detrimental. Conflict may symbolize vitality and may represent the opening wedge for break-through achievement. It can be argued that a society ought to strive to reduce internal conflict only when such conflict clearly leads to outcomes that are themselves evidently meretricious, such as when, for instance, they lead to the harming of innocent persons. But the rote reduction of conflict, it may be said, hardly ought to be a cate-goric goal.

On the other hand, conflict, like neurosis, can be inordinately enervating, and given the fact that there ultimately will be winners and losers, it can be notably alienating for those whose views fail to prevail. Consensus, as the Second World War indicated for the United States, can produce a kind of unity of effort that allows a high level of achievement·of mutually agreed-upon ends. The sum-mary point seems clear enough, however: The imposition of penal sanctions upon those who differ in attitude and behavior in order to attempt to achieve consensual well-being hardly seems a decent social goal.

In terms of its consequences for social strength, the use of moder-ate amounts of marihuana in the United States appears to pose dangers in three major areas, as the 1971 HEW report to Congress noted: (1) The possibility of progression to the use of either more or stronger marihuana, or to other stronger drugs; (2) The possi-bility of development of psychic dependence and/or psychotic reac-tions; (3) The possibility of the commission of crimes while under the influence of marihuana.[131]

Psychological Consequences of Marihuana Use

It seems reasonable that a society, if it has reasonable alternatives, ought not to allow psychological harm to an individual of so thoroughgoing and unmitigated a nature that it causes irremediable and perhaps lethal harm. Such a judgment must be made, of course, on the basis of individual evaluations of available facts, and predic-tions of future consequences.

In regard to marihuana, there have been recent speculations insisting that relatively regular—two or more cigarettes smoked

---

[131] *Marihuana and Health, op. cit.,* n. 118, p. 88.

two or three times a week—use of marihuana can produce very
serious psychological sequelae. In a May 1971, article in the *Journal
of the American Medical Association*, two psychiatrists reported
that such usage can cause grave psychiatric ills, including psychosis,
even in young persons who were previously stable. They said that
all 38 patients in their study had been adversely affected by smoking
marihuana. Of eight who became psychotic, four tried to kill themselves, and of the 13 unmarried girls who became promiscuous (some
with other girls and some with both sexes) seven became pregnant.
Eighteen were said to have developed anxiety, depression, apathy,
or "poor judgments." None of the patients, who were from 13 to 24
years old, was believed to have used any drug but marihuana and
none had a history of serious mental illness. The two doctors maintained that marihuana accentuates problems that concern most
adolescents: changing physiology, awakening sexual interests and
similar developmental matters. Marihuana was said to cause difficulty
because it interrupted "normal psychological adolescent growth
processes." [132]

Critics quickly pointed out that there were no controls in the
study; that is, there was no group matched against the subjects
involved in the reported inquiry, so that it was impossible to maintain that the problems reported were not indeed routine manifestations of difficulty among persons similar to those in the study group,
whether or not they used marihuana. The small number of cases
and the exceedingly impressionistic nature of the diagnosis also
called the report into serious question. It was perfectly likely too
that the therapists were seeing youngsters suffering from normal
guilt responses to their use of an illegal drug and not from the drug
itself. That they had been referred and had gone to a psychiatrist
indicated that someone had defined their behavior as abnormal;
psychiatrists, it was suggested, are professionally adept at locating
symptoms, whether indeed they exist or not. That the marihuana
usage was found to have occurred prior to the referrals, critics also
suggested, hardly allowed causal inferences of so sweeping a nature
to be drawn. Perhaps the general intellectual arrogance and sloppi-
ness of the *J.A.M.A.* report, which was very widely quoted in the
press, can be discerned from its concluding paragraph:

> We are aware that claims are made that large numbers of
> adolescents and young adults smoke marihuana regularly with-

---

[132] Harold Kolansky and William T. Moore, "Effects of Marihuana on Adolescents and Young Adults," *Journal of the American Medical Association*, 216
(April 19, 1971), pp. 486–492.

out developing symptoms or changes in academic study, but since these claims are made without the necessary accompaniment of thorough psychiatric study of each individual, they remain unsupported by scientific evidence . . . .[133]

For most social scientists, the belief that "thorough psychiatric study" is equivalent to the gathering of "scientific evidence" would be regarded as a certain indication of the child-like, rather magical quality of the thinking that went into the overall *J.A.M.A.* report. Medical consequences of marihuana use as these bear on social vitality have, as we have noted, most usually been related to what has been called the "amotivational syndrome." The sociopolitical issue inherent in amotivational behavior has been summarized by a Federal official in the following terms:

> If we should ever, in a wild moment, decide to legalize marihuana, I think we could sap the strength and energy of a whole nation. Any disrespect for law could be minor compared to the lack of drive, goals, and ambition that legalization could produce. I really think it could make the United States a second-rate nation.[134]

The difficulty with demonstration of the linkage between marihuana usage and a subsequently developing "amotivational syndrome," however, is not unlike that between indicating an onset of psychosis and maintaining that it was "caused" by marihuana smoking. As the HEW report to Congress notes, "It is not certain to what degree this 'amotivational syndrome' is the result of marihuana use per se or of a tendency for those who lack conventional motivation to find drugs unusually attractive." [135]

All told, the evidence seems to indicate that marihuana does not represent any serious threat to the well-being of American society, certainly in terms of present dosages and, extrapolating from foreign data, in terms of heavier dosages. That American society would prefer to have fewer dropouts is evident (though not beyond cavil, for no one has clearly established the proper amalgam of social types for the "best" kind of a society). But that the United States cannot afford the number of dropouts that might ensue without criminal sanctions against marihuana—after all, a considerable percentage of the youth population now uses the drug at least once—seems highly

---

[133] *Ibid.*, p. 492 ; A critique of the study may be found in Erich Goode, "Ideological Factors in the Marihuana Controversy," *Annals of the New York Academy of Sciences*, 191 (December 31, 1971), pp. 246–260.

[134] Eugene Rossides, quoted in "Marihuana : Is It Time for a Change in Our Laws?", *Newsweek*, September 7, 1970, p. 27.

[135] *Marihuana and Health, op. cit.*, n. 118, p. 8.

unlikely. For one thing, if it is demonstrated that marihuana produces personal problems—be they of a psychotic nature or in the form of an "amotivational syndrome"—then it may be presumed that a considerable number of persons would become more cautious about use of the drug—this is clear from experience with behavior following widely circulated reports of chromosomal damage from use of LSD. If, on the other hand, marihuana were found to be not at all or only slightly causative of psychological disorganization, it could then take its place among an endless array of social circumstances and agents with similar or more devastating consequences, and society would go on much as it has, or, at least, much as it will.

It might be noted, in this context, that marihuana use may also have consequences that reasonably could be regarded as socially advantageous. The best data to this point is found in a 1967 study by Herbert Blumer and his colleagues which was designed to induce youthful drug users in the flatlands of Oakland, California, an area populated primarily by lower-class blacks and Mexican-Americans, to abstain from further usage, a mission that totally failed. "The real reason for lack of success," the project workers noted, "were the strong collective belief held by the youths that their use of drugs was not harmful and their ability to put up effective arguments, based usually on personal experience and observation, against claims of such harm." Two major types of drug users—the *rowdy* and the *cool*—were identified among the youths. Rowdies, a small majority, used any and all drugs, but preferred alcohol. Cool youths included pot heads (or weed heads), exclusively marihuana users, described as follows:

> He used no drugs other than marihuana and may even prefer soda pop to drinking alcohol. He is respected by other adolescents, presenting an image of a calm, sensible, solitary figure, soft-spoken, personable, and thoroughly knowledgeable about what is "happening" in the adolescent world. He takes pride in his appearance, always wearing sharp slacks and sweaters, is interested in taking things easy, having a good time, and fostering relations with the opposite sex. He is likely to be involved in conventional life activities, participating in various school functions, athletics, and conventional work.[136]

Initiation into marihuana use was regarded by the researchers as something other than a fulfillment of a personality predisposition or a motivational syndrome. Various conditions were found to keep

---

[136] Herbert Blumer, Alan Sutter, Samir Ahmed, and Roger Smith, *The World of Youthful Drug Use* (Berkeley, Calif.: School of Criminology, University of California, 1967), p. 79.

the neophyte from access to drugs, primarily conditions relating to other's estimate of his integrity and his "coolness." Many pot heads were "turned on" by older brothers, intent on preventing them from "sniffing glue, drinking wine, or risking the chances of being arrested." [137] The Oakland study team assailed standard personality theories of drug use, finding them "ridiculous." It is "primarily the defining response of associates that leads to the formation of whatever motives may be attached to drug use," they claim. For them the study evidence showed "overwhelmingly that the great majoriy of youngsters become users not to escape reality but rather as a means of embracing reality" in a setting in which drug use is extensive and deeply rooted.[138] It was the guess of the research group that most pot heads will be assimilated into conventional life as adults, although their drug experience might lead a few of them into more serious narcotics involvement.

Progression From Marihuana to Other Drugs

The argument is often made—as it was in the preceding sentence—that initiation into marihuana use is apt to foster later use of more dangerous drugs or heavier use of higher potency marihuana. The argument is much like that which insists—with truth—that kissing is a precursor to sexual intercourse and that, therefore, illegitimate births are a consequence of kissing. Under such circumstances, it would be argued, the most efficacious method of reducing illegitimate pregnancies is to level criminal penalties against kissing.

There is no gainsaying that the marihuana user is also apt to indulge in other kinds of drug activity, partly because he is likely to be an exploratory kind of person and one not constrained from such experimentation. In addition, it is perfectly possible that the results of marihuana use might encourage a person to seek experiences with different kinds of pharmacological agents.

The major social fear concerns "graduation" from marihuana use to heroin use. Here the evidence is not clear, though it is obvious that there is no natural relationship between use of the two drugs, only that involvement with a marihuana culture that is by definition engaged in illegal activity might lead more readily to association with persons with access to heroin and attitudes favoring its use. The unresolved issue concerns whether legal access to marihuana might cut down on those users of the drug who later use heroin, or whether it would instead increase such use, by bringing larger groups

[137] *Ibid.*, p. 49.
[138] *Ibid.*, p. 59.

of persons into the drug culture with no possibility of exercising
penal sanctions to inhibit them. Tom Wicker, in a *New York Times*
column, opts for the view that the danger of heroin involvement is
accentuated by criminal definitions attached to marihuana use, and
that, given the nature of marihuana, the danger of such multidrug
involvement is a serious argument for removal of the ban against
marihuana:

> Driving the pot-smoker underground, after all, also drives
> him nearer the hard-drug culture and the criminal world that
> feeds it; and what is to be gained by ruling his life with long
> imprisonment and a criminal record when the nature of his
> "crime" is not even known? Waiting for science is not a substi-
> tute for sensible action.[139]

The evidence on "graduation" from marihuana has been clearly
summarized by Richard Blum in a report included in the publications of the President's Commission on Law Enforcement and
Administration of Justice. In essence, it appears that the relationship between marihuana and heroin is rather spurious, not much
different from that existing between beer and the "harder" beverages:

> With reference to the belief that marihuana causes heroin use
> in the sense that it predestines its user to go on to bigger things,
> there are two critical tests: one asks what proportion of mari-
> huana users do not go on to heroin; the other test asks if
> marihuana use is an inevitable and necessary precondition of
> heroin use, that is, can it be shown (a) that all heroin users
> first took marihuana, (b) that such marihuana use is the only
> factor common to heroin users, and (c) that the presence of
> this common factor can be shown experimentally to be a deter-
> minant of heroin use. The results of such tests are, of course,
> negative. Most persons who experimented with marihuana do
> not try heroin, some heroin users even in slum cultures . . .
> have not first tried marihuana, and among heroin users first
> trying marihuana a number of other common factors are also
> likely to be present. Among these may be experimentation with
> other illicit drugs reflecting a general pattern of drug interest
> and availability.[140]

Criminality and Marihuana

The HEW report to Congress disposes of the alleged relationship
between the use of marihuana and the commission of crime traceable

[139] Wicker, *op. cit.*, n. 97.
[140] Richard Blum and Lauraine Braunstein, "Mind-Altering Drugs and Dangerous Behavior: Narcotics," in President's Commission on Law Enforcement
and Administration of Justice, *Task Force Report: Narcotics and Drug Abuse*
(Washington, D.C.: Government Printing Office, 1967), p. 53.

to such use with the summary observation that "on balance, it would seem that cannabis abuse is a relatively minor contributor to major crimes and violence in any country in the world in which it is used." [141] Indeed, the relationship here raises some interesting semantic issues, for there are a number of prominent persons who suggest that by defining marihuana use as a "crime" the society itself is committing a worse kind of "crime." Given the legal character of the definition of crime, the matter might be otherwise stated by saying that the criminalization of marihuana use creates situations more morally reprehensible than any that could be said to be associated with use of the drug. "I know of no clearer instance in which the punishment for an infraction of the law is more harmful than the crime," Stanley Yolles, former head of the National Institute of Mental Health, maintained in testimony on marihuana laws before a Congressional committee.[142] Similar views came from a prominent anthropologist, summarized in a newspaper headline as: "Dr. Mead Calls Marihuana Ban More Perilous Than Marihuana." Margaret Mead, the anthropologist, had told the Senate Subcommittee on Monopoly that in the United States our attitudes represent a mixture of Roman, puritan, and the "distinctive American belief that if something is wrong you ought to fix it, against the European belief that if something is wrong you should fix your character." Mead maintained that use of marihuana ought to be legalized because present conditions create a dangerous friction between the young and the old in our society.[143] Part of this generational antagonism was said to arise from attempts by adults to create attitudes antipathetical to marihuana use by employment of alleged factual depictions of marihuana which conflict with the ideas and the experience of the actual user and those of his friends. As one member of the younger generation put it:

> I remember seeing movies when I was a kid, and they showed movies on drug addicts and everything, you know, little dramatizations of junkies and people that smoked marihuana and they painted a really bad picture like, look kids, don't ever get involved in this . . . this is what it's like, really bad people sitting around, shooting up dope, or smoking pot, really criminal type people. And they'd actually come out with lies, you know. They'd say, "Well marihuana was addicting and that if

---

[141] *Marihuana and Health, op. cit.,* n. 118, p. 94.

[142] Stanley Yolles, in U.S. Senate, Subcommittee to Investigate Juvenile Delinquency, 91st Cong., 1st Sess., "Narcotics Legislation," *Hearings,* (1970), p. 275.

[143] Paul Delaney, "Dr. Mead Calls Marihuana Ban More Perilous Than Marihuana," *New York Times,* October 28, 1969.

you take it twice, you automatically turn into a raving maniac or something . . . ." And then you find out, well these people lied to me, society in general has really lied to me. . . . They said a lot of things about drugs that weren't true.[144]

Current conditions are also said to create a considerable disrespect for law in the United States, a consequence of erratic enforcement in regard to marihuana based upon arguable social and medical premises. John Kaplan, who has written the most articulate statement advocating repeal of laws criminalizing marihuana use, sees such laws creating basic problems for the system of criminal justice in the United States:

> Although, like many Americans of my generation, I cannot escape the feelings that drug use, aside from any harm that it does, is somehow wrong, I am deeply moved by the consequences of our present policy. As a lawyer and teacher of law, I regard it as a matter of desperate urgency to repair the damaged integrity, credibility and effectiveness of our criminal law; and as one who is constantly in contact with students I am deeply upset by anything that increases their alienation from traditional American values.[145]

Kaplan has maintained that the legalization of marihuana is inevitable, and he predicts that it will take place within the next 7 years, and that it will include provisions for strict licensing and for taxation. He finds the situation in regard to the history of alcohol control an apt parallel to marihuana. "We don't know of any drug that isn't harmful," Kaplan notes, "including marihuana. But prohibition wasn't repealed because alcohol was suddenly found harmless . . . . It was because the law was doing much more harm than the drug itself." [146]

It should be noted, however, that there are those who reject the ideological linking of marihuana to alcohol and the polemical insistence that what is reasonable regarding one is proper regarding the other. Their position has been stated by a Department of Justice official in the following terms:

> It has become popular with those who would legalize marihuana to claim that its use is no worse than the current use of alcohol. However, any comparison of marihuana with other sub-

---

[144] James T. Carey, *The College Drug Scene* (Englewood Cliffs, N.J.: Prentice-Hall, 1968), p. 51.

[145] John Kaplan, *Marihuana—the New Prohibition* (Cleveland: World, 1970), p. x.

[146] Quoted in Jim Broady, " 'Pot' Laws Do More Damage Than the Drug, Prof. Claims," *San Jose (Calif.) Mercury*, February 24, 1971.

stances such as alcohol is extremely tenuous at best, and in a basic sense, such efforts are pointless. Surely it is not valid to justify the adoption of a new vice by trying to show that it is no worse than a presently existing one. It is true that alcohol abuse constitutes a major social problem; but the social damage which would result from a permissive use of marihuana cannot, like some finely balanced equation, be canceled out by placing a measure of social damage resulting from alcohol opposite it. The result can be only additive.[147]

Marihuana Report in Great Britain

In 1968, an Advisory Committee on Drug Dependence presented a report of its conclusions regarding marihuana to the British Home Office. Its observations come from a jurisdiction with an uncommon concern for individual rights, and one in which Governmental commissions have been particularly concerned with issues such as those confronting us here, issues which must balance individual versus social rights.

Interestingly, the British Committee went to the history of tobacco control for its analogy to the present situation in regard to marihuana. It notes that in the 17th century a number of countries had tried unsuccessfully to restrict or forbid the use of tobacco. In 1606, Philip III of Spain issued a decree forbidding tobacco cultivation. In 1610, in Japan restrictions were issued against planting and smoking tobacco, and records indicate that at least 150 people were apprehended in 1614 for buying and selling tobacco contrary to the Emperor's command, and that they were "in jeopardy of their lives." At the same time, tobacco users in Persia were tortured and in some instances beheaded. In 1634, the Czar of Russia forbade smoking and violators had their noses slit, with persistent violators being put to death.[148]

Other ingested agents have also come in for their share of historical obloquy. Of one item it was written in a standard textbook written about 1900 by the Regius Professor of Physics at Cambridge in collaboration with the most distinguished pharmacologist of the time:

> . . . the sufferer is tremulous and loses his self-command; he is subject to fits of agitation and depression. He has a haggard appearance . . . . As with other such agents, a renewed dose of

[147] Donald E. Miller, quoted in *Facts about Marihuana: An Instructional Bulletin* (Los Angeles City Schools, Division of Planning and Services, Pub. No. GC–17, 1968), p. 14.

[148] Great Britain, Advisory Committee on Drug Dependence, *Cannabis* (London: Her Majesty's Stationery Office, 1968), p. 16.

the poison gives temporary relief, but at the cost of future misery.[149]

And of another substance it was written:

> (It) has appeared to us to be especially efficient in producing nightmares with . . . hallucinations which may be alarming in their intensity . . . . Another peculiar quality . . . is to produce a strange and extreme degree of depression. An hour or two after breakfast at which (it) has been taken . . . a grievous sinking . . . may seize upon a sufferer, so that to speak is an effort . . . . The speech may become weak and vague . . . . By miseries such as these, the best years of life may be spoilt.[150]

The substances: The first was coffee, the second tea.

Nonetheless, the British Committee was hesitant to break very deeply into new ground in regard to marihuana. In a long, soul-searching review of the philosophical conditions moving it, the Committee noted the difficulty of balancing individual freedom with social requirements—"If, generally speaking, everyone is entitled to decide for himself what he will eat, drink, or smoke, the fact remains that those who indulge in gross intemperance of almost any kind will nearly always become a burden to their families, the public authorities or both." [151] All told, it seemed that the Committee members paid their greatest heed to the restraints of public opinion, and to the limits public attitudes might set upon their recommendations in regard to marihuana. They would only go so far as to observe that "existing criminal sanctions intended to curb . . . use are unjustifiably severe" and that "imprisonment is no longer an appropriate punishment for those who are unlawfully in possession of a small amount (of marihuana)." [152]

New Directions

It has been noted that "the marihuana situation is awkward at best—legally untidy, geographically inconsistent, medically unresolved and morally perhaps a bit unfair. But it appears to be the best the Nation can manage for some time." [153]

For some persons the introductory statement in the preceding quotation may appear abrasive when read in conjunction with the passive, shoulder-shrugging concluding statement. In the current jargon,

---

[149] *Ibid.*
[150] *Ibid.*
[151] *Ibid.*, p. 4.
[152] *Ibid.*, pp. v–vi.
[153] *Newsweek, op. cit.*, n. 133, p. 27.

the statement's tenet of "oh, well" might be regarded as something of a political and moral "cop out."

For some persons—and the present writer is persuaded to their view—current conditions are much more unsatisfactory than being "perhaps a bit unfair." John Kaplan summarizes these conditions as follows: (1) The penal code automatically turns at least one-third of the younger generation—the marihuana users—into criminals. (2) Hostility towards the police has gone up in relation to escalation of marihuana use. "To smoke the stuff today," Kaplan observes, "automatically makes a policeman your enemy." (3) There is a tremendous money drain associated with futile attempts to control marihuana. In California alone, the cost is estimated to be $72 million each year. (4) Marihuana laws make a mockery of drug education, because teachers generally have no choice but to (a) give pupils the old moralistic propaganda and be laughed at, or (b) tell them the truth and lose their job. (5) By keeping marihuana illegal, yet being unable to eliminate it, society has turned over the marketing of the drug to the members of the drug culture.[154]

To change the direction of some of the items cited by Kaplan as characteristic of current conditions, other persons have spelled out details of a reform movement which would begin with the general decriminalization of marihuana use. Then laws would be enacted forbidding sales to children under 18 years of age, banning advertising, proscribing the driving of automobiles while under the influence of marihuana, instituting Federal quality controls, imposing severe penalties for illegal pushing, and establishing high excise taxes.[155] That such possibilities are neither remote nor visionary may be gathered from the editorial support by a professional journal, the *Massachusetts Physician*, in August 1970, of a program placing marihuana under the same controls as alcohol.[156]

There are two summary statements that appear worthy of notation here. One, by the author Gore Vidal, is fairly brief and at its conclusion not a little whimsical:

> It is possible to stop most drug addiction in the United States within a very short time. Simply make all drugs available and sell them at cost. Label each drug with a precise description of what effect—good and bad—the drug will have on whoever take it. This will require heroic honesty. Don't say that marihuana is addictive or dangerous when it is neither, as millions of people know—unlike "speed," which kills most unpleasantly, or heroin which is addictive and difficult to kick.

[154] Quoted in Broady, *op. cit.*, n. 145.

[155] *Time, op. cit.*, n. 128, p. 78.

[156] "Marihuana," *Massachusetts Physician*, 29 (August 1970), p. 14.

The United States was the creation of men who believed that each man has the right to do what he wants with his own life as long as he does not interfere with his neighbor's pursuit of happiness (that his neighbor's idea of happiness is persecuting others does confuse matters a bit).[157]

It seems doubtful that Vidal's idea that his proposal would "stop most drug addiction in the United States within a very short time" ought to be taken seriously, though his views have merit on other grounds. The second statement, to be presented below, is a quite long, rather impassioned plea entered by student writers in the *Virginia Law Review* after they had made an intensive review of legal, medical, and social evidence concerning marihuana. It is quoted at length because it bears not only on the problem of marihuana legislation, but also on the fundamental issue of the proper manner in which a democracy ought to employ its criminal law:

1. *The Premise*—Whatever the constitutional mandate, we believe legislators ought to begin as a matter of policy with the assumption that conduct harmful only to the actor is not a legitimate subject for the criminal law. In the first place, notions of blameworthiness, if not immorality, should underlie any criminal statute. Yet contemporary western man increasingly regards as blameworthy only that which directly or indirectly harms others; the presumption ought therefore to be that conduct harmful only to the actor should be deterred through means other than the criminal law.

Second, to the degree that the society continues to render moral judgments regarding purely personal conduct, we do not agree with Lord Devlin that the criminal law is ever the appropriate vehicle for the imposition on the minority of the dominant personal moral code. In this day of rampant relativism, imposition on the minority of the dominant personal morality is presumptuous and suspicious.

We . . . share Justice Brandeis' warning that government is most dangerous when it purports to "help" the individual citizen. In fact, we believe that contemporary society is ill advised to insist on homogeneity of conduct, even where the majority continues to attach moral blame. The danger of regimentation and stultifying conformity is one of the paramount disutilities of modern technological society. We feel it encumbent on the legislators as designers of the social order to promote the widest possible latitude for private conduct so as to encourage the diversity that fosters the creative element in any productive society.

A third related reason for this policy premise is that the benevolent societal goal of protecting the actor from his own

---

[157] Gore Vidal, "Drugs: Case for Legalizing Marihuana," *New York Times*, September 26, 1971.

folly, if it should be effectuated at all, can be achieved by means other than the criminal law. Indeed, use of the criminal law for this purpose is generally less effective than other means because of the difficulty of enforcement, which itself is our final rationale for the initial premise. Laws prohibiting purely personal or consensual conduct have an ancillary effect which causes more harm to the social fabric than the mere offensiveness of deviant personal conduct—the inevitable collision of law enforcement techniques with constitutional limitations. Sacred protection of the individual's right to privacy is, to us, a far more noble end than the protection of the individual from his own folly, as defined by the dominant segment of society.

We do not pretend to have settled or even enriched the continuing philosophic debate regarding "crimes without victims." However, since the only rationale remaining for marihuana prohibition is that it is harmful to the user, legislative adoption of our position on this issue would dictate partial or total repeal of existing law. It should be noted that an increasing number of lawyers, philosophers and social scientists have taken this position. We recommend it to the state and federal legislatures.

2. *Statutory Recommendations*—We offer first a statutory scheme which might be palatable to legislators who still fear that further study will reveal that marihuana use has long-range ill effects. While we do not think this fear justifies perpetuation of existing statutes, it will justify a scheme which permits those who choose to smoke marihuana to do so but which inhibits spread of the conduct; that is, it simply takes the users of marihuana out of the criminal process.

For this minimal solution, we propose:

(a) prohibiting possession of more than 4 ounces of marihuana unless the defendant can show that it was possessed solely for personal use;

(b) prohibiting public use of the drug;

(c) proscribing driving or operating any other dangerous machine while under the influence of the drug;

(d) proscribing transfer to any one party of more than 4 ounces of marihuana;

(e) prohibiting transfer of any amount to persons below the age of 16;

(f) punishing all violators as misdemeanants.

The prohibiting of possession or sale of more than 4 ounces of the drug fulfills the possibly justified legislative goal of limiting mass distribution and proselytizing the use of marihuana. We feel that none of the important values of right to privacy or individual freedom are involved when one individual goes beyond his own private use of the drug to proselytize. However, as we have seen above, the realities of the marketplace are such that the average user might sell to friends to support his own use. Our arbitrary choice of 4 ounces as the cutoff point for the criminal process reflects an assumption, based on current trade practices, that it will keep the small seller out of the criminal process while ensnaring the mass distributor. Of course, this figure should be raised or lowered if prevalent market conditions change . . . .

It should be reiterated that we view the above statutory scheme as a minimal response that protects what might be perceived as legitimate public goals while not infringing the right to privacy. However, some form of legal dissemination of the drug accords philosophically and practically with the logic of the authors' views. To this end we both predict and urge that each state adopt a regulatory scheme—either the licensing or state monopoly models—to control cultivation, distribution and consumption of marihuana in the same way those states now regulate the use of alcohol. The benefits of such a system, especially if a state monopoly controls cultivation and distribution, are manifold: First, the state can regulate the quantity and the potency of the drug produced. Second, the state can restrict the age and other eligibility of the purchaser. Third, and most important, the state can tax the purchaser providing a valuable source of revenue to the states in a time when lack of revenues is becoming a more and more serious problem. As a corollary, to the limited extent that organized crime is involved in the marihuana trade, any such regulatory scheme would both divert the revenue from the coffers of the Mafioso and eliminate possible contact between the marihuana users and its henchmen.[158]

These views, articulate and carefully reasoned, are more than adequate to summarize our discussion of marihuana.

---

[158] Bonnie and Whitebread, *op. cit.*, n. 56, pp. 1177–1178.

V. Prostitution

Prostitution in the United States today is a nationwide industry that is believed to gross more than a billion dollars a year and to involve between 100,000 to 500,000 women. This is one of the items of information reported by Charles Winick and Paul M. Kinsie in a book titled *The Lively Commerce: Prostitution in the United States,* which is said to be the first comprehensive study of prostitution in almost 50 years.[1] An earlier study, it might be added, had been done by Mr. Kinsie in his younger days.[2]

Winick, a sociologist at the City University of New York, and Kinsie, who works for the American Social Health Association, had at their disposal more than 2,000 interviews with prostitutes and their clients, judges, probation officers and others associated with the lively commerce.

Some of the things that Winick and Kinsie report about prostitution are the following:

Most prostitutes are physically unattractive; some of them have flagrant physical defects. In the last three decades prostitutes apprehended by the police tend to be overweight and short, with poor teeth, minor blemishes and untidy hair.[3] Some are tatooed with

---

[1] Charles Winick and Paul M. Kinsie, *The Lively Commerce: Prostitution in the United States* (Chicago: Quadrangle, 1971), with the summary given here largely drawn verbatim from Anatole Broyard, "More Commercial Than Lively," *New York Times,* May 5, 1971. See also Jean Crafton, "The Sociology of the Sidewalk: A New Look at the Oldest Profession," *New York Daily News,* May 5, 1971; "Prostitution Today," *Family Life,* 31 (October 1971), pp. 1–4.

[2] Paul M. Kinsie was director of field work for the study: League of Nations, *Report of the Special Body of Experts on Traffic in Women and Children* (C. 52.M.52. 1927, IV), (Geneva: 1927).

[3] This finding calls to mind the early work by Cesare Lombroso, often regarded as the "father of criminology," who observed that prostitutes, when gathered en masse, could be seen to be terribly obese. To what are we to attribute this peculiarity? Lombroso asked. He proceeded, with tortured logic, to offer and rebut a number of possible explanations, such as the easy lives led by prostitutes and their use of mercury preparations for venereal ills. Finally, Lombroso concluded inanely that prostitutes were similar to Hottentots, women who became simply "monsters of obesity," and that both prostitutes and Hottentots were atavistic groups, that is throwbacks, or inferior products of the evolutionary regimen. Cesare Lombroso and William Ferrero, *The Female Offender,* trans. by W. Douglas Morrison (New York: Appleton, 1895), pp. 113–114.

legends like "Keep off the grass" and "Admission 50¢." They are usually indifferent to men, regarding them simply as "trade." They are rarely rebels in any conscious or deliberate sense. In contrast to the dramatic coloration they are given on stage, in films, or novels, the majority have relatively uninflected personalities. In describing her work, a typical prostitute said it was "a little more boring" than her former job as a file clerk. Prostitution pays poorly: At three $10 tricks a day, 6 days a week, the average prostitute may gross about $9,300 per year and net from $5,000 to $6,000.

The suicide rate among prostitutes is seen by Winick and Kinsie as indicating a high degree of alienation and unhappiness. Seventy-five percent of a sampling of call girls were said to have attempted suicide, and 15 percent of all suicides brought to public hospitals are reported to be prostitutes. Though "baby pros" between the ages of 12 and 16 are said to be increasing in numbers, the median age for prostitutes is 25 to 40. While folklore has them going directly from defloration to the trade, there is usually a 2-year gap. Their three tricks a day may reflect the declining vigor of the working class: in the 1920's and 1930's, prostitutes averaged between 15 to 30 tricks daily.

The Lively Commerce defines the pimp as an occupational disease of the prostitute, her punisher or flatterer, her superior or inferior, as the occasion demands. He may be her lover, or he may be impotent. Helping her feel human, spying out the land, dealing with drunks, supplying drugs, breaking in new girls—these are some of the pimp's jobs. The madam—that larger-than-life personality—is almost as obsolete as the piano player, since most girls are entrepreneurs now and the brothel is only a nostalgic memory, a subject that has been elsewhere addressed by one of America's Nobel Prize winners:

> At the present time the institution of the whorehouse seems to a certain extent to be dying out. Scholars have various reasons to give. Some say that the decay of morality among girls has dealt the whorehouse its deathblow. Others, perhaps more idealistic, maintain that police supervision on an increased scale is driving the houses out of existence. In the late days of the last century and the early part of this one, the whorehouse was an accepted if not openly discussed institution. It was said that its existence protected decent women. An unmarried man could go to one of these houses and evacuate the sexual energy which was making him uneasy and at the same time maintain the popular attitudes about the purity and loveliness of women. It was a mystery, but then there are many mysterious things in our social thinking.

These houses ranged from palaces filled with gold and velvet to the crummiest cribs where the stench would drive a pig away. Every once in a while a story would start about how young girls were stolen and enslaved by the controllers of the industry, and perhaps many of the stories were true. But the great majority of whores drifted into their profession through laziness and stupidity. In the houses they had no responsibility. They were fed and clothed and taken care of until they were too old, and then they were kicked out. This ending was no deterrent. No one who is young is ever going to be old.

Now and then a smart girl came into the profession, but she usually moved up to better things. She got a house of her own or worked successfully at blackmail or married a rich man. There was even a special name for the smart ones. They were grandly called courtesans.[4]

In the Winick-Kinsie study of the contemporary prostitute, clients were seen as being attracted to the girls by drunkenness, curiosity, restlessness, bravado, "perverse" desires, or a need for reassurance. In less than 15 minutes, the client must find whatever it is he is seeking; if he takes longer, he may be handed his hat, which may be all that he has taken off. His first preference is fellatio, but he may also fancy himself a "lover"—an unpopular type with most girls—who kisses, dawdles and tries to arouse his partner with "marriage manual" techniques. The authors are inclined to think that the prostitute's client probably paid for his sex because he can't fuse the tender and the sensual in his feelings, and here he can forget about tenderness. Afterwards, however, he may become more human and talk about his wife and children until the prostitute turns him off. Once in a while, he'll cry. The prostitute does not "drain off" his antisocial impulses for very long: statistics show that when prostitution declines, crime does too.

America is not yet ready to repeal its laws against prostitution, Winick and Kinsie maintain, though they find the trade firmly operating in practically every city of consequence in the Nation. They conclude that prostitution has "stabilized" in the United States, but that it has not been particularly curtailed by the sexual revolution because "the change in attitudes has primarily been on the part of young people and prostitution customers are primarily older men."

Supplementing the countrywide overview of prostitution by Winick and Kinsie are several investigations based on specific aspects of the job of being a prostitute. Paul Gebhard's study of 127 prostitutes, for instance, suggests that their trade is misperceived

---

[4] John Steinbeck, *East of Eden* (New York: Viking, 1952), pp. 90–91.

in a number of ways. Gebhard notes that few prostitutes are unwillingly led into their business. Only 4 percent of the girls he interviewed fell into this category, Gebhard notes; even then, these girls were presented with alternatives. As he observes: "The female who says her husband or boyfriend forced her into prostitution is saying she chose prostitution rather than lose her mate and possibly experience a beating. Even the brothels," Gebhard points out, "would not want the problem of confining a captive beseeching her clients for rescue."

Absence of heavy drug use was another characteristic of the women Gebhard interviewed. Only 4 percent were ever addicted to "hard" drugs while another 5 percent had experimented with them without becoming addicted. Use of amphetamines and marihuana was found to be more frequent, but the cost of these drugs, Gebhard points out, would not be so high as to force a girl into prostitution in order to secure money for their purchase. In regard to the reasons why a girl becomes a prostitute, Gebhard's interviews disclosed the following:

> The major motivation for becoming a prostitute is financial. Nine out of ten of our sample listed money as the prime motivation. Second, one can meet a diversity of males, some of them interesting, and one may enter a social milieu otherwise inaccessible.[5]

There were several additional "misconceptions" which Gebhard sought to correct on the basis of his data. He concluded that the common view that prostitutes hate men was erroneous. "The truth is that the prostitute's attitude toward her clients is not unlike that of anyone providing services to a diverse clientele. Some clients are disliked, toward some one feels neutral, and a few are liked." He also reported that most prostitutes—two-thirds in the case of his sample—indicate no regrets with their choice of work. Finally, Gebhard takes exception to the prevalent view that prostitutes are basically frigid and homosexually inclined women. "In their coitus with friends and husbands, the prostitutes are somewhat more responsive in terms of reaching orgasm than other females," it is noted. Nor do the data support the notion of homosexuality. "Prostitutes so effectively compartmentalize their lives that their profession does not interfere seriously with their heterosexuality, orgasmic capacities, or ability to form affectional relationships with men."[6]

---

[5] Paul H. Gebhard, "Misconceptions About Female Prostitutes," *Medical Aspects of Human Sexuality*, 3 (March 1969), p. 29.

[6] *Ibid.*, p. 30.

The voluntariness and the relative "normality" of the trade of prostitution underlies most contemporary writing on the subject. In some measure, this conclusion appears to be based on the absence of coercion involved in leading girls into prostitution. "There are certainly many exceptions," a United Nations worldwide survey noted as far back as 1959, "but the trend appears to be toward a freer prostitute whose relationship with those living on her earnings is more or less voluntary." [7]

Indeed, in some respects prostitution has been regarded as a more attractive enterprise than many of those occupations otherwise available to its practitioners. Characteristic of this appraisal is the report of a psychiatrist in an American juvenile court who granted that the sale of her sexual favors by a young girl probably represented a rational resolution of the difficulties with which she was confronted:

> If she has not already been getting clothes, etc., through her sexual life I expect that she will soon begin doing so. To be quite frank, I am not half so disturbed about this as I am about her realistic approach to the problem. She knows that she stammers, she knows that she is poor, she guesses that she is illegitimate, she knows that she is dumb, and in a rather cold way she looked me in the eye and asked me whether I wouldn't do the same thing.[8]

In addition, prostitution may be regarded as an entrepreneurial endeavor, at least on certain levels of its pursuit, replete with all of the advantages that self-employment offers (including the opportunity to easily avoid the payment of income taxes). One has no bosses, and retains the right to choose whether one cares to work at given times. Perhaps, in an ironic way, prostitution can be seen as much as anything else as fulfilling the vocational wish, expressed today by so many altruistically inclined young persons, that they "like to work with people."

Whether prostitution is chosen for reasons such as these or whether it becomes the resort of females merely following a path of least resistance—as so many of us do in our own endeavors—is a moot issue. But the freedom connected with the occupation should not be underestimated, any more, of course, than its more sordid aspects and its dangers should be overlooked. The independence of attitude that might be related to a career as a prostitute has been indicated

[7] United Nations, *Study on Traffic in Persons and Prostitution* (ST/SOA/SD/8), 1959, p. 7.

[8] Quoted in Jay Rumney and Joseph B. Murphy, *Probation and Social Adjustment* (New Brunswick, N.J.: Rutgers University Press, 1952), pp. 33–34.

in a fiery outburst by a New York schoolteacher who doubled as a call girl. She is explaining her refusal of an office job in the institution where she was incarcerated:

> . . . "Why don't you work in the office?" I was asked. "Because I don't want to think her [the supervisor's] thoughts," I said. "I can scrub floors and keep my mind to myself. In her office I'd have to listen to her talk about her work and her problems. They can't control my mind even if I do have to sit around here for 3 months." [9]

It needs to be stressed that there exist many different kinds of prostitutes. Gebhard's definition of the female prostitute provides the operational standard by which all may be delineated: "A female prostitute is a person who for immediate cash payment will engage in sexual activity with any person (usually male), known or unknown to her, who meets her minimal requirements as to age, sobriety, cleanliness, race, and health." [10] Within this general rubric, there is a range running at one end from the expensive call girl, operating out of a luxury apartment, to the haggard streetwalker, working waterfront bars.

Most prostitutes, regardless of their status in the trade, are likely to explain their choice of occupation using, as most of us do, indices of social acceptability to demonstrate their own adequacy. One study—conducted by the present writer in collaboration with Norman Jackman and Richard O'Toole—noted that the prostitutes interviewed, in this instance primarily call girls working hotels in Oklahoma City, were apt to select a number of middle-class values in terms of which they regarded their performance as outstanding, and to stress these values as explanations for their choice of work. [11] None of the girls, to our surprise, insisted that she had been tricked or otherwise led into prostitution, nor did any blame poor upbringing, neglectful parents (rather they tended to see themselves as spoiled and indulged children), early seduction, or others of the standard cliches for their present work.

The girls interviewed by us in Oklahoma City were apt to express the view that "everyone is immoral," and that they could therefore hardly be regarded as worse than other persons, that they were, in fact, a good deal less hypocritical. During one episode in which call girls met with students in an undergraduate course at the University,

[9] Virginia McManus, *Not for Love* (New York: Dell, 1961), p. 192.

[10] Gebhard, *op. cit.*, n. 5, p. 24.

[11] Norman R. Jackman, Richard O'Toole, and Gilbert Geis, "The Self-Image of the Prostitute," *Sociological Quarterly*, 4 (Spring 1963), pp. 150–161.

this viewpoint came forth angrily when one of the call girls flared
out at a coed that she was "only selling what you're giving away."
Quite astonished, the coed turned with puzzlement to the rest of the
class. "I don't understand her," she said. "I don't give anything
away."

There was also, not surprisingly, considerable stress by the prostitutes on their financial success, and few saw anything anomalous
about these pretensions and the fact that they were often being
interviewed in the city jail, where they had been stored because they
were unable to pay a $12 fine. One told us, for instance, about

> a very wealthy businessman who pays me 25 to 30 dollars an
> evening just for my company. He takes me to the best places
> in town for a dinner and dancing, and buys me expensive gifts.
> And I've never been to bed with the man. He told me that I
> mingled well with the finest people. He said once, "You act like
> a lady." [12]

The concern with attributions of ladylike behavior was common
among many of the prostitutes interviewed. They were apt to dero-
gate their colleagues who worked the less resplendent hotels as girls
who wore pants (slacks), while they themselves always wore dresses.
In one of the more poignant interview episodes, one of the call girls
told us that the vice squad officers (she called them "Mr. Jackson"
and "Mr. White") always treated her like a lady, that they—and
she said this with great pride—always held the door of the squad
car open for her when they arrested her. In fact, this particular call
girl had an ongoing arrangement with the vice squad team under
which she would telephone them to let them know whether or not
she was working on a given day. If she was working, they were
free to arrest her on sight, under any conditions; if she said that
she was not working that day, they would not interfere with her
regardless of how suspicious her behavior appeared. In this way, she
managed to go places unmolested with male relatives and dates who
had no idea of her true vocation.

There were also stories about the extraordinary fees paid by
fathers for the initiation of their male sons into sex, and each of
the girls managed to let us know how much she earned in a good
week, or at least the amount that she would have us believe she
earned, and the most money she had ever received from an individual
client. In addition, new television sets, mothers in expensive rest
homes, children in exclusive private schools, and plane trips—the
girls always said that they "flew" someplace, never that they "went"

---

[12] *Ibid.*, p. 155.

there—dotted our interviews, at least with the "higher class" of call girls. A rather typical story concerned a call girl who had been visited one night by a regular customer. He told her that his wife had just had a miscarriage, and that the doctor had sent him to the drugstore to get some medicine. Instead, he had decided to stop off for a brief sexual interlude. "I told him to get right out of here," the girl said righteously, "and get that medicine and get back to his wife."

Similarly, a number of the girls, those whom we defined as *dual world* prostitutes—girls with middle-class orientations—avoided the topic of sex completely. They justified their prostitute role as a self-sacrificing necessity to maintain those who were helpless and dependent upon them. One girl claimed to be supporting six persons and herself.

> They don't know what I do for a living, except my husband. I see my little girl often. About once a week. I don't work weekends so I can see her.[13]

Another married prostitute also claimed to be supporting her unemployed husband, two children, and her mother. Her mother takes care of her children and none of them knew that she was a prostitute:

> I think that I am a good mother who takes care of her chil-dren. I love my family very much. I have a normal family life other than being a prostitute. I hope my husband can find a job and gets to working steadily again so I can be an ordinary housewife.[14]

Of the unmarried prostitutes in the dual worlds group, one had five children by a previous marriage and the other had never been married. The first strongly identified with her children, and the second with her parents. Neither of them associated with other people much. Both claimed that they had become prostitutes to support others:

> I am very proud of my family. Even though the mother is a prostitute it doesn't reflect on her family—this business doesn't keep you from having good children. I keep my children in the best private schools and colleges in Texas. One of them married very well. They don't know what I do.[15]

The respondent who identified with her parents maintained that her father had given her the best of everything as a child, but she

[13] *Ibid.*, p. 157.
[14] *Ibid.*
[15] *Ibid.*, p. 158.

had failed to live up to his expectations because she was too much like him. Nevertheless, she helped both parents financially:

> My parents are the most wonderful people alive. I like 'em both but my mother is easier to get along with. Dad and I fight like cats and dogs. Both alike. He thinks I'm 2 years old. He said, "I knew the day you was born you'd be just like me." He's got suspicious of my work, but not my mother. She had an operation—cancer of the brain. I gave him [father] $400 and $300 more after I came back from Chicago. He said, "Myra, I know what you're doing, but for God's sake don't let your mother know." [16]

There are, of course, many other prostitutes who accept the role without much attempt to justify either its middle-class attributes or their own admirable traits. And there are many who regard themselves and their behavior with nothing but contempt. One girl interviewed in a nightclub observed, for instance:

> I live by myself and have no friends. I just sleep and hustle at the night club. No, TV shows and books just bore me. Daydreams? Why daydream when you can't be out doing the things you daydream about? . . . Just before you came in, I was out standing in the rain watching the world cry because it's been so screwed up by all the bastards in it. [17]

Nonetheless, the point needs to be stressed that prostitutes tend to be satisfied with their calling, and that they have chosen it with some awareness of the options available to them. That later options which can be employed to leave the trade ought to be maximized, given the not unreasonable American viewpoint that there appear to be more worthwhile ways for a woman to spend her time, seems to be an obvious element of any social policy in regard to prostitution. Other components of such policy will be suggested on the basis of a following review of the history and present status of prostitution in the United States and elsewhere. We will also examine the apparent impact of prostitution on the girls involved in it, on those connected to them, including their pimps, and its apparent impact on the social system.

In regard to prostitution, there are important questions concerning the precise manner in which weak and relatively disenfranchised minorities are able, if they are able, to translate their interests into legislation. Abortion law reform has a power base among articulate and well-to-do women, whose own vested interests are involved.

---

[16] *Ibid.*
[17] *Ibid.*, p. 159.

Similarly, homosexuals often are found in the powerful and sophisticated segments of society. Reform of the laws concerning drug use only became a matter of intense public concern, as we have noted earlier, when marihuana began to be used by a great number of middle-class, suburban, and college youngsters. Prostitutes, we will find, are rather déclassé and dispossessed. With growing sexual openness and the availability of (as the prostitutes call them) "freebees" in American society, the traditional whore, initiating "respectable" youngsters into sexual experience, has lost her strongest customer base. Gebhard, for instance, has found a drop from 25 to 7 percent in the past two decades in the number of male students who experienced their first sexual intercourse with a prostitute,[18] and two marriage counselors at Yale University recently observed that the contact between students and prostitutes was "zilch."[19]

It is in such terms that issues regarding prostitution must be seen. They concern not the right to sexual freedom, providing such freedom does not impose upon equivalent rights of others, but they involve questions about the kinds of support necessary for such freedom to be translated into legislative mandate.

The Wolfenden Report

At the same time that it inquired into the question of the proper legal attitude toward homosexuality, the Wolfenden Committee in Great Britain reexamined the country's laws bearing upon prostitution. As noted earlier, it took nearly a decade, from 1957 to 1966, for the Committee's proposal that there ought not be any legal restrictions upon adult consensual homosexuality to be translated into public policy by Parliament. The Wolfenden Committee's recommendations regarding prostitution—that public solicitation of prostitutes be dealt with more severely, and that those living on the earnings of prostitution be criminally punished—found almost immediate legislative favor.[20] The Wolfenden Committee did not recommend any alteration in the British policy that prostitution itself should not constitute a criminal offense. On this point it observed:

It will be apparent, from the recommendations we have made, that we are not attempting to abolish prostitution or to make

---

[18] Quoted in Lester Graham, *No More Morals: The Sexual Revolution* (New York: Pyramid, 1971), p. 141.

[19] Judy Klemesrud, "Yale Students Have Own 'Masters and Johnson,'" *New York Times*, April 28, 1971.

[20] Street Offences Act, 1959 (7 & 8 Eliz. 2, c. 57), Halsbury, 2d ed., Vol. XXXIX, pp. 262–267.

prostitution in itself illegal. We do not think that the law ought to try to do so; nor do we think that if it tried it could by itself succeed. What the law can and should do is to ensure that the streets of London and our big provincial cities should be freed from what is offensive or injurious and made tolerable for the ordinary citizen who lives in them or passes through them.[21]

At the time the Wolfenden Committee sat, soliciting on the streets for the purpose of prostitution was punishable by a fine of 2 pounds, about $5.80 in American money.[22] The Committee noting that this sum had been established more than 100 years earlier, asked that it be raised to a maximum of 10 pounds ($28) for the first offense, 25 pounds ($70) for a second offense, and that there be a penalty of 3 months' imprisonment for a third and any subsequent offenses.[22] The reasoning behind the recommendation was expressed in the following terms:

> . . . we have two purposes in mind. The first is straightforward deterrence. We believe that most of the prostitutes loitering in the streets are those who are well established in their habits, whom repeated fines have failed to deter. We therefore feel justified in recommending that deprivation of liberty, which would be particularly unwelcome to those offenders, should be available as a sanction when, in an individual case, monetary fines have failed.[23]

The Committee did not specify quite what it meant by the idea that prostitutes, more than other offenders, would be "particularly" inhospitable to a term of imprisonment. But it did indicate that it was not imprisonment that it sought but supervised postconviction arrangements for the girls:

> We do not deceive ourselves into thinking that a short term of imprisonment is likely to effect reform when repeated fines have failed. But we believe that the presence of imprisonment as a possible punishment may make the courts anxious to try, and the individual prostitutes more willing to accept, the use of probation in suitable cases.[24]

Finally, the Wolfenden Committee proposed a penalty of 2 years'

---

[21] Great Britain, Committee on Homosexual Offences and Prostitution, *Report* (Cmnd. 247, 1957), p. 95.

[22] Walter H. Wagoner, "Vice Reform Urged in Britain," *New York Times*, September 5, 1957; Wagoner, "British Map Curb on Prostitution," *New York Times*, November 27, 1958; Wagoner, "New British Curb in Effect on Vice," *New York Times*, August 16, 1959.

[23] Committee on Homosexual Offences and Prostitution, *op. cit.*, n. 21, p. 93.

[24] *Ibid.*

imprisonment for the offense of "living off the earnings of a prostitute." It is noteworthy that the three female members of the Wolfenden Committee united in rejecting the 2-year penalty for pimping on the ground that it was too lenient. "The law must," they wrote in their dissenting statement, "have regard to the worst case that could arise." They thought that 2-year sentences were "quite inadequate to deal with a person who makes a business of exploiting prostitution on a large scale." Instead, they would have preferred a 5-year maximum.[25]

The manner in which the Wolfenden Committee made its case for handling prostitution is worth indepth review here, for it tells what this sophisticated group, after considerable study, found to be factually accurate and how it used such facts to reach its policy recommendations.

"From the evidence we have received, there is no doubt that the aspect of prostitution which causes the greatest public concern at the present time is the presence, and the visible and obvious presence, of prostitutes in considerable numbers in the public streets of some parts of London and of a few provincial towns," it began. Then the Committee attempted to determine from available information whether the problem of prostitution had been growing worse or improving in recent years, but, like any group looking at the statistical data that passes for an overview of criminal activity, the Wolfenden members found the endeavor futile. "We have," it decided, "no reliable evidence."

Committee members granted that there might be something to the view that "the mere presence of prostitutes carrying on their trade was no more, and no less, a matter for police intervention than the presence of street photographers or toysellers." But they were not taken with the argument sufficiently to endorse it. Rather, the Committee concluded that "the right of the normal, decent citizen to go about the streets without affront to his or her sense of decency should be the prime consideration and should take precedence over the interests of the prostitute and her customers."

There was a passing amount of difficulty involved in the fact that the "normal, decent citizen" subjected to annoyance by a prostitute was almost never able to be persuaded to provide evidence in court concerning the indignity he had suffered. The Wolfenden Committee members hurried by this issue, never quite confronting the possibility that one might conclude that since such cooperation was not readily provided the annoyance might not have been serious enough

---

[25] *Ibid.*, p. 128.

to be punished as criminal. Instead, the Committee endorsed the principle that the annoyance of prostitution was to "inhabitants and passengers in general" and not to any given individual who had personally been accosted. The opinion that the Committee ended with, it can be observed, was exactly that with which it had begun, so that an arguable proposition became endorsed on the ground that its ingredients were "self-evident":

> In our view both loitering and importuning for the purpose of prostitution are so self-evidently public nuisances that the law ought to deal with them, as it deals with other self-evident public nuisances, without calling on individual citizens to establish the fact that they were annoyed.[26]

The question of whether the prostitute's male customer ought to be punished was another major issue that occupied the Committee. The result was again more of a semantic slight-of-hand than a direct response to the question. It was not prostitution with which it was concerned, the report noted. Prostitution was immoral, but not illegal. The purpose of the state was to legislate against "those activities which offend against public order and decency or expose the ordinary citizen to what is offensive and injurious." "The simple fact," said the Committee, on a matter far from simple, "is that prostitutes do parade themselves more habitually and openly than their prospective customers."

The Wolfenden group was rather more forthright in its review of "an increasingly prevalent form of solicitation, commonly called 'kerb crawling.' " Kerb crawlers, it was observed, were motorists who drove slowly, overtaking women pedestrians, and halting by them with the intention of inviting them into the car. The Committee granted that such solicitation might be a nuisance to some women, but it concluded that the difficulties of proof were so burdensome that it did not appear worthwhile, at least at that time, to make such behavior a criminal offense. Besides, "the possibility of a very damaging charge being leveled at an innocent motorist must also be borne in mind." The same possible objection had already handily been dealt with in regard to prostitutes. A woman would be cautioned first, and only on a later offense would she be able to be labeled a "common prostitute" and charged with solicitation. That other persons might just as readily be warned first and then defined as "common kerb crawlers" did not seem to have occurred to members of the Committee.

The Committee was not impressed by arguments favoring licensed

---

[26] *Ibid.*, p. 87.

brothels, which would, perhaps, reduce the amount of public solicitation by prostitutes. They thought such places would be apt to
encourage white slavery, and that they would represent an unwise
state endorsement of the practice of prostitution. Nor was the Committee swayed by the view that licensed brothels, duly inspected,
might provide safeguards against the spread of venereal infections
by prostitutes. "It is obvious," the Committee noted, not quite meeting the issue (as was its tendency whenever it pronounced something
"obvious" or "self-evident"), "that a woman who is absolutely
healthy at the time of examination may be infected shortly afterwards and infect others before her own infection is detected." In
the view of the Committee, tolerating brothels would be a "retro-
grade step" by the state.

The Committee took great pains to point out that its best information indicated that the pimp—"commonly known as a 'ponce' or
souteneur"—was voluntarily supported by the prostitute, with neither coercion or physical force figuring into their financial arrangements. Each took from and gave to the other, in a relationship
providing mutual satisfactions. Therefore, the Committee concluded
that there existed no reason to increase the 2-year penalty for the
criminal offense of "living on a prostitute's earnings." It was noted
in passing that the offense itself was usually difficult to prove;
prostitutes often worked in one district and lived with their pimp
in another. Finally, in a somewhat irrelevant flight of rhetoric, the
Committee suggested that it really was not the pimp who was basically responsible for the allure of prostitution, nor, most certainly,
was it an "irresistible demand of natural instinct" which kept the
trade flourishing. Rather:

> At the present time, entertainments of a suggestive character,
> dubious advertisements, the sale of pornographic literature,
> contraceptives and "aphrodisiac" drugs (sometimes all in one
> shop), and the sale of alcoholic liquor in premises frequented
> by prostitutes, all sustain the trade, and in turn themselves
> profit from it.[27]

It was not the law most fundamentally which would see to the
eradication of prostitution, but a change in attitudes and values:

> With most of these evils the law attempts to deal so far as
> it can without unduly trespassing on the liberty of the indi-
> vidual; and, as in the case of prostitution itself, it is to edu-
> cative measures rather than to amendment of the law that
> society must look for a remedy.[28]

[27] *Ibid.*, p. 100.
[28] *Ibid.*

Finally, the Wolfenden Committee recommended that persons who knowingly rent premises to prostitutes and/or their agents should be prosecuted as persons "living on the earnings of prostitution." Curiously, though, the Committee seemed to have only a recommendation of forbearance and a few words of sympathy for those who might be annoyed by finding themselves residing in neighborhoods where in-house prostitution was taking place. It did note that there might be civil remedies if such premises constituted a nuisance, but it neglected to observe that recourse to such remedies, particularly for persons living in such kinds of areas, rarely is feasible. Apparently, then, the Wolfenden Committee thought that persons obligated to live in the vicinity of prostitution activity ought to be sympathized with, while those given esthetic and moral offenses by prostitutes in the street ought to be protected from such offense by the police. That such recommendations appear notoriously to favor one social class as against another seems (to borrow a word from the Committee, but to use it, hopefully, more felicitously) "self-evident."

Post-Wolfenden Developments

The recommendations of the Wolfenden Committee in regard to prostitution were in large measure translated into law by enactment in 1959 of the Street Offences Act. Given the lengthy study and the considerable concern of the Committee in creating a set of conditions which its members regarded as superior to those prevailing, a key question is: How has the Street Offences Act worked?

The answer is summarized in the lead sentence of an article in *New Society* in 1969:

> The decline of the Street Offences Act is a setpiece study of how legislation can be limited in its effects.[29]

Parliament had attempted to overcome the danger of inadvertent harassment of respectable women and to permit the neophyte prostitute to mend her ways by writing into the first section of the Act a provision that required two cautions before a girl could be arrested for soliciting in public. The result of this approach, as best as could be ascertained, seemed to be an increase in the mobility of prostitutes, but no particular decline in their activity. "What the most professional girls do," the *New Society* observed, "is to get their two cautions in one town and then push off under a different name elsewhere."

One of the problems which the Wolfenden Committee had been

---

[29] Nicholas Swingler, "The Streetwalker Returns," *New Society*, 13 (January 16, 1969), p. 81.

reluctant to tackle out of fear of encouraging undue harassment had come home to roost a decade later. Those very "kerb crawlers" whose reputations the Wolfenden group had been so insistent upon protecting were now in great numbers using their vehicles to solicit prostitutes. For the girls, such arrangements allowed them to transact business in the car and to avoid problems associated with having special working premises or having to rent an apartment or motel or hotel room.

Use of automobiles as roving whorehouses had also undercut many of the approaches devised by the Wolfenden Committee to regulate and to circumscribe the practice of prostitution. Taxi drivers and other men were chauffering prostitutes about the cities, acting as touts for them and soliciting business from likely male pedestrians, with the intercourse taking place in the automobiles. In addition, despite the Wolfenden report proposals and the provisions of the Street Offences Act, certain areas of London were unofficially being sanctioned for on-the-street solicitation by prostitutes. Interference by the police occurred only when the informal geographic boundaries of the areas were crossed by the girls. In this regard, England was following the practice of several continental countries, most notably Germany, where "red-light" districts exist for tourists and others interested in the merchandising that is allowed to take place therein. In England, prostitutes were also working immigrant neighborhoods, attempting to find replacements for the dwindling number of armed forces customers.

The somewhat offhanded dismissal of the male as only an incidental appendage to the problem of prostitution also proved to be something of an oversight by the Wolfenden group, given its intent to reduce the amount of public nuisance associated with prostitution. Cases were arising in which men were blatantly soliciting women in public places, but police action against the men proved impossible following a 1966 judicial verdict which overturned one such prosecution on the ground that it was not supportable under provisions of the Street Offences Act. In regard to pimps, the Street Offences Act, undoubtedly combined with many other innovations in the life style of the contemporary prostitute, had led to a separation between the business life of the prostitute and her emotional relationship to a pimp. "Girls with lighted bell-pushes in the Soho area [the conventional calling card of the prostitute there] prefer to use independent touts to bring in men at dry times," the *New Society* study observes. "The modern prostitute . . . tends to employ others rather than to be employed." [30]

---

[30] *Ibid.*, pp. 81–83.

The inability of the Street Offences Act to achieve its stipulated purposes was most evident from examination of arrest figures for prostitution. In 1965, there were 1,552 arrests, and that number jumped to 2,422 within 2 years, with the latter number believed by observers to be a considerable underestimation of the true extent of the increase in prostitution in England. The statistical and survey results led to a growing belief, quite common as a reaction to reform efforts in such an area, that the matter being attacked is impervious to much change. Thus, the former chief of the vice squad in London now writes:

> The dominant conclusion resulting from our inquiry into the vice of London, and more particularly into the incidence of prostitution in all its aspects, is the somewhat axiomatic and self-evident inference that, while the sex appetite might be temporarily curbed, it can never be eradicated by legislation. The theorists who imagine that the oldest profession in the world can be put out of business by Act of Parliament are perpetuating a doctrine that is far removed from reality . . . .[31]

It is, of course, not possible to indicate the level of prostitution that would have taken place had the Wolfenden Committee not met and had the Street Offences Act not taken the form that it did. Without the Act, it can be claimed, prostitution might have been considerably more rampant than it is in London, and might constitute an even more serious affront to public morality and personal modesty. On the other hand, it seems apparent that the Act was not able to provide continuing inhibition of the activity that it sought to regulate and that it left a considerable number of loopholes by means of which persons were able to offend against the values the Act sought to protect. It can hardly be maintained, however, that laws can be expected to eliminate totally the behavior they are addressed to, especially when that behavior is as resistant as prostitution has proven to be. In such terms, the verdict on the impact of the Street Offences Act must be a Scottish "not proven." There has been some readjustment in the methods by which prostitution is carried on, but there has been no apparent improvement along the lines that had been anticipated.

Other Countries

The historical record is a grab-bag of diverse kinds of arrangements under which prostitution has existed and been sanctioned or outlawed. The lesson from history appears to be that when there

[31] John Gosling and Douglas Warner, *The Shame of a City: An Inquiry Into the Vice of London* (London: Cassell, 1965), p. 103.

are women willing to exchange sexual contact for financial reward prostitution will find a way to manifest itself. The literature on the subject, however, is notably silent on the consequences of the different manners in which society has responded to such conditions. There are, in addition, no decent studies of the career patterns of cohorts of prostitutes, but only stray anecdotal versions of this or that satisfactory or tragic conclusion to an individual life. Nor, on a grander scale, are there attempts to determine the impact of different kinds of definitions of prostitution on the social health and integrity of different countries. Perhaps, indeed, such an attempt would be vainglorious, and prostitution represents only a minor and very insignificant aspect of any society's way of life.

The historical record, therefore, is primarily a recital of exotica and a description of the ingenuity of man in satisfying erotic concerns. Prostitutes have ranged from the streetwalking harlot, often glamorized in the disproportionate amount of literature devoted to her, to the courtesan who bestows her favors upon only royalty and near-royalty. In ancient Rome, where prostitutes were regarded with indulgence, they were nonetheless required to wear distinctive clothing and to have their hair dyed yellow, red, or blue.[32] In Greek society prostitutes were of several types, with the *hetairae*, or "good friends," occupying the highest position. Demosthenes noted: "We have *hetairae* for pleasure; concubines for daily use, and wives to provide us with legitimate children and to grow old faithfully in the interior of the house." [33] The concubine, a purchased or rented slave, was part of the Greek household. The *hetairae* had their own luxurious district, while the Piraeus, a segregated area along the wharves, was the territory of the plebian prostitutes.[34]

The Old Testament took a firm stand against prostitution to establish a tradition that, despite considerable ambivalence, appears to be the dominant motif in American society today. The Old Testament contains many warnings against the pagan world harlot whose wantonness was seen as threatening the Hebrew theocracy. Solomon cautioned against the prostitute, saying that "her house is the way to hell, going down to the chambers of death." Jewish fathers were forbidden to turn their daughters into prostitutes (*Leviticus* 19:29), and the daughters of Israel were forbidden to become prostitutes (*Deuteronomy* 23:17).

[32] Eustace Chesser, *Live and Let Live: The Moral of the Wolfenden Report* (London: Heinemann, 1958), p. 69.

[33] Demosthenes, *In Neaeram* [c. 373–339 B.C.], sect. 122, trans. by A. T. Murray (Cambridge: Harvard University Press, 1939), pp. 445–447.

[34] "Prostitution in Early Times," *Massachusetts Physician*, 29 (September 1970), p. 41.

Early Christian writers were more inclined to regard prostitution as a necessary, even vital, evil. "Early Christian obsessions with chastity," it has been observed, "were born of an age when every nunnery was liable to become a brothel." [35] Saint Augustine, the spokesman for the period, believed that what the prostitute did was morally wrong, but that still worse evils would arise if she did not provide an outlet for human lust; in fact, Augustine declared that the prohibition of prostitution would threaten a society's existence, writing: "Suppress prostitution and capricious lusts will overthrow society." [36] Saint Thomas Aquinas, the medieval theologian, reiterated this position. The prostitute, he wrote in *Summa Theologica*, "is like the filth in the sea or the sewers in the palace. Take away the sewer and you will fill the palace with pollution and likewise with the filth in the sea. Take away prostitutes from the world and you will fill it with sodomy." [37] This attitude, more tolerant than that of the Old Testament, may perhaps find its roots in the story of Christ and Mary Magdalene, the prostitute who was forgiven her errant ways. Prostitution was well-nigh omnipresent throughout the Middle Ages, according to Benjamin and Masters. "There were frequent attempts at regulation and suppression, with the former inefficient and the latter unsuccessful. Also characteristically unsuccessful were a variety of attempts to rehabilitate prostitutes." [38]

Historical materials such as these do not, however, penetrate to the core of evaluative issues. The *London Times*' review of the most thoroughgoing treatise on the subject, Fernando Henriques' two-volume *Prostitution in Europe and the New World* summarizes aptly the author's inability to draw firm conclusions from his historical survey:

> Is prostitution a response to repression? Does legislation against sexual immorality provoke the evil it seeks to control? Or is human nature such that only the forbidden is attractive and greater freedom merely encourages more esoteric sexual diversions? Dr. Henriques inevitably raises questions of this kind but does no more than hint at the answers, though he provides plenty of evidence to support both sides of the argument.[39]

---

[35] Fernando Henriques, *Stews and Strumpets: A Survey of Prostitution* (London: MacGibbon, 1961), Vol. II, p. 43.

[36] Quoted in Harry Benjamin and R. E. L. Masters, *Prostitution and Morality* (New York: Julian Press, 1964), p. 51.

[37] Quoted in Chesser, *op. cit.*, n. 32, p. 71.

[38] Benjamin and Masters, *op. cit.*, n. 36, p. 52.

[39] "Chasing Too Few Men," *The Times* (London), August 29, 1961.

The contemporary experience of foreign countries other than Great Britain is equally inconclusive, though it points clearly to the fact that repressive efforts that have been undertaken to control prostitution invariably seem to boomerang.

Italy did away with licensed brothels in 1958, but in 1971 reports were indicating that "just as much [prostitution] is going on." According to a *Los Angeles Times* reporter, the level of venereal disease had tripled in Italy since the control legislation had become effective, with an estimated 30 percent of the prostitutes in Rome allegedly venereally infected. Under the former system, prostitutes had been required to undergo periodic examinations. Most of the traffic in prostitution was now run through switchboards, in apartments, or on sidewalks, with very few of the girls said to be doing business in clandestine houses of prostitution.[40] According to the chief press officer of the Rome prefecture, "All hopes for moral rehabilitation, sincere or otherwise, which came to the fore immediately after the law was approved, have remained merely pious hopes."[41]

A review of conditions in Italy during the years following passage in 1958 of the Merlin Act, which outlawed brothels, indicates the grounds for the verdict of the prefecture official:

> For 10 years, as a member of the Italian Senate, Angelina Merlin had badgered and pestered her fellow parliamentarians to close down the nation's "houses of tolerance" and to outlaw an industry that paid the state $20,000,000 a year in taxes. An end must be made to "this terrible form of slavery," the little senator would shrill. And finally, she got her way . . . and red lights blinked out across Italy.
>
> But *Signora* Merlin's delight was soon dimmed. First of all, the indignant males in her constituency voted her right out of the Senate. Worse yet, the majority of the 18,000 prostitutes she had redeemed from the bondage of the bordello refused to seek redemption in her "centers of social reeducation" and took to streetwalking. No longer bothered with police registration or enforced medical checkups and subject to only 8 days in jail if caught soliciting, Italy's prostitutes flourished as never before—and drew eager recruits to their ranks.
>
> Today, barely 7 years after Angelina's great victory, an estimated 200,000 Italian women earn their living by prostitution . . . . In Rome, 12,000 prostitutes stalk the avenues and streets, with the more successful ones plying their trade in

expensive Alfa Romeos. Said a Roman hotel director: "They're
so thick in the historic part of the city, you've got to wade
through tons of makeup and bumps and grinds to get to the
monuments.". . .
   [Prostitutes] were hopeful that the lawmakers would eventually . . . put them back in their brothels. "I get so tired of this
same beat," one of them sighed. "In a nice warm house, I
wouldn't have to stand and wait and take all those insults from
hypocrites."
   And many thoroughly respectable Italians share these sentiments; at least they believe they will never be able to clear the
prostitutes off the streets of their cities until Italy's Parliament
abolishes the Merlin Law in its entirety and once again insists
that a prostitute's home should also be her house.[42]

The story of prostitution in France reads much like that for Italy.
At first, there was registration of prostitutes, and the trade was, as
Harry Söderman notes, circumscribed by many regulations. Prostitutes were not allowed to walk near military barracks or near places
of entertainment, and they were forbidden to pick up clients either
by speaking or gesture. "Violation of this rule," Söderman observes,
"was technically called *racolage*—crimping or soliciting—a word
which is also used when a French barrister tries to attract clients by
unethical means." [43]
   Then the brothels were closed by law, largely as a result of strenuous lobbying efforts by Marthe Richard. Thereafter, Mme. Richard
became the most articulate opponent of her own reform. "The houses
of prostitution are necessary," she wrote, after surveying what she
had wrought by her reform effort. Residents of the houses, Mme.
Richard now maintained, should be considered "as some kind of
social workers," and vice squad officers should cease their "rule
through fear." This turnabout was a result of a conviction that the
closing of the brothels had had no impact upon morality, and that
the venereal infection rate had risen astronomically, presumably
because of the freelance nature of prostitution.[44]
   The verdict of Benjamin and Masters on the French experience
is almost completely negative:

   The French attempt to close down the brothels, and otherwise
   greatly restrict the operations of prostitutes, seems to have produced more whores, more pimps, more venereal disease, more

[42] "Italy: House and Home," *Newsweek*, November 8, 1965, pp. 53–54.
[43] Harry Söderman, *Policeman's Lot* (New York: Funk and Wagnall's, 1956),
p. 150.
[44] Hefner, *op. cit.*, n. 41, p. 159.

crime, and no benefits apart from such satisfaction as may be derived from the existence of the ban.[45]

The situation in Asia with regard to prostitution offers little in the way of other kinds of information which would allow a broader interpretation of methods used to control prostitution or of the consequences of unchecked prostitution. In Japan, the Government outlawed prostitution in 1957. "Japan's new law making prostitution illegal went into effect today," an observer on the scene noted. "Under the new law offending brothel operators, prostitutes, and their patrons will not be punished for another year. In that time the Government expects all those displaced from the profession to have found new means of livelihood." [46]

The Government's expectation proved other than soundly based, however. Of the 150,000 prostitutes believed to have been operating in the red-light districts in Japan when the new law took effect, the majority today, according to a member of the Rehabilitation Commission of the Japanese Ministry of Welfare and Health, "are now either in a disguised form of their past practices or in forced prostitution systems operated by gangsters." [47] The verdict of this official is similar to that of French and Italian commentators:

> It is clear that prostitution is a problem of such social complexity that it cannot be resolved by passage of legislation. As indicated by experience in Japan and other countries, disguised prostitution—with all its attendant evils—may quickly become a substitute for the old red-light districts.[48]

In India, the situation is more complex, but the conclusions rather similar to those reached elsewhere. Caste traditions are sometimes tied to prostitution in India. In Malabar, for instance, grownup girls are kept in purdah, and it is customary to expel them if they are seen or touched by an outsider. An offending—or offended—girl is pushed out of the main gate by servants, and anyone can take her

---

[45] Benjamin and Masters, *op. cit.*, n. 36, p. 437.

[46] Robert Trumbull, "Prostitution Ban Scored in Japan," *New York Times*, April 2, 1957.

[47] In a similar vein, note the following quote concerning prostitution in the U.S.: Detroit has given up on a plan to rehabilitate its prostitutes because the girls do not seem to be interested. The Common Council voted Thursday to terminate a $151,191 Model Cities program [designed] to offer job training to 60 inner-city prostitutes in its first year because no one had yet entered the program. "Prostitutes Ignore Rehabilitation Plan," *Los Angeles Times*, November 20, 1971 (AP).

[48] Quoted in Hefner, *op. cit.*, n. 41, p. 72.

away.[49] A 1956 report of the Central Social Welfare Board also notes another form of customary prostitution in India:

> Communities exist in many parts of India unrelated to each other but having similar traditions, i.e., the daughters of the house automatically become breadwinners of the family, the sons may marry but serve their sisters and help them to carry on the profession as pimps and instrumentalists if they belong to the dancing and singing class. There was nothing clandestine about it and families approved of and made arrangements for a newly matured girl to enter into the profession with due pomp and ceremony.[50]

Attempts to control brothels in India also began in 1958, the year which saw the wave of similar reform movements throughout the world. And the verdict a decade later matched that rendered elsewhere. After futile years of attempted enforcement, an observer noted, the result "is a marked decline in moral values and the spread of disguised forms of prostitution." [51]

The lesson from overseas nations, it should be said, is hardly unequivocal, except to the extent that it indicates rather clearly the results that may be expected from attempts only to close brothels. The foreign experience does not address itself to the question of very heavy penalties for prostitution, or to issues of reclamation subsidies, intensive reeducation efforts, or to similar approaches which have sometimes been suggested. The foreign experience does indicate a widespread initial disapproval in legislatures of brothel-based prostitution, followed by an even stronger dissatisfaction with the consequences of outlawing such arrangements.

PROSTITUTION IN THE UNITED STATES

Three areas within the United States will be examined to obtain information on prostitution. Each offers particular kinds of data on the institution of prostitution in America, and on public and police response to the practice. In Nevada, prostitution may be legal if a county decides to take advantage of this option offered under State law. In New York City, judicial resistance to the prosecution of prostitutes, among other things, has led to a blatant increase in overt streetwalking and to an obvious geographical concentration of prostitutes in the midtown area. In San Francisco, a recent Crime

---

[49] United Nations Secretariat, "Prostitution in Selected Countries of Asia and the Far East," *International Review of Criminal Policy*, 13 (October 1958), p. 48.

[50] A. M. Rosenthal, "India to Attempt Prostitution Ban," *New York Times*, April 27, 1958.

[51] Om Prakasha Kahol, quoted in Hefner, *op. cit.*, n. 41, p. 72.

Commission recommendation that prostitution be legalized focused attention upon the extent and character of the practice and the attitudes of different officials toward the proposed approach.

Nevada

Prostitution is legal in 15 of Nevada's 17 counties, providing, as Charles Winick and Paul M. Kinsie note, "the most unusual legal arrangements for prostitution in America." [52] The two excepted counties are Clark County, which includes the city of Las Vegas, and Washoe County, in which Reno is located. There were said to be about 60 brothels operating in Nevada during 1971.

The only county in the United States where prostitution is officially endorsed, to the extent of being licensed, is Nevada's Storey County, which imposes a $1,000 a month fee upon its only house of prostitution. The County has fewer than 700 residents and the license fee provides about one-fifth of its annual budget.

The licensing law in Storey County went into effect on the first of January in 1971. The brothel, open 24-hours-a-day and employing 20 girls, is located 7 miles east of Reno, and is known as the Mustang Bridge Ranch. To operate it pays the County an $18,000 yearly fee.[53] Customers are charged $10 for about 20 minutes with a girl, and the prostitutes are reported to earn between $500 and $1,000 a week. One-half of the Ranch's customers are said to be local residents, the other half to be tourists. The male operator of the Ranch defines its success in the following terms: "Do you think that all the home cooking in the world will close all the good restaurants?" [54]

Another Nevada brothel is called the Cottontail Ranch, and is situated in Esmeralda County, about 150 miles south of Las Vegas. Daily airplane flights take customers to the 3.75-acre plot of land rented by the madam for $100 a year from the Department of Interior.[55]

Girls working in brothels in Nevada are usually fingerprinted and made to carry identification cards, obtained from the police or the district attorney. County laws generally require the women to have weekly medical examinations, and prostitutes usually are not permitted to leave the brothel and mingle with other residents of the

---

[52] Winick and Kinsie, op. cit., n. 1, p. 221.

[53] David Lamb, "Brothels Test Anti-VD Drug," Los Angeles Times, November 13, 1971.

[54] Steven V. Roberts, "Expansion of Legal Prostitution Weighed by Counties in Nevada," New York Times, February 14, 1971.

[55] Charles Hillinger, "Uncle Sam is the Landlord of a Bawdy House in Nevada," Los Angeles Times, April 5, 1971.

community. State laws require that houses of prostitution cannot be located on principal business streets or within 400 yards of a schoolhouse or church, and that they do not disturb the peace of the neighborhood. The operation of the system in a relatively large town is described by Winick and Kinsie:

> Perhaps typical is the situation in Winnemucca, a town of 3,000. It has five brothels with an average of five women each. They sit in the windows of the brothels and smile at male passersby. The brothels are open from 4 p.m. to 5 a.m. Police drive by every half hour in case any customers get rowdy. The brothels generally refuse to admit servicemen in uniform in order to avoid possible trouble. One Winnemucca minister lost his job because he spoke out against prostitutes. Such is the general attitude toward prostitution that in a nearby community a school and a brothel were in adjacent buildings. A local paper editorialized, "Don't move the brothel—move the school." The school was moved.[56]

New York

Perhaps the most important lesson from New York concerns the failure of relatively lenient penalties for prostitution to reduce the aggravation associated with it to the point that it ceases being a matter of public and official concern.

In 1930, the Seabury investigation uncovered widespread corruption in New York's Women's Court. There were documented instances of payoffs and extortion, notorious episodes of entrapment of innocent women, and numerous cases of bribery. The scandal led the district attorney to withdraw his assistants from the Women's Court, with the police taking over the prosecution of prostitution.[57] There were promised reforms, but a 1940 inquiry indicated that little had changed. Ten lawyers were found to represent most of the prostitutes and to charge exorbitant fees. Usurious bail bondsmen operated flagrantly in Women's Court and the ubiquitous practices of police entrapment continued apace.[58]

It was not for another 10 years, according to Judge John M. Murtagh, that judicial procedures improved much with regard to prostitution. In 1950, Legal Aid lawyers were introduced into Women's Court to represent indigent defendants. But Murtagh and many of his colleagues were still doubtful about the police practices

---

[56] Winick and Kinsie, *op. cit.*, n. 1, p. 223.

[57] Cf., Herbert Mitgang, *The Man Who Rode the Tiger: The Life and Times of Judge Samuel Seabury* (Philadelphia: Lippincott, 1963).

[58] J. Anthony Lukas, "City Revising Its Prostitution Controls," *New York Times*, August 14, 1967.

used to get prostitutes before the courts, and they tended to be
lenient when they heard the cases. This judicial bias is evident in
Murtagh's observations about the fundamental importance of the
1950 changes:

> Again, reformers and newspapers, eternal optimists today as
> yesterday, hailed the court's cleanup as a milestone toward hon-
> est vice control. But they did not stop to think that inasmuch
> as the vice squad still employs its traditional methods of arrest
> and the court was still merely a way station between the jail
> and the street, basic conditions were little improved.[59]

This uneasy relationship between the courts and the police in New
York regarding prostitution continued unresolved through the years.
The police developed harassment tactics which kept the streets relatively free from blatant solicitation, then they eased off until a flagrant situation again focused attention on prostitution. Thus, in 1961,
the *New York Times*, taking a role as one of the "eternal optimists,"
reported that "a new and apparently effective campaign to rid midtown Manhattan streets of prostitutes has been put into operation
by the police." [60] If the campaign changed anything for the moment,
it was not evident a moment later.

A major change did take place in New York in 1967, however.
That year, largely on the incentive of the judiciary, an experiment
was inaugurated which involved rather light punishments for prostitution. The behavior was redefined from a criminal offense to a
"violation," and punishment was set at a maximum of 15 days in
jail or a maximum fine of $250. In practice, offenders often were
allowed to settle three or four charges with a fine of $150 and no
jail term.[61]

The impact of the new approach may have been to make prostitutes less bitter and to have kept them from being further criminalized by long stretches in jail. But the changes in the law
obviously did not cut into the extent of prostitution. In 1969, the
New York City police reported (indicating in their report the
belief that these conditions were a function of the more lenient
statute) that there had been a 70 percent increase in prostitution
arrests and that women, many of them teenagers, were flocking to

---

[59] *Ibid.*

[60] Walter Carlson, "Police Open Drive on Prostitution," *New York Times*,
September 10, 1961.

[61] Pamela A. Roby, "Politics and Prostitution: A Case Study of the Revision,
Enforcement, and Administration of the New York State Penal Laws on Prostitution," *Criminology*, 9 (February 1972), p. 439.

midtown Manhattan from all sections of the United States to engage in prostitution.[62]

Prostitution, however, was reported to be operating without much organized crime control involvement in New York, perhaps a benefit of the relaxed statutes and the lesser need for protection on the part of the girls. But syndicated criminals were said to be impinging on the trade through ownership of the bars in which many of the prostitutes worked. Police studies showed a typical pattern of "revolving door" justice for the girls themselves. Of 795 women arrested for prostitution in midtown Manhattan during the first 6 months of 1967, 525 had been arrested before for the same offense and together they had a total of 5,568 arrests—an average of more than 10 for each woman.[63] Typical was the case of Matilda F.:

> Shortly after midnight on May 19, as red neon lights danced in a fine mist on West 85th Street, a policeman watched a man and woman whisper in a darkened doorway and then enter a hotel.
>
> Half an hour later the man left. After briefly questioning him on the street, the policeman walked into the hotel and arrested Matilda F. for prostitution.
>
> When she appeared a few hours later in Women's Court, a clerk called, "Hi, Matilda. Back home again, eh?" Matilda laughed weakly and said, "Yeah, I love you so much I can't stay away."
>
> Matilda's May court appearance was her 81st on prostitution charges since 1943. Age 44 years old, she has spent 12 years and 10 months in the Women's House of Detention—most of it in sentences of 10 to 90 days. "She's doing life on the installment plan," a clerk remarked.[64]

An unsuccessful attempt was made during the 1968 legislative session to change the prostitution law. Despite rather intense police lobbying, the bill was stalled in the Committee on Codes. An analysis by Pamela Roby of the legislative maneuvering in regard to prostitution in 1968 indicates that in large measure the bill was blocked because Committee members, all 16 of whom were lawyers, felt that the 1967 reform had been made only after considerable study, and that there had not been enough time yet to determine the impact of the milder penalties. There was also a feeling among Committee members that 1-year sentences for prostitutes, called for

---

[62] Edmund C. Burks, "New Prostitution Law Increases Maximum Penalty to 90 Days," *New York Times*, August 31, 1969.

[63] Lukas, *op. cit.*, n. 58.

[64] *Ibid.* See also Lesley Oelsner, "World of the City Prostitute is a Tough and Lonely Place," *New York Times*, August 9, 1971.

by the bill before them, would overcrowd the jails. Lastly, there
was a belief that the act of prostitution did not warrant a sentence
as long as 1 year.[65]

The action of the legislative committee proved to be only a delay-
ing tactic, however, and the following year proponents of sterner
measures had their way as prostitution again became a criminal
offense. The maximum jail sentence was raised from 15 to 90 days
and the maximum fine was changed from $250 to $500.[66] The new
measure—seemingly in the manner of all new measures dealing with
prostitution—was seen by some as a potential cure for the problem.
"Street girls and the hustlers and pimps working with them are a
focal point for crime in midtown," a criminal court judge noted.
"The girls push dope, pick pockets, carry knives and take their
customers to cheap 'trick houses' or cheap hotels where they get
assaulted by the pimps." The judge suggested that, hopefully, aware
of the new fines and stiffer jail sentences, the girls would stop
behaving this way.[67]

That was 1969. By March 1971, newspapers in New York were
noting that "strengthened police patrols, both uniformed and plainclothes, toured the district between Times Square and Central Park
yesterday in a drive against prostitutes." This new cleanup had been
set into motion after the mugging of a former West German government official and the fatal stabbing of a south European industrial-
ist, both incidents involving prostitutes. The German had been
robbed in front of his hotel by two women, who leaped from a taxi-
cab, grabbed him and took his wallet. Arrested later, both women
proved to have prostitution records. The other man had been stabbed
by a prostitute after an argument that seemed to involve, as best
police could determine, a language misunderstanding. Police reports
noted that "dangerous riffraff types" had been drifting north from
the midtown area of Manhattan, and a police captain observed that
on the average his officers were arresting 20 to 40 prostitutes a night.
"We know that for that night, at least, they won't be mugging or
robbing anyone," he said.[68]

The lesson seems quite clear. Neither under the first rather stringent law, nor under the second, more moderate law, nor under
the present, even more stringent law, has prostitution apparently
changed very much in New York. "Dressed in flamboyant pants or

[65] Roby, *op. cit.*, n. 61, p. 442.

[66] *Ibid.*

[67] Amos S. Basel, quoted in Burks, *op. cit.*, n. 62.

[68] Charles Grutzner, "Prostitute Drive Pressed by Police," *New York Times*,
March 18, 1971.

microminiskirts, most of them turned out to be remarkably young and frequently pretty beneath their heavy makeup and bouffant hairdos or wigs," an observer wrote after a 1971 tour of New York's Eighth Avenue. Prostitutes on the Avenue were charging $20 plus the cost of a hotel room for their sexual favors. Some 427 women had been arrested during April, with 16 of them being fined and 276 receiving jail sentences. The rest had their cases dismissed. Those going to jail, it was reported, did so only for a "short" time.[69] In all, the summary by Winick and Kinsie seems to catch the tone of opinion on the situation in regard to prostitution in the Nation's largest city:

> In 1969 New York ended its 2-year experiment with a lenient prostitution law. Policemen began picking up suspected or known prostitutes on sight. As one vice squad member said, "The best we can do is to harass them." Most such arrests were thrown out of court for insufficient evidence. Some prostitutes would clear up several charges with a single plea of guilty and a token fine. As Criminal Court Judge Jack Rosenberg said, when the maximum penalty was increased from 15 to 90 days on September 1, 1969, "The prostitutes have no respect for the court. They come in here like it is a supermarket." [70]

San Francisco

Appropriately—and deliberately—the seventh report of the San Francisco Committee on Crime was bound between lavender covers. The Committee had been established late in 1968 by the Mayor and the Board of Supervisors, and its 28 members represented a wide variety of professions and minority groups. That seventh report, issued on June 3, 1971, only a few weeks before the group was to cease functioning, was, the local papers observed, its "blockbuster." The 107-page document, titled *A Report on Nonvictim Crime in San Francisco*, called for less police emphasis on "morality" offenses and more on "serious" crime. Among other things, the report advocated "discreet" trafficking in pornography, "discreet" gambling, and "discreet" prostitution.

Speaking to a reporter from the San Francisco *Examiner*, the executive director of the Crime Committee underlined the philosophy that had dictated the Committee's conclusions:

> "We don't condone or approve any of these activities. But we have to stop cluttering up our criminal justice system with unenforceable laws." [71]

---

[69] Thomas F. Brady, "Prostitutes, Most of Them Young, Now Work the Day Shift Along Eighth Avenue," *New York Times*, May 29, 1971.

[70] Winick and Kinsie, *op. cit.*, n. 1, p. 226.

[71] Irving Reichert, quoted in Ernest Lenn, "Crime Board Report Backs 'Discreet Vice,'" *San Francisco Examiner*, June 3, 1971.

Among the basic principles which had guided the Committee, its executive director noted, were the following:

—The law cannot successfully make criminal what the public does not want made criminal.

—Not all the ills or aberrancies of society are the concern of the government. Government is not the only human institution to handle the problems, hopes, fears or ambitions of people.

—Every person should be left free of the coercion of criminal law unless his conduct impinges on others and injures others, or if it damages society.

—When government acts, it is not inevitably necessary that it do so by means of criminal processes.

—Society has an obligation to protect the young.

—Even where conduct may properly be condemned as criminal under the [above] principles, it may be that the energies and resources of criminal law enforcement are better spent by concentrating on more serious things. This is a matter of priorities.[72]

The summary by the Committee regarding the character of prostitution in San Francisco is worth extended quotation because it represents the best available contemporary overview of conditions in a large American city:

The range of prostitution in San Francisco is fantastic. Practitioners may be male or female; black, white, or oriental. They may be 14-year-olds hustling as part of a junior high school "syndicate" operation; they may be hippies supporting the habits of their "old man" (or their own habits); they may be moonlighting secretaries who sell their favors on a selective basis through legitimate dating services. Places of assignation range from rundown hotels to luxurious hilltop apartments. A few houses still exist (under elaborate covers) in spite of the red-light abatement laws.[73]

Most of those who seek prostitutes in San Francisco are returning servicemen or merchant seamen, conventioneers and other visitors looking for the "fun" that San Francisco has a reputation for providing. The middle-class tourist works through a cab driver, hotel clerk or bellhop who will put him in touch with the $100-a-night call girl. She is generally not a native of San Francisco, and she does not stay long enough to get caught; she is shrewd, versatile, and usually white. Affluent "swingers" may also find sexual partners at some massage parlors and "breakfast clubs," the latter a euphemism for sleazy early morning catchalls of vice-prone buyers. Less affluent visi-

---

[72] San Francisco Committee on Crime, *A Report on Non-Victim Crime in San Francisco* (*Part II: Sexual Conduct, Gambling, Prostitution*), June 3, 1971, p. 3.

[73] *Ibid.*, p. 19.

tors pick up bar girls or streetwalkers, the latter considered by other prostitutes to be of the lowest caste.[74]

Customers do not wish to get involved with a prostitution arrest. When a police officer apprehends a prostitute and customer on the street, the customer is likely to give the officer a false name and address . . . . Even if the customer gives his correct name, the chances are slim that he will be willing to go to court. One Municipal Court judge in 1970 set all cases (where the customer was supposed to testify) for trial on the same day, because he knew that only one in a hundred would ever go to the trial and others would "fold up." This practice became widely known around the Hall of Justice as "trick day." [75]

Streetwalkers—because they are so flagrantly visible—have provided the greatest source of public outcry and consequent political pressure. As competition increases, there is strong rivalry for "territory" and approaches to the customer become more aggressive. Hotel owners in the downtown area complain that respectable tourists are shocked by the aggressive tactics of streetwalkers in the heart of town.[76]

No doubt some prostitutes do rob or "roll" their clients by the use of force or the threat of force. [But] one pimp has told us that it is necessary to protect the girls from being robbed or beaten by the customer. More frequently, however, prostitutes rely on their customer's naivete or stupidity.[77]

These conditions were seen as essentially immutable. "No person conversant with reality believes that prostitution can be eliminated, certainly not in a city like San Francisco—with its port, tourists, conventions, etc.," the Committee observed.[78]

An analysis of arrest and court statistics showed that during 1969, 50 percent of all arrests in San Francisco had been for nonvictim offenses, while more than 13 percent of the killings, forcible rapes, robberies, aggravated assaults, burglaries, larcenies, and auto thefts went unsolved.[79] The Crime Committee report hit at "the cost and futility of antiprostitution enforcement." It was estimated that in 1967 it had cost the city more than $375,000 to process the 2,116 arrests for prostitution—more than $175 for each arrest.[80]

Prostitution was illegal, the Committee declared, "because of a wide and historical feeling that it is immoral and sinful." But this did not seem to the Committee members to be adequate substantia-

[74] Ibid., pp. 18–19.
[75] Ibid., p. 22.
[76] Ibid., p. 19.
[77] Ibid., p. 28.
[78] Ibid., p. 16.
[79] Ibid., p. 1.
[80] Ibid., p. 20.

tion for involving the criminal law in the behavior. Besides, political pressure and enforcement whims pervaded the entire realm of police dealings with prostitutes. Rousting prostitutes was regarded as a "flamboyant" method of police "streetcleaning." No arrest pattern was "more ritualized and superficial, nor any more apparently ineffectual" than that used with prostitutes. Pressures to harass prostitutes became particularly intense during election years and arrest figures clearly indicated the crazy-quilt pattern of enforcement. In 1960, there were fewer than 300 arrests for prostitution in San Francisco; 9 years later the figure soared to 3,221, but no one believed that there was either much more prostitution or many more prostitutes in one or the other of the years.[81]

Police statistics for 1969 were said to tell an entire story of their own, except for the drama and melodrama of human involvement, about the control of prostitution in San Francisco. There were 1,556 arrests of adults (including 286 males) for either soliciting or engaging in acts of prostitution. Charges were dismissed in 683 cases. Only 246 defendants went to jail, and most of these were sentenced for fewer than 4 months. Another 1,938 adults were arrested for "obstructing the sidewalk," the usual charge in a streetsweep operation where no attempt is made to prove prostitution. Of these, 334 persons went to jail, usually for less than 30 days. All told, during 1969, only about 15 percent of all persons arrested for prostitution in San Francisco ended up in jail. Not surprisingly, prostitutes were said to regard such statistical outcomes as the cost of doing business, an occupational hazard.[82]

The San Francisco Crime Committee was blunt in its conclusion:

> The reason that current enforcement practices have not worked is that the statutes are unenforceable and the courts congested. The appearance of efforts at enforcement goes on because it offers the public the *appearance* of "controlling" prostitution. The whole process resembles a game.[83]

Reasons for the failure of the police part of the game were said to lie in motivation, and in the intricacies of making an arrest for prostitution stick. To avoid entrapment requires delicate kinds of maneuvering by vice squad officers. The requisite verbal skirmishing deceives none but the neophyte prostitute; in addition, the street grapevine is apt to identify a plainclothes officer in almost no time and undercut his effectiveness.

---

[81] *Ibid.*, pp. 14–16.
[82] *Ibid.*, pp. 20–21.
[83] *Ibid.*, p. 21.

The members of the San Francisco Crime Committee were not impressed with the argument that prostitution, left alone, would encourage the spread of venereal disease. They argued, contrariwise, that the very criminality of prostitution serves to discourage women from seeking cures for venereal infections, and they suggested that medical researchers ought to be encouraged to develop preventive approaches to venereal diseases.

It was also believed that the criminalization of prostitution played into the hands of the pimp:

> The pimps . . . have a large amount of economic leverage, and most of this is supplied by the criminal justice system itself. The pimp allows his girls enough money so that they can keep themselves looking good but not enough so that they can keep themselves out of jail. The girls need the pimp to pay bail and to hire a lawyer. Thus a direct consequence of our current law enforcement practices is that they provide the pimp with economic power over his girls.[84]

Nonetheless, the Committee would not endorse a system of licensed prostitution, "forceful . . . as arguments were" in its favor. It felt that history had shown this procedure to be no more efficacious than present policies. The Committee preferred to follow the Wolfenden report by advocating that prostitutes should be kept off the streets, though "tolerated" elsewhere. "We find it difficult to imagine that tolerating them off the streets would recruit more women than pimps are doing now," it was argued. Therefore, "discreet, private, off-the-street prostitution should cease to be criminal," the Committee recommended. Its members did not believe it likely that the legislature would be able to endorse such an approach, however. They suggested, therefore, that a policy of "selective enforcement" should be established by all agencies of criminal justice to accomplish the recommended goals.[85]

Support for the Committee recommendations came immediately from the *San Francisco Chronicle*, which liked the "thrust and particularly the premises on which the committee based its conclusions," especially the idea that the law cannot successfully make criminal what the public does not want made criminal. The *Chronicle* thought that further debate was essential to be certain that the young and those persons with particular sensibilities on moral issues could be adequately protected, but its inclination was toward the view that "the committee makes a strong case for its position."[86]

---

[84] *Ibid.*, p. 35.
[85] *Ibid.*, pp. 40–46.
[86] "A New Look at Sex and Gambling," *San Francisco Chronicle*, June 4, 1971.

The chief of police in San Francisco was a good deal less enthusiastic about the Crime Committee's report, telling the press that its contents has "flabbergasted" him. In particular, he insisted that the recommendations advanced, if translated into public policy, would encourage rather than discourage crime. The chief was especially indignant about the idea that "discreet" prostitution be made legal:

> There is no such thing as discreet prostitution. This would be the epitome of hypocrisy. The commodity they are talking about are (sic) human beings. Some people on the Crime Committee I know personally. They would never in a million years advocate prostitution for their daughters, relatives, or friends.
> And where would this 'discreet' prostitution occur? Would members of the committee want to see it in the neighborhoods where they live. . . . ? [87]

The chief thought that the Crime Committee report reflected a "defeatist attitude." He denied that any bordellos existed in San Francisco, as the Committee had alleged, and said that if anyone knew anything to the contrary, he would, if supplied with the appropriate information, see to it that such houses ceased operating.

The chief was joined the following day by the Mayor in his criticism of the report:

> I would not support any legislation that would legalize prostitution in any way at all. I think something happens to the moral tone of communities when you legalize prostitution. All you have to do is take a look, for example, at what effect it has had on a state like Nevada.
> This is a moral community and moral leadership is going to be exercised. [88]

Similarly, the Presiding Municipal Court judge took issue with the Committee's views on prostitution, especially its statement that prostitution "is essentially a business transaction between a willing buyer and a willing seller."

The judge thought that this observation was "cynical and shocking," adding: "This coldblooded premise ignores the human values damaged and destroyed by prostitution." He thought that "discreet" prostitution would "give the cloak of respectability and legality to conduct which is a serious social evil" and that moving solicitation indoors "would simply make the activity more surreptitious and increase telephone solicitation." [89]

---

[87] Lenn, *op. cit.*, n. 71.

[88] Dale Champion, "Alioto Tough on Crime Proposals," *San Francisco Chronicle*, June 5, 1971.

[89] Gerald O'Gara, quoted in *ibid*.

The outcome of the work of the Crime Commission in San Francisco, in summary, might be regarded as something of a prototype of the Nation's stand on the issue of prostitution at the moment. There is apparently a considerable core of reputable opinion moving toward advocacy of relaxation of statutes dealing with so-called victimless crimes. These persons are willing to be counted publicly on a side that not so many years ago would probably have been regarded as irredemiably heretical. The proponents are people of some social and political consequence and they appear in camps where they might not have been expected. Thus a man with 30 years of experience on the police force in San Francisco, a member of the Crime Committee, noted: "I subscribe to the report 100 percent. It's creative and dynamic and very realistic. That's the way things are working out anyway. It's the trend. I see no reason why the report's recommendations cannot be completely accepted." [90] But, it needs to be stressed, the officer had been retired from the police force for more than a year, and was now teaching police science at a junior college. On the official front, among persons whose professional existence was believed to depend·upon "proper" responses, condemnation of moves toward relaxation of existing laws regarding prostitution remained immutable. The defense of such positions tended to be couched in terms of moral "givens," with little examination of the consequences of the policies in force, but categoric belief that more lenient policies would be more deleterious. It is not altogether fair to maintain that a man's subtlest views on complicated social matters may be gleaned from a two-paragraph newspaper quotation, especially if the man is a politician or public official who has learned the art of quickly capturing the attention of mass media audiences, but it seems fair to observe that the opposition to the San Francisco Crime Committee recommendations was put in quite banal terms. The view advanced by the chief of police that the Committee members would not approve of their kinfolk being prostitutes as an argument against the report is the quaintest kind of nonsense, though his observation that relaxation of the laws against prostitution might lead to more serious crime obviously merits some attention.

SOME IMPACTS OF PROSTITUTION

The police chief's allegation will, therefore, be one of the matters to which we will attend in this section. We will attempt to summarize the impact of prostitution under diverse sets of legal arrange-

---

[90] William Osterloh, quoted in "Members of Crime Group Back Report," *San Francisco Chronicle*, June 5, 1971.

ments upon the women engaged in the behavior, others involved with them (pimps and customers most notably), and on the society in general.

The Prostitute

Research studies regarding prostitution indicate that in contemporary times it is an occupation entered into voluntarily. It offers a considerable range of vocational advantages, including flexible hours of work, contact with diverse kinds of persons, a heightened sense of activity, and the opportunity to make substantial sums of money. Such consequences do not accrue to all practitioners, nor perhaps to very many. For those women whose involvement is the most tawdry, prostitution represents a dirty and dangerous enterprise. There are beatings, ugly copulations, little financial reward. The loss of self-esteem that seems to attend upon the practice of prostitution is, of course, a function of broader social attitudes, which themselves are likely conditioned in part by legal sanctions. It seems likely, at any rate, that legalization of prostitution would not harm the self-esteem of its practitioners and might help them convince themselves more easily that they are engaged in a worthwhile occupation.

The harm that will accrue to the individual prostitute from her choice of occupation clearly seems to be neither so vicious nor so totally inexorable that social constraints ought reasonably to operate on these grounds. If the society prefers women to follow what it regards as more admirable kinds of endeavors, we would, again agreeing with Mill, suggest that it provide such outlets and make access to them attractive enough to counteract whatever appeals prostitution offers. If the society cannot accomplish its goal by such means, or by propagandizing adequately for its values as against those of prostitution, it might reasonably conclude that its arguments and the techniques legitimately available for their advance are not sufficient to the end sought, and let the matter stand there.

Unfortunately, there exist no studies of which we are aware concerning the outcomes of the lives of prostitutes; whether, as in the fictional portraits which tend to portray them as golden-hearted, prostitutes ultimately marry above their original social position and settle down comfortably in suburbia, there to condemn their neighbor's wife-swapping, or whether they end up as premature corpses, lying anonymously on city morgue tables. Such information ought to be sought in order to make public policy decisions more informed.

We would be inclined to believe that legalizing prostitution—or, more accurately, decriminalizing the behavior—would tend toward increase in the number of its practitioners, unless we could be persuaded to the view that in this realm the law is so peripheral an element that its character has no impact on recruitment. On the basis of our own values, we would regard it as unfortunate if more girls than otherwise would seek out prostitution because of the absence of legal constraints. But we have no certainty that ours is not a senseless opinion, based on an archaic morality that differentiates sexual matters from other kinds of matters. After all, writing toothpaste advertisements hardly seems more ennobling than catering for profit sexually to a lonely, perhaps crippled man. In any event, we are hard pressed to see that this is a matter of concern to others than the girls themselves, given for the moment their possible harm as the only consideration. The interesting use of a race relations analogy by the chief of police in San Francisco (i.e., "Would you want your daughter—wife, friend, relative—to be a prostitute?") provides its own, and easy, answer in a society valuing freedom. "This is her business, her choice."

Supporters of the Women's Liberation movement might come to rest on either of two ends of the continuum in regard to prostitution—either that the prostitute represents a typical illustration of the worst and most vicious kind of male exploitation, or, conversely, that the prostitute is the freest of women, honestly engaged in doing what her sisters do dishonestly, exchanging sexual favors for coin of the realm.

It is the second of these two stands that in fact strikes the Women's Liberation leaders as the more accurate one. The reasoning behind the Women's Liberation position on prostitution can be found in the statement of a female law student, speaking at a symposium, who said that the law on prostitution regards the woman as "naive, a half-person." Prostitution statutes, the speaker maintained, look upon the woman as "being beyond redemption."

> She's a menace, an outcast. The law appraises her as being steeped in crime. The man receives no punishment, although the prostitute is only filling his desire, doing something there is a demand for.[91]

Similarly, Ti-Grace Atkinson, regarded as the theoretician of the radical feminists, at a public meeting urged women to "support the prostitute" as the model of the new, independent woman. "We have to go out on the street to help her," she was quoted as saying, though there was no indication of what form such assistance ought to take.

---

[91] Judy Bakal, quoted in Michele Willens, "Legal Discrimination Hit," *Los Angeles Times*, May 23, 1971.

"My impression," Miss Atkinson said, "is that the prostitute is the only honest woman left in America." For Miss Atkinson, the suppression of women was equivalent to forcing them into prostitution. A liberated woman, therefore, would not succumb "for free" but would "up the charges." A marriage contract forces a female to work for life without pay; prostitutes, more honest, charge for their services.[92]

In such terms, it can be argued that decriminalizing prostitution represents a move toward equality for women, and thus fulfills one of the stipulated social and political objectives of our society.

Customers

A society with a dedication to monasticism and sexual abstinence might suggest that the abatement of prostitution would encourage chastity and sexual inhibition among those who now use prostitutes for purposes of sexual outlet. America is not, however, such a society. The assumption here would be that the absence of prostitutes for sexual activity would lead men who now have recourse to prostitutes to other means of releasing what are regarded as strong, demanding sexual energies. Masturbation could be one such outlet; sex by force another; or encouragement might be had of various kinds of things that psychiatrists call inhibitions and sublimations, involving, most generally, the transfer of sexual energies into pursuits not generally regarded as sexual, such as the drive for power.

The possibility exists that the availability of sexual liaisons with prostitutes discourages marriage, which some men may find more demanding than impersonal sexual contact. But American society is not that dedicated to the encouragement of marriage; otherwise, we could readily subsidize it so heavily that its avoidance would be economically devastating. Therefore, to argue that prostitution undermines marriage is to use a value that is not otherwise vigorously encouraged.

It is around the possibility that the absence of prostitution would lead men to seek sexual satisfaction by force that much discussion centers. In many respects, forcible rape and prostitution are similar. Both are illicit, both often involve brutality, and both have about them an atmosphere of humiliation of the female. In neither behavior is the woman viewed as a person requiring sexual satisfaction, nor as one apt to achieve such satisfaction. In neither instance, too, are demands for sophisticated sexual performance placed upon the male.

---

[92] Lacey Fosburgh, "Women's Liberationist Hails the Prostitute," *New York Times*, May 29, 1970.

Information regarding the relationship between prostitution—
legal or otherwise—and crimes of sexual violence is inconclusive,
perhaps necessarily so, given the number of confounding variables
that would enter into such a determination. Societies probably
encourage or discourage both rape and prostitution as a consequence
of commitments to certain attitudes and values, and it is likely that
these commitments, rather than legal codes, influence the rates for
both behaviors.

There are, however, some statistical data available from Australia,
though the numbers involved and other methodological difficulties
make definite conclusions impossible. Between the early 1950's and
the middle 1960's the rape rate rose steadily in the Australian state
of Queensland, from a level of 1.07 per 100,000 population in the
1949–1952 period to 3.70 per 100,000 population in the 1964–1967
period. The increase was particularly precipitous after 1961, and
it was characterized by a sharp rise in the number of gang rapes,
or "pack" rapes, as they are known as in Australia.

During this period, policies regarding prostitution were altered.
Brothels had been tolerated by the Queensland police until late in
1959. Thereafter, they were closed down, though sex remained available for money for men of the more affluent classes in connection
with various "drinking clubs" attached to Queensland hotels. Rape
rates jumped 149 percent following the closing of the brothels,
though offenses against the person committed by males rose only
49 percent. Statistical analysis indicates that the likelihood of such
discrepancies in crime increase for the two types of offenses occurring by chance is but one in 1,000. The Australian writer, however,
is reasonably cautious in his interpretation: "This, of course, does
not of itself prove that the increase in the number of convictions
for rape and attempted rape was caused by the closing of the brothels in Queensland, but it does show clearly that there was a remarkable increase in the conviction rate for these two crimes after this
closing—an increase that was not found in convictions for offenses
against the person by males in general." [93]

Some support for the hypothesis connecting rape rates and the
availability of prostitutes can be found in Kinsey's work, in which
it is maintained that a major reason for visiting prostitutes is the
desire for immediate and uncomplicated intercourse, with "romance"
seen as the major complicating factor in nonprostitution sex. "At

[93] R. N. Barber, "Prostitution and the Increasing Number of Convictions for
Rape in Queensland," *Australian and New Zealand Journal of Criminology*, 2
(September 1969), pp. 169–174.

all social levels men go to prostitutes because it is simpler to secure a sexual partner commercially than it is to secure a sexual partner by courting a girl who would not accept pay," Kinsey observes. Kinsey also suggests that intercourse with a prostitute is apt to be a good deal cheaper than intercourse ensuing from the courtship pattern prevalent in other heterosexual relationships, which could involve, in Kinsey's inventory, "flowers, candy, 'coke dates,' dinner engagements, parties, evening entertainments, moving pictures, theaters, night clubs, dances, picnics, weekend house parties, car rides, longer trips, and all sort of other expensive entertainment . . . ." before the male "might or might not be able to obtain the intercourse he wanted." [94] The Australian researcher, approaching the matter from another viewpoint, also suggests that persons who perpetrate forcible rape share to a considerable extent the socioeconomic traits of those who most often deal with prostitutes. It is this group, he argues, that was most severely hit by the closing of brothels, and this group—presumably in fact some of the same individuals—whose members turned to rape when denied a brothel sexual outlet.

The Australian study, it might be said in summary, is suggestive, but hardly conclusive. We would, pending further research, be inclined toward endorsement of the brief summary statement on the matter that appears in Kinsey's work:

> There is constant rumor of an increase in the frequency of forced intercourse or outright rape among the girls of a community where prostitution has been suppressed. We have no adequate data to prove the truth or falsity of such reports.[95]

The issue, even more than forcible rape, that dominates discussions of prostitution is that of venereal disease. It is argued that prostitutes are conduits of venereal infections. Given so high a level of intercourse with so diverse a clientele, it is regarded as inevitable that many prostitutes will sooner or later acquire a venereal infection and that they will pass the disease on to other customers who, in turn, will pass it on to other females—girl friends, wives, or other women—with whom they have sexual contact.

That such a chain of events occurs can hardly be doubted. The issue concerns the rate at which it occurs under different social arrangements and the manner in which it might more adequately be dealt with. There is also the question, of course, of whether pro-

[94] Alfred Kinsey, Wardell B. Pomeroy, and Clyde E. Martin, *Sexual Behavior in the Human Male* (Philadelphia: Saunders, 1948), p. 607.
[95] *Ibid.*, p. 608.

posed cures for this situation are reasonably related—ethically and politically—to the disorder.

In numerical terms, venereal diseases stand first among those medical conditions which by law are required to be reported to public authorities. A 1971 report on venereal disease issued by the American Social Health Association indicated that more than 500,000 persons in the United States suffer from undetected syphilis and are "in urgent need of skilled medical attention." The national rate of reported gonorrhea per 100,000 population in 1970 was 285.2 cases; the figure for reported syphilis per 100,000 population was 10. Actual cases were estimated to be about 4 times the reported rates.

The ASHA report noted that the United States, among the western nations, had a very high rate of undetected syphilis. Among the cities, San Francisco reported the highest gonorrhea rate and Shreveport the highest rate of infectious syphilis.[96]

These figures are supplemented by reports on America's youth culture today, some segments of which have been labeled a combination of "Sodom and gonorrhea." [97] Part of the youth problem is said to be related to the fact that only 14 States allow infected minors to be treated by doctors without the consent of their parents, and that many minors, adding distrust of their parents to the general embarrassment associated with venereal disease, prefer to hide rather than treat their condition. Besides youth, another major source of the disease is in the military. Authorities report that some 45,000 soldiers have contacted venereal infections in Vietnam each year since 1965, a figure that represents 16 cases per 100 soldiers, and one that is 5 times above the reported domestic rate.[98]

In New York City, approximately 50,000 venereal disease cases are reported each year. Estimates are that only 10 percent of the gonorrhea cases are reported, but that 90 percent of the syphilis cases becoming known to laboratories or physicians are brought to the attention of the public authorities. An investigator for the venereal disease control board in New York City suggests that the reported rates of venereal infections are probably related more to matters of social policy than to changes in patterns of sexual behavior. He believes that when venereal diseases were brought under some degree of control in the 1950's and 1960's, the response of governmental authorities was to decrease available funds; thereafter, unattended, the problem again escalated, and the public became more concerned

[96] American Social Health Association, "ASHA Releases National Survey on VD," *Social Health News*, 46 (April 1971), pp. 1–2.

[97] Quoted in Graham, *op. cit.*, n. 19, pp. 18–19.

[98] *Ibid.*, p. 228.

and appropriated more funds for control. These funds were used to discover more cases, thereby rapidly inflating the reported rates.

When the authorities learn of a syphilis case in New York, they attempt to interview the carrier and to insist that he seek medical treatment either from his own physician or from a City clinic. Most often, in large part because syphilis is more readily ascertainable in a male, it is a man with whom the authorities initially deal. If there is a suspicion that a man's wife has been infected by him after he acquired the disease elsewhere, the authorities are willing to "go along with some pretext to get the wife examined." As one investigator notes: "We're not purists." The same investigator provides the following responses regarding the relationship between venereal diseases and prostitution:

> Question: Are prostitutes often a source of syphilis?
> Answer: Statistically, prostitutes are not a significant syphilis problem. They're far more of a gonorrhea problem. This is because of the nature of the diseases. Let's say a prostitute has acquired syphilis and doesn't recognize it. You have to understand that syphilis is only spread in two brief periods of time— when a patient is in a primary state which may last for a week or two, and when a patient is in the secondary stage.
> Q.: But in a week she can infect perhaps 50 people.
> A.: That may be. But if she has gonorrhea, the chances are that she will be infectious for a far longer period, for months and months and months, rather than weeks. She may not even know she has the disease.
> Q.: Do prostitutes, to your knowledge, take prophylactic doses of penicillin?
> A.: A lot of them do. A lot of them are under the care of private physicians. But it's a misleading kind of prophylaxis. A lot of girls will go to a doctor once a week, or once every 10 days, for a shot of penicillin. But unfortunately the shot of penicillin they get is not in sufficient dosages to treat either gonorrhea or syphilis, and yet is more than sufficient to beautifully mask or hide the symptoms of both diseases.[99]

The key phrase in the above dialogue may be the one that indicates that "prostitutes are not a significant syphilis problem." The thrust of the investigator's answers seems to be that prostitutes, professionally threatened by the prospect of acquiring venereal infections, take precautionary measures. The best information indicates that venereal infections are primarily a function of nonprofessional promiscuity, spread among young persons whose moral codes see

---

[99] Norman J. Scherzer, quoted in "Interview with a VD Investigator," *Sexual Behavior*, 1 (June 1971), pp. 25–26.

little wrong in casual sexual intercourse.[100] To inhibit the spread of the diseases among such persons would require either a medical breakthrough which would produce a vaccine against venereal infections and/or intensive educational campaigns. For prostitutes, possibilities of relatively effective control of venereal infections could be arranged by various methods, including those proposed at the end of this section.

Pimps

The fear that prostitutes represent innocent victims of vicious males often forms part of the arsenal of arguments raised against abandonment of attempts to control and ameliorate the practice of prostitution through use of the criminal law. In fact, it has been observed that official and public attitudes toward the prostitute have become increasingly tolerant, while the public attitude toward the men with whom prostitutes live "remains relentlessly intolerant." [101]

There appears to be general agreement among researchers that the relationship between the pimp and the prostitute represents a mutual exchange, in which both parties provide and secure things important to themselves. The standard psychiatric reasoning is that the pimp serves symbolically for the prostitute as a debased person, someone even lower than herself, since he offers little in the way of service, but lives parasitically on her earnings. Other writers, less inclined toward symbolic interpretations of such things, suggest that prostitutes, like all of us, rather prefer to be loved and to love, and that the pimp happens to represent the person with whom they form such an attachment. That the pimp exists on the work of women, and often of several such women is, by definition, his condition. It need only be mentioned that some of us manage the same achievement by the fruit of cashing dividend checks accompanying inheritances or equivalently "parasitic" activities.

Pimping, in fact, has sometimes been described as something of an art. "It's a skull game," one pimp explained to a graduate student in anthropology preparing a doctoral dissertation on the business. "It's a brainwashing process. When you turn a chick out, you take away every set of values and morality that she previously had and create a different environment. Instead of bookkeepers or secre-

[100] See, generally, R. R. Wilcox, "Proportion of Venereal Disease Acquired from Prostitutes in Asia : A Comparison with France, the United Kingdom, and the United States of America," *British Journal of Venereal Diseases,* 38 (March 1962), pp. 37–42.

[101] Louis Blom-Cooper, "Prostitution : A Socio-Legal Comment on the Case of Dr. Ward," *British Journal of Sociology,* 15 (March 1964), p. 66.

taries for friends, you give her professional hos [whores]." [102] Indeed, this description sounds not unlike the self flattery of many entrepreneurs, rather overrating their performance. Note might be made, too, in the quotation of the kinds of associates prostitutes might have had prior to their entering the trade—these are the Kitty Foyles of the urban areas.

Pimps, we noted earlier, seem to be disappearing as their social and emotional functions decrease in a more sexually free society. It is our guess that pimping tends to be enhanced by stringent laws against prostitution and to decline with the elimination of such laws. In any event, to the extent that a female chooses of her own volition to affiliate with a pimp, the liaison should be regarded, it would seem, much as any other formed freely by two persons who have reached the age of consent.

The Impact of Prostitution Upon Society

Illegal prostitution exists in large measure as a function of the efforts of our society to regulate sexual behavior, so that, in a sense, prostitution is created by the attempts to see that it does not occur. That paradox can perhaps be best understood by imagining a society in which sexual relationships were readily obtainable by all who sought them, in whatever form. Such an "ideal" society is not likely to exist, any more than is any kind of society in which all persons are easily able to secure whatever it is that they desire. Prostitution then functions to provide things not otherwise available, as Kingsley Davis indicates in the following functional explication:

> In short, the attempt to control sexual expression, to tie it to social requirements, especially the attempt to tie it to the durable relation of marriage and the rearing of children, or to attach men to a celibate order, or to base sexual expression on love, creates the opportunity for prostitution. It is analagous to the black market, which is the illegal but inevitable response to an attempt to control the economy. The craving for sexual variety, for perverse gratification, for novel and provocative surroundings, for ready and cheap release, for intercourse free from entangling cares and civilized pretense—all can be demanded from the woman whose interest lies solely in the price. The sole limitation on the man's satisfactions is in this instance not morality or convention, but his ability to pay.[103]

Kinsey, speaking of the extent of prostitution in the United States,

---

[102] "The Pimping Game," *Time*, January 11, 1971, p. 54.

[103] Kingsley Davis, "Sexual Behavior," in Robert K. Merton and Robert A. Nisbet (editors), *Contemporary Social Problems*, 2d ed. (New York: Harcourt, Brace, and World, 1966), p. 360.

seems startled at the attention the behavior has received when it is measured against the importance that it plays numerically as a sexual outlet:

> The world's literature contains hundreds of volumes whose authors have attempted to assay the social significance of prostitution. For an activity which contributes no more than this does to the sexual outlet of the male population, it is amazing that it should have been given such widespread consideration. Some of the attention [has] undoubtedly been inspired by erotic interest; but a major part of the interest has centered around this question of the social significance of prostitution. The extent of the attention which the subject still receives in this country today is, as we have shown, all out of proportion to its significance in the lives of most males.[104]

The Kinsey quotation is, however, itself rather puzzling, seeming to imply that the extent rather than the quality of behavior should be the criterion by which its importance may reasonably be measured. More people are killed by a variety of means—including traffic accidents—and many more die of the avoidable lethal conditions that go to make up the infant mortality rate than are murdered each year in the United States. Nonetheless, murder is considered, and reasonably so, a very important matter. So too is capital punishment, though very few persons have been executed in the United States in the past decade. Some things, like prostitution, contain elements cutting to the core of social commitments, and the attitudes taken toward them may be regarded as reflective of a wide range of attitudes toward all sorts of behavior in our social system.

The impact of legal or illegal prostitution, under the diverse kinds of arrangements sometimes suggested (e.g., prostitution in brothels, licensed or otherwise, in circumscribed areas of a city, by telephone solicitation) upon the moral fiber of the Nation is one of those questions that we would not pretend to be able to respond to adequately. We would only observe that moral fibers include a large number of strands, and that the encouragement of hypocrisy by outlawing a trade that nonetheless is covertly allowed to continue may be just as, or more, damaging to a social system as the tolerance of sexual variation. So too encouragement of a philosophy of live-and-let-live could be a contribution to democratic vitality.

As far as public opinion is concerned, the most recent poll, conducted by Mervin D. Field in California in late May 1971 indicates that "legalized prostitution today seems to have more support than opposition among the California public." In its statewide poll, the

---

[104] Kinsey, *op. cit.*, n. 94, p. 605.

Field organization found that one-half of the respondents (50%) thought that the legalization of prostitution was a "good idea." Less than half (42%) believed that it was a "poor idea" and 8 percent had no opinion on the subject.[105]

The poll was taken after a State assemblyman had introduced a bill which would provide State-sanctioned houses of prostitution. Under the terms of the bill, individual prostitutes would be licensed by the State Department of Public Health and counties would have the option of permitting legalized prostitution within their boundaries.[106]

The prolegalized prostitution argument among the California public was supported by a variety of arguments, Field noted, including the fact that respondents were "troubled by the hypocrisy of a society which says prostitution is sinful but allows it to exist and flourish so long as it is out of view." Many respondents also believed that sanctioning prostitution would allow for better control over venereal disease and crimes said to be associated with prostitution.[107]

Unlike similar matters, legalization of prostitution found less favor, according to the Field Poll, with youngsters than with older persons. Thus, it was the group in the 30–49-year age bracket and the men who most strongly favored the legalization of prostitution, as Table V–1 shows.

Two other items need to be noted here. These involve the arguments that uncontrolled prostitution would result in a heavy increase in public annoyance on the streets and residential disturbances in neighborhoods in which prostitutes were located. The first of these two matters we are inclined to dismiss out of hand. Solicitation on public streets by prostitutes, we believe, is distasteful only because of public prejudice against prostitutes. If the matter becomes too "outrageous" we would not object to business zoning regulations which specified the areas in which the activity may reasonably be engaged in—and the same may be said regarding house-based prostitution.[108]

That prostitution tends to encourage derivative kinds of criminal activity can hardly be denied, any more than it can be denied that

---

[105] Mervin D. Field, "Legalized Prostitution Has More Support Than Opposition," (The California Poll, May 28, 1971) ; "Poll Reports 50% Favor Prostitution," *Los Angeles Times*, May 28, 1971 (UPI).

[106] "Legal Brothels Defeated," *Los Angeles Herald-Examiner*, July 14, 1971 (AP).

[107] Field, *op. cit.*, n. 105.

[108] See Lesley Oelsner, "Prostitute Neighbors Vexing Tenants, Especially Those in Luxury Units," *New York Times*, August 22, 1971.

Table V–1

Responses to Question: Legalizing prostitution to provide more tax revenue and help control the disease and crime that now results from uncontrolled prostitution is a . . . .

	Good Idea	Poor Idea	No Opinion
Totals _____	50%	42%	8%
Sex			
Male _____	57	37	6
Female _____	44	47	9
Age			
18–20 years _____	42	54	4
21–29 _____	43	50	7
30–49 _____	56	38	6
50–69 _____	51	39	10
70 and over _____	44	47	9

Source: The California Poll, May 28, 1971, p. 2.

kissing may tend to lead to illegitimate births. One would suggest that such crimes attendant upon prostitution ought to be prosecuted vigorously, and that the halfhearted measures now used for dealing with prostitution itself ought to yield to a more intensive effort to see to it that prostitutes stick to their basic business. Indeed, a clearer directive toward law enforcement might contribute to more effective personnel use and particularly to the elimination of the ugly practices that now pervade the manner in which prostitution tends to be dealt with. In a recent novel regarding the Los Angeles police department, written by a sergeant on that force, for instance, there is a detailed, obviously accurate, portrait of a roundup of prostitutes, more as a police recreational adventure than as anything else. The girls are dumped into the paddy wagon, teased some, driven about the city, and then deposited far from the places where they had been "arrested." The police officers observe that this is done because there is no chance of gaining a conviction in court, and this procedure is the best that they can think of.[109]

In summary, we are suggesting that some state concern with prostitution, in the manner that the state concerns itself with such trades as barbering, would be in order. We have learned in Vietnam—most

[109] Joseph Wambaugh, *The New Centurions* (New York: Dell, 1970), pp. 78–86. See also Albert J. Reiss, Jr., *The Police and the Public* (New Haven: Yale University Press, 1971), pp. 43–44.

recently from the revelations in the "Pentagon Papers"—what may happen when the leadership of a society uses its moral persuasions ("We have got to stop the spread of Communism") to dictate policy without overt debate and discussions regarding the matters being decided. Prostitution should be examined, debated, regularized. Its practitioners should be offered reasonable opportunities to pursue other callings, and reasonable methods of persuasion should be utilized—if we so desire—to convince them that their self-interest lies in such other callings. That done, it would seem a good idea to let the matter proceed as it will.

PROS AND CONS

It seems worth including here the sophisticated listing of arguments for and against the question of whether prostitution ought to be regarded as a criminal offense, as these arguments were put together by a United Nations study team about a decade ago.

The advocates of the prohibitionist system generally advance the following arguments in support of their view:

1. It is the responsibility of the Government to regulate public morals in the interest of public good; hence, to declare prostitution a punishable offence.

2. If prostitution *per se* is not made a punishable offence, the abolition of the regulation of prostitution will merely replace controlled prostitution by clandestine prostitution.

3. It will be difficult strictly to enforce legal provisions proscribing the exploitation of the prostitution of others when prostitution itself is not considered a punishable offense.

4. Many women and girls on the borderline may be encouraged to take up prostitution by the fact that the law does not proscribe such a calling.

5. The absence of any legal provision against prostitution may be interpreted by the public as meaning that the Government tolerates commercialized vice because it is a "necessary evil."

The following counterarguments are generally advanced by the advocates of the abolitionist system:

1. The prohibitionist legislation would necessitate the formulation of a definition of "prostitution." If the term "prostitute" were to be given wide scope, the fact of making prostitution a legal offence would entail unwarranted interference in private life which would be contrary to Article 12 of the Universal Declaration of Human Rights.[110] If, on the other hand, the term

---

[110] Article 12 reads: "No one shall be subjected to arbitrary interference with his privacy, family, home or correspondence, nor to attacks upon his honour and reputation. Everyone has the right to the protection of the law against such interference or attacks."

"prostitute" were to be given too restricted a legal connotation, then it would be difficult to establish the charge against the culprit.

2. Prostitution is an act which is committed by the prostitute and her client. Both are equally responsible. It would be a discrimination against the woman for the law to be directed only against her. Further, whenever the law inflicts penalties on the client as well as on the prostitute, experience shows that, in practice, the repressive measures are enforced on the prostitute alone.

3. Between prostitution and other sexual relations outside wedlock there is only a difference of degree and it would be unjust to limit the penalty only to persons who meet the arbitrary criteria set forth in a legal definition of prostitution.

4. The penal law should not take cognizance of every immoral act. To protect minors, and to maintain public order, prostitution with and of minors, as well as soliciting for the purpose of prostitution, may be proscribed. But adult prostitution should not be singled out from all other moral sins and be brought within the realm of the penal law.

5. In terms of the results achieved, experience teaches that prostitution cannot be eliminated by mere enactments and that making prostitution a criminal offense generally leads to clandestine prostitution and to a ruthless underworld organization for the exploitation of the prostitution of others. As long as a demand for prostitution exists on the part of men, there will undoubtedly be a corresponding supply on the part of women, despite the penalties inflicted on the latter.

6. The prohibitionist policy depends for its effectiveness upon a system of police espionage and entrapment which is itself detrimental to the common good.

7. By making prostitution *per se* a criminal offense, the prohibitionist system creates among persons engaged in prostitution a collective as well as an individual antagonistic attitude which hamper the chances of their rehabilitation.[111]

In the end, the United Nations group was more persuaded by the arguments against declaring prostitution a criminal offense. "The above objections indicate clearly the problems inherent in a prohibitionist policy," it was observed. "Legal provisions proscribing prostitution should not therefore be considered as preventive measures to be taken in conjunction with the abolition of the regulation of prostitution." Rather, the UN group recommended a sweeping array of educative and retraining programs for prostitutes and persons who might become prostitutes.[112]

---

[111] United Nations, *op. cit.*, n. 7, pp. 10–11.
[112] *Ibid.*, p. 11.

VI. Gambling

The absence of explicit sexual content in gambling is surely what most differentiates it from the other "crimes without victims" that we have considered. An emphasis on sexual regularity, defined as marital heterosexual genital-introjective sex, stands behind legal bans on homosexuality and prostitution. Abortion concerns, among other things, the consequences of failure to exercise due restraint in sexual relationships, and a large measure of public opposition to legalized abortion lies in the fact that traditionally it is regarded as the birth-avoidance tactic of the promiscuous unmarried girl.

"Abuse" of narcotics, like gambling, has no overt sexual content, though outlawing some drugs has been justified on the ground that their use reduces sexual inhibitions. Visions of mass orgies, triggered by drug ingestion, often are at the root of arguments raised against freer access to drugs. The mythology of opium-smoking orientals wildly raping pristine white girls dies hard. So, too, marihuana usage and the more lax (or relaxed, depending upon one's manner of looking at the situation) sexual morality of the young are often a combined affront to supporters of prohibition of the drug. That heroin, like liquor, deters sexual performance, is now only beginning to become generally known.

Gambling shares with drugs an ingredient that probably underlies the laws which make it legal only under special conditions and, because of this, only for special persons. Gambling toys with and teases certain imperatives of our culture, particularly those concerned with what has been called the Puritan ethic, a set of postulates about human existence which maintain that man should prosper and enjoy the good (i.e., conspicuous consumption) only by means of his own efforts, and not through the sheer intervention of chance or providence. The roots of contemporary viewpoints about gambling can be found in a 1767 court order issued in Virginia, which ruled that only the gentry may enter horses in a race and bet upon the outcome of that race:

> James Bullocke, a Taylor, having made a race for his mare
> to run with a horse belonging to Mr. Matthew Slader for 2,000
> pounds of tobacco and caske, it being contrary to the Law for

a Labourer to make a race, being only a sport for Gentlemen, is fined for the same 100 pounds of tobacco and caske.[1]

Similarly, Cotton Matther, the fire and brimstone preacher in the American colonies, explained how lotteries and similar games of chance were an arrogation by man of rights that were God's alone:

> . . . lots, being mentioned in the sacred oracles of Scripture are used only in weighty cases, and as an acknowledgement of God sitting in judgement . . . cannot be made the tools and parts of our common sports without, at least, such an appearance of evil, as is forbidden in the word of God.[2]

For our purposes, current problems surrounding the issue of gambling concern the effect of criminal bans and/or alternative methods of dealing with gambling upon individuals who gamble or who might gamble, upon other persons involved with the behavior (such as sponsors of gambling operations, persons who run "legitimate" business enterprises, and members of the gamblers' families), as well as upon the society in general. It is sometimes alleged, for instance, that holding out the legal prospect of sudden, striking improvement in one's lot by an act of chance might undercut incentive toward involvement in more mundane, less exciting and less prospectively lucrative enterprise. Why work for $100 a week when a winning lottery ticket can reward you with more money than you will ever be able to earn in a lifetime of labor?

Surprisingly, however, (and perhaps it tells a great deal about American society), winners of large sums in the State-run lotteries to date have often remained at their jobs and insisted that the deluge of cash had made little difference in the way they intended to live. The response of a winner of $1 million in the New Jersey lottery is rather typical: "You can only play so much golf or lay on so many beaches," he said, noting that he will keep his $11,000 a year job as a telephone technician, will plan no spending orgies, and intends to place the money in safe investments. Another $1-million winner replaced his 10-year-old car with a 1-year-old one and bought an $11,750 house. A winner of $1 million in the New York lottery, a buyer of women's dresses, told news reporters that he is thinking about donating the receipts for medical research. "Money never meant that much to me," he said.[3]

---

[1] Henry Chafetz, *A History of Gambling in the United States from 1492 to 1955* (New York: Potter, 1960), p. 12.

[2] *Ibid.*, p. 19.

[3] Les Gapay, "A Million Dollars Isn't Ticket to A New Life, Lottery Winners Find," *Wall Street Journal*, May 17, 1971. See also Martin Arnold, "Baker and Son Win $1-Million; Lottery Mixed Blessing to Some," *New York Times*, December 22, 1971.

There are both semantic and boundary-setting problems involved in the issue of gambling that do not present themselves quite so sharply with some of the behaviors we have considered earlier. Gambling—the word itself is derived from the Middle English *gamen*, to amuse oneself—involves the taking of a chance on the occurrence of some event, with rewards flowing from an accurate estimate and deficits from an inaccurate one. All human behavior, however, is predicated on a calculated risk that it will bring about a desired result, and most all human behavior entails an estimate that is based on something less than all the relevant information necessary for an accurate choice. Making no choice—that is, remaining passive—is in itself a choice, and it too involves certain consequences of variable likelihood.

In this sense, all human behavior is gambling, though only certain kinds of activities are officially said to be "gambling." One writer, psychiatrically inclined, has observed that "The compulsive gambler is one who will take no real risks—he gambles on the throw of the dice or the luck of a horse, because he is afraid to gamble on himself, to wager his character against the monumental indifference of the world." [4] So it may be. But without entering into adjudication of the aptness of this diagnosis, there is no gainsaying that life itself does involve risks, and that its players can take large chances with the possibility of large gains or losses or, in a different style of living, they can always hedge their bets.

Major concern in the United States today centers about four kinds of gambling operations: (1) numbers; (2) casino-style gambling; (3) lotteries; and (4) parimutuel betting at race tracks and its extension, offtrack betting. Numbers remain illegal throughout the United States; casino gambling is legal only in the State of Nevada; lotteries have recently been started in New Hampshire, New York, New Jersey, Pennsylvania, and Massachusetts; and offtrack betting was inaugurated in New York City in April 1971, in a move that has been watched with special care by other jurisdictions, particularly those—and there are but few which do not fit the category—looking desperately for new sources of revenue. After some brief introductory observations about gambling in general, we shall examine each of these forms.

PERSPECTIVES ON GAMBLING

Gambling represents an invocation of the ethos of luck that pervades our society and serves as an important cultural ingredient in

---

[4] Sydney J. Harris, *Leaving the Surface* (Boston: Houghton Mifflin, 1968), p. 405.

providing continuing motivation for the putative failure. Hard
work, touched with vital portions of luck, is regarded as the key to
success, and few persons of prominence fail to pay obeisance to luck
when they recount stories of their achievements. If luck plus work
represent the mainspring of success, then luck alone represents the
major shortcut to success. This is the promise offered by gambling,
a promise that also introduces an element of anticipatory hope into
what otherwise are often drab existences. The New York Offtrack
Betting program deliberately tapped this theme with its citywide
advertisement: "Nothing Brightens the Rat Race Like a Horse
Race." [5] As Irving K. Zola has pointed out, in the lower classes
gambling also serves as a vehicle by means of which a person is able
to achieve recognition for his accomplishments by demonstrating
ability in the selection of horses or numbers.[6]

It is claimed that psychologically gambling serves as a ritualistic
flirtation with an unknown fate. Gambling has been called "a kind
of question addressed to destiny," and it has been maintained that
the fascination of gambling is that it is "a simulation of life itself."
"Speaking pessimistically," Clyde Brion Davis writes, "you might
say that life itself is a one-armed bandit slot machine which, in the
end, takes all your nickels"; in pointing to the many aspects of
everyday living that constitute forms of gambling, Davis notes that
the insurance company "bets you at what might be called parimutuel
odds that your house will not burn down within the next 3 years." [7]

Success at gambling is supposed to be transposed by the gambler
into a general sign of favor from otherwise inscrutable gods, somewhat in the manner of, for instance, the prize fighter who traces his
success to the fact that "Somebody Up There Likes Me," rather than
to a fast right hand and an unusual ability to withstand punishment.[8] It was this mental transposition, as Max Weber has shown
while tracing the purported origins of capitalism, that led financially
successful persons in early Calvinistic societies to credit their wealth
to divine approval of their total person and thus to regard it as an
indication of a future place in heaven.[9]

Gambling shows an elaborate history through the annals of civili-

[5] Steve Cady, "Offtrack Betting," *New York Times*, April 4, 1971.

[6] Irving K. Zola, "Observations on Gambling in a Lower-Class Setting," *Social Problems*, 10 (Spring 1963), p. 360.

[7] Clyde B. Davis, *Something for Nothing* (Philadelphia: Lippincott, 1956), p. 12.

[8] Rocky Graziano, *Somebody Up There Likes Me* (New York: Simon and Schuster, 1955).

[9] Max Weber, *The Protestant Ethic and the Spirit of Capitalism*, trans. by Talcott Parsons (London: Allen and Unwin, 1930).

zation. Stone-Age people are known to have tossed painted pebbles and to have cast knucklebones, though it is not certain whether their attempt was to win somebody else's stone axe or to invoke magic and to facilitate prophecy. We have records from India from as early as 321 B.C. showing the existence of a governmental department that regulated gambling, with a Superintendent of Public Games who supplied dice for a fee of 5 percent of the receipts.[10] Public lotteries were common in the United States from early colonial times until the 1830's. Many institutions of higher learning, including Columbia, Harvard, and Yale, were financed by public lotteries. Reactions against State-sponsored gambling were due to numerous scandals connected with its operation as well as to a growing sense of moral outrage.[11]

NUMBERS

It is worth noting, in regard to the moral outrage often brought to bear on gambling, that the only important form that is not allowed anywhere in the United States is that favored by the ghetto resident. Suburbanites with the leisure and wherewithal may travel to the race track and bet legally in many states, and the lottery is available now in several jurisdictions to those who have learned, as good middle-class citizens have, to wait for their rewards and postpone their pleasures. Persons intent on trying their luck at blackjack need but have the fare for a trip to Las Vegas or Reno, where the gaudy, graceless gambling palaces also compete for the customer's slot-machine bets and his outlay at the roulette tables.

For persons such as the Harlem black, however, gambling means "numbers" or, as they are sometimes known, "policy," "bolita," "the figures," or "the digits." Unlike the lottery player, the numbers player gets to make his own choice, so that winning may be regarded as a testament to personal skill and/or insight. The dominant position of "numbers" in gambling today is evidenced by the changing pattern of arrests for gambling in New York City. In 1969, the police made 6,331 arrests for policy transactions as compared to 2,663 for bookmaking. In contrast, there were 6,480 arrests for policy in 1948 compared with 6,297 for bookmaking.[12]

---

[10] Will Durant, *Our Oriental Heritage* (New York: Simon and Schuster, 1954), p. 444.

[11] John S. Ezell, *Fortune's Merry Wheel: The Lottery in America* (Cambridge: Harvard University Press, 1960).

[12] Emanuel Perlmutter, "Cheaper Lottery Tickets and More Drawings Are Not Expected to Cut Into Numbers Play," *New York Times*, April 26, 1970.

Officials in New York estimate that there are 500,000 daily policy players in the city, who wager about $200 million per year with the "policy banks." [13] There are said to be 100,000 numbers workers employed in the five boroughs of New York, with the bulk of them active in Harlem. They range in a strictly ordered hierarchy from layoff persons to pickup men and finally down to runners, who take bets directly from customers. Odds normally are 600 to 1 against a person selecting the winning, three-digit number, though in fact the payoff is 540 to 1 since the winner is obligated to give a 10 percent bonus to the runner. Some numbers are regarded as "cut"—digit combinations such as 111, 222, and 325 which, because of their popularity, are paid off at lower rates.[14]

Winning numbers are derived from several sources. In Chicago, policy wheels, designated by different names or colors, are spun a number of times daily, and winning combinations are drawn from them.[15] Other cities use the last three digits of the total amount of money bet at a designated race track, the final numbers of the last dollar bills printed at the mint, the payoffs on specified horse races, or various other sources.

The integral role of numbers in certain neighborhoods is underlined in St. Clair Drake and Horace Cayton's study of the Black Belt of Chicago, where the authors found many residents defending the pervasive numbers game as crucial to the economic security of the community because of the jobs it provided.[16] In the Boston slum, women would send their children to the grocery store for milk, giving them an extra nickel to put on a number.[17] Publications, so-called "dream books," were sold openly, each claiming to provide clues to winning numbers.[18] "Policy is not only a business—it's a cult," Drake and Cayton note.[19] Competition was eliminated either by mergers or by police action against newcomers, instigated by the organization that controlled the area. Police were paid off regularly, at a "union wage," with a sliding scale for patrolmen, plainclothes-

---

[13] *Ibid.* See also Charles Grutzner, "Dimes Make Millions for Numbers Racket," *New York Times,* June 26, 1964.

[14] Thomas J. Johnson, "Numbers Called Harlem's Balm," *New York Times,* March 1, 1971.

[15] Frederick W. Egen, *Plainclothesman* (New York: Greenberg, 1953), Chap. 4.

[16] St. Clair Drake and Horace R. Cayton, *Black Metropolis: A Study of Negro Life in A Northern City* (New York: Harcourt, Brace, 1945), pp. 493–494.

[17] William F. Whyte, *Street Corner Society: The Social Structure of an Italian Slum,* 2d ed. (Chicago: University of Chicago Press, 1955), p. 116.

[18] See George J. McCall, "Symbiosis: The Case of Hoodoo and the Numbers Racket," *Social Problems,* 10 (Spring 1963), pp. 361–371.

[19] Drake and Cayton, *op. cit.,* n. 16, p. 474.

men, and headquarters' officers. Honest law-enforcement officers often found themselves transferred to the cemetery beat. "It's lonely out there in the cemetery," one resident noted wryly. "Nothing ever happens out there." [20]

The arguments concerning criminalization and decriminalization of numbers gambling involve an intricate evaluation of competing values and arguable consequences. Many insist, for instance, that the present arrangement most benefits the ghetto dweller, since it involves a mutually beneficial rapprochement among law enforcement personnel, numbers operators, and the slum dweller. Numbers provide jobs for blacks who otherwise would not be able to earn nearly as much money. The law enforcement charade, it is said, harms no one, and if public pressures against "vice" intensify they can always be becalmed by a sham arrest. "I take a wino down to the Salvation Army or a rummage sale or pawn shop and buy him some good clothes, shave him and make him presentable and then let the cops arrest him," a numbers chieftain says, explaining how the system works.[21] Most importantly, the argument is made that the numbers, as they now operate, satisfy the emotional needs of the ghetto dweller. The moods associated with playing the numbers are admirably caught in the following writeup, which also indicates the potentialities for social mobility inherent in winning:

> The numbers player pays far less attention to what happens to the dollar he presses into the hand of a runner than to the excitement of a possible hit. This was found to be true of the hardened bartender who bet the same number daily on credit with a runner and also with churchgoing grandmothers who determine their plays by giving numerical significance to daily events, birthdays, dreams and sermons.
> A black professional man, who reminisced recently about the time years ago his mother had hit the numbers said: "There was money all over the bed and spilling over on the floor. I laid down on the bed and tried to cover myself with it. My mother watched me and she was laughing and crying at the same time. It was just unbelievable."
> The hit took the family from the slums of Brooklyn to a two-family house in Queens and into partnership in a restaurant. The man's parents, both hard-working, church-going people, continue to play the numbers daily.[22]

The argument is also made that the numbers, by remaining an indigenous slum activity, provide fluid cash for legitimate business activities in places such as Harlem, where banks and financial lend-

[20] Whyte, *op. cit.*, n. 17, p. 125.
[21] Johnson, *op. cit.*, n. 14.
[22] *Ibid.*

ing institutions have not seen fit to underwrite such costs. The psychologist, Kenneth Clark, has said that the numbers are "a vital and indestructible part of the Harlem economy," [23] and the writer, Fred J. Cook, has estimated that some 60 percent of Harlem's economic life depends upon the cash flow from numbers.[24]

There also tends to be a close relationship built up over the years between the collector of numbers and his customers. The numbers man represents a model of success, a person worthy of emulation, and a friend in need. He can serve as a breakwater between the tenement dweller and what may seem to be menacing, anonymous, and immutable outside forces. Often the slum resident finds that he cannot communicate comfortably with the agents of the society, such as the social workers, who may be defined as both condescending and prim. Leaders of the numbers operation, on the other hand, pass no moral judgments and can deliver real services. When a slum child gets into trouble with the police, the social worker may map out a long-range plan involving the community center, deliver a lecture on the responsibilities of parenthood, or review the financial position of the family to derive a "more meaningful" plan of living. But often the numbers operator sees to it that the child receives adequate (i.e., shrewd and somewhat unprincipled) legal defense, so that he is soon returned home. When a father loses his job, the family is likely to turn to the numbers boss, with his financial resources and connections. It becomes singularly irrelevant that, by other standards, the major society regards these persons as undesirable citizens. Such a judgment carries little weight when it conflicts with the more immediate and real experience of power, opulence, and good will that the numbers men can demonstrate.

For such reasons, there are persons who insist that the status quo of numbers ought to remain undisturbed. "Unlike narcotics," one writer observes, "which creates droves of criminals who prey on the generally poor black community, the numbers game seems to many people to be just a potent, daily titillation for poor people seeking a rainbow's end." Almost every day, the same writer notes, "someone in the tenement dweller's block, family, or neighborhood will 'hit' and the excitement—the rags-to-riches explosion of joy by someone close by—is enough to renew the faith of those who were not so lucky." [25] Politicians from Harlem tend to agree: "For the average

[23] Quoted in *ibid.*

[24] Fred J. Cook, "The Black Mafia Moves into the Numbers Racket," *New York Times Magazine*, April 4, 1971, pp. 24–27ff.

[25] Johnson, *op. cit.*, n. 14.

Harlemite, playing numbers is like bingo is to the Catholic Church," one has noted. "It's moral and it's a way of life." [26] "There is no way in God's earth to keep folks from playing numbers," another has said.[27]

There are others, however, who insist that the idea that the money from numbers gambling remains in the community and invigorates its economy is pure myth. They insist that the profits of numbers are channeled by organized criminals—primarily whites—out of the slum communities. Such criminals, they say, suck every vestige of pride out of the community along with its money. Then, having power, they keep the community subjugated, with the numbers part of the diversion from the realities of oppression. A Harlem minister, speaking to this point, and to the point that the numbers contribute to further deprivation, has noted that "It is another example of how the powerlessness of poverty helps complete a cycle that makes the original condition worse." [28]

It is also said that the corruption of the police in regard to numbers introduces hypocrisy that taints all relationships between the political system and its ghetto constituents. This view can be employed to buttress calls for forceful control of the numbers gambling or to support appeals for its legalization. An articulate statement on the subject of the relationship between law enforcement conditions and crimes such as numbers has been put forward by Patrick Murphy, New York City's Police Commissioner:

> The policeman would be more effective in his crime prevention duties and he would be held in higher public esteem if he were not required to enforce so many regulations which attempt to control morals—the so-called victimless crime.
>
> By charging our police with the responsibility to enforce the unenforceable we subject them to disrespect and corrupting influences. And we provide the organized crime syndicates with illicit industries on which they thrive.[29]

Today, the main thrust is toward persuading legislators that they ought to extend legal gambling to the numbers game, with the State itself operating the game. So far, the only real discussion of the subject has been in New York, since it is there that offtrack betting first—and only recently—became legal. The proponents of legalized numbers say that the State should hire the runner, and should use the proceeds realized to provide revenue earmarked for slum im-

---

[26] Charles B. Rangel, quoted in Perlmutter, *op. cit.*, n. 12.

[27] Guy R. Brewer, quoted in Johnson, *op. cit.*, n. 14.

[28] Johnson, *ibid.*

[29] *Ibid.* See also Nicholas Gage, "Legal Gambling Proposed by Murphy to Curb Police Graft," *New York Times*, September 13, 1971.

provement. Small merchants in the area have been proposed as sales agents for numbers, with the proceeds from their gambling transactions steadying their usually faltering income.

It is said that legalizing other forms of gambling without permitting numbers to be bet will never have any discernible impact on the gambling behavior of the ghetto resident. "My customers want daily action," a numbers man has said. "They want to be paid daily. And they ain't interested in going to a store to buy a ticket—not when I come to them." Numbers players also avoid having to pay taxes on their profits as long as the game remains illegal.[30] On the other hand, proponents of legalizing numbers point out that a State-run operation could easily pay bigger prizes than those currently offered. In this way, it is said, they would drive organized crime out of the gambling business in the slums.

LOTTERIES

The early history of legal gambling in the United States concerns a series of State- and franchise-run lotteries which were promoted with great fanfare. Proceeds were used for various benevolent purposes, with franchises often going to private promoters upon payment of licensing fees. As noted, these flamboyant enterprises disappeared from the American scene one by one as immense scandals surfaced in regard to the way in which they were being operated and the excessive percentages being taken by their promoters.

The appeal of a lottery lies in the relative ease with which it may be run, and in the painless way it offers to raise money for beleaguered state budgets. The "immorality" of gambling on a lottery tends to be blunted since the transaction involves the purchase of tickets at reputable business sites. Particularly, the long wait between the purchase of a ticket and the announcement of the drawing results hardly makes for intensive emotional involvement in the enterprise for most persons.

All of these considerations—with the financial one probably predominant—coalesced to convince some American jurisdictions again to look favorably upon State-sponsored lotteries. Thus, in 1964—70 years after the last legal lottery had taken place in the United States—the voters in New Hampshire approved a State-run scheme by a referendum margin of four to one. First prize in the New Hampshire lottery is $100,000. Proceeds are directed primarily to school districts, which received $.28 million in the first year of the

---

[30] Perlmutter, *op. cit.*, n. 12.

lottery and $1.4 million during each of the following 2 years—about
$50 for each school pupil in the State.[31]

The New York lottery, given the size and prominence of the State,
has been the one that has attracted the most attention throughout
the Nation. Original speculation was that the lottery would bring
in several hundred thousand dollars each year, but early returns
have been far below this estimate. It is now alleged that the enabling
legislation in New York undercut effective revenue raising tactics.
The legislature, it is said, attempted to have the best of both worlds,
establishing gambling and yet cocooning it so thoroughly that it was
a lollipop kind of enterprise. Sales were at first restricted only to
banks (though this site was later declared unconstitutional), hotels,
motels, and local governmental offices. Advertising emphasized the
educational benefits that would accrue from participation in the
lottery. Lottery players had to fill out cards, indicating their name
and address on them, and the drawings were held but once a month.

After a disappointing first year sales of $47.2 million, New York
authorities were permitted to hold "diversified" drawings. There
were two with prizes up to $1 million, and the usual $1 sales price
for a lottery ticket was at times reduced to a 50-cent minilottery
standard. The result was an increase of 50 percent in sales, to $70.5
million in the fiscal year that ended on March 30.[32]

New Jersey—the third jurisdiction to join in the lottery business—
began its drawings in 1971. It had learned a lesson from New York,
and immediately began realizing sales of $1 million higher than its
neighboring State.[33] Drawings in New Jersey are held weekly, tickets
are sold in strips like motion picture admissions, and each ticket is
adorned with a large four-leaf clover.[34]

The lesson is clear and predictable. Soon there was the report
that the Connecticut general assembly had approved legislation
allowing a State lottery. "Statewide polls have consistently shown
widespread public support for gambling," it was noted. And then
there was the observation, rather surprisingly, that "there has been
no organized opposition."[35] In addition, in September 1971, the

[31] John H. Fenton, "The New Hampshire Sweepstakes, Its Dreams Unrealized,
Begins 3d Drawing of Names," *New York Times*, July 14, 1966.

[32] "State Lottery Sales Climb to $70.5-Million," *New York Times*, May 29,
1971.

[33] Joseph B. Treaster, "Passage of Betting Bill Expected in Connecticut," *New
York Times*, May 29, 1971.

[34] Ronald Sullivan, "Jersey Lottery Exceeding Hopes," *New York Times*,
March 7, 1971.

[35] Connecticut, Public Act 865, January Session, 1971 (Connecticut Legislative
Service, No. 5, 1971, p. 1232).

Massachusetts legislature overrode the Governor's veto to join the ranks of States sanctioning lotteries.[36] A month earlier, Pennsylvania had become the fourth State to legalize lotteries.[37] Perhaps the most intense puzzlement was that of the ghetto numbers player who remained unclear about the difference between what he was doing surreptitiously and illegally in his neighborhood and what the State was encouraging all its residents to do openly.

OFFTRACK BETTING

The legislative mandate in Connecticut for the establishment of a State-run lottery also endorsed the principle of offtrack betting as a State operation. In providing immediate, that-day rewards for customers, offtrack betting moves into the realm of gambling that carries the heaviest emotional loading. On the other hand, the discrepancy between allowing bets to be made at the racetrack and forbidding wagering on the same horse races to be done elsewhere has stood out as a blatant piece of discrimination. Class-differentiated morality is always in jeopardy in a working democracy, particularly when the theological justification for its existence begins to come into question.

At present, 28 States permit parimutuel betting at their racetracks. It is noteworthy that such betting has rarely brought about scandal and fraud. Some persons insist that the States realize only limited funds from the parimutuel operations, and that those persons running the racetracks exercise extraordinary influence in the political processes of their jurisdictions. There are no strong allegations, however, that parimutuel betting involves things such as fixed races, avoidance of stipulated taxes, and similar kinds of criminal machinations. Given their rather calm operation, the extension of betting to offtrack installations, again appreciating the desperate need for new sources of taxes, seems foreordained.

OFFTRACK BETTING IN NEW YORK

Unlike the lottery promotion in New York, there has been nothing shy and backward about the program of the State's Offtrack Betting

---

[36] "Lottery Becomes Law Despite Veto in Massachusetts," *Los Angeles Times*, September 28, 1971 (AP) ; Massachusetts, State Lottery Law, Acts 1971, chap. 813, §2 (Advance Legislative Service, No. 8, 1971).

[37] "Lottery Bill OKd in Pennsylvania," *Los Angeles Times*, August 27, 1971; "Pennsylvania Adopts a Lottery to Cut Taxes for Elderly," *New York Times*, August 27, 1971; Pennsylvania, State Lottery Law, Act No. 91, 1971 Session (Purdon's Legislative Service, No. 3, 1971).

Corporation. The Corporation has attempted to make an exuberant thing out of its business, rather than to have it regarded as a shady, shoddy kind of deal, to be engaged in only because of an inability to control one's more despicable impulses. "Start a new morning routine," an OTB advertisement proclaims. "Coffee and doughnuts and the daily double." Another advertisement announces: "There's a new game in town," and a third suggests: "If you're in the stock market you might find this a better bet." [38]

This last bit of waggery brought forth a not altogether unanticipated response from the head of the New York Stock Exchange (writing "on behalf of the more than 31 million shareholders who own stock in America's publicly owned corporations"), who "strenuously" protested the "ill-considered slogan." [39] Political experts might have predicted a political response from OTB, begging forgiveness and charging the ad to an overzealous impulse. Instead, the betting corporation counterattacked: "On behalf of the more than 48,972 horses that raced in this country in 1971," the head of the Corporation answered, "I am sure that some of the horses feel they have been a better investment in the past few years than some of the investments on the New York Stock Exchange." [40] Finally, a newspaper reader entered the discussion, and tried to put matters into perspective—with a slight tilt in the direction of the horses:

> Both [the stock market and offtrack betting] spawn touts . . . . Both thrive to some extent on decisions by wishful thinking out of impulses and by tipsters. Both are susceptible to rumors, hearsay, half-truths, undisciplined emotionalism and expert straddling in analysis and prophecy.
> There is this to be said for horse racing. When you lose—whether because of bad luck or bad judgment—you know it within minutes, whereas it might take months to discover that you've picked a loser in the market. And time, too, is money.
> Perhaps a balanced, diversified portfolio of racing bets and market purchases might be the best bet after all. [41]

Offtrack betting in New York had gotten its incentive from a citywide referendum conducted in 1963 by then Mayor Robert Wagner which showed that the voters approved of such a move by a 3 to 1 margin. Given legislative sanction to inaugurate offtrack betting, New York City authorities spent some $5 million drawing

[38] "City Betting Agency Sets March 29 Goal," *New York Times*, March 3, 1971.
[39] Emanuel Perlmutter, "City is Told Betting Ad Sells Big Board Short," *New York Times*, March 4, 1971.
[40] *Ibid.*
[41] Reuben Gabel, Letter to the Editor, *New York Times*, March 15, 1971.

public attention to their program and attempting to establish a much-heralded computerized betting system that during the first months of the program remained truculently inoperative. The off-track betting system, one writer observed, "began with labor pains, financial nausea, and even charges of illegitimacy." [42] But it began— on April 8, 1971—with the Mayor playing a hunch and betting on a seventh-race horse called Money Wise, which finished fourth.[43] A month later OTB was still calling forth inelegant metaphors, but notes of success were also beginning to be heard. "Offtrack betting lurches into its second full month of operation tomorrow," a reporter noted, "a hornblowing jalopy steadily picking up speed despite locked brakes, defective safety belts and smoke-billowing exhaust pipe." The initial response of the public had been "overwhelming— even more solid than anticipated." [44]

Reviewing the early period of offtrack betting, another writer found it to be a "remarkable phenomenon." It had been made to function by "a group of people, with all the intense loyalties, aggressive marketing ideas and giddy enthusiasm of a worthwhile political effort." They were "actually waging a campaign to get people to bet," operating on the principle that "betting can be a normal, legal—and enjoyable—part of city life." The comment of a patron standing in line at one of the betting booths in Grand Central Station was regarded as epitomizing public response to OTB: "This is the only fun thing in Fun City." [45]

The early triumph of the OTB system with the Kentucky Derby was largely responsible for such enthusiastic reactions. The State had realized a profit of $100,000 on betting in connection with the Derby and persons fortunate enough to select Canonero II to win had received $59 for their $2 bets. The "large action" and "honest payoff" of OTB in the Derby so impressed a Michigan legislator that he issued a call for his State to look into offtrack betting as a source of revenue.[46]

The OTB authorities also continued their aggressive campaign to define their activities as perfectly proper and reasonable. Accused of "taking" money from the poor, the head of the OTB Corporation asked, rather rhetorically: "Who's to say what's gambling and

---

[42] Cady, *op. cit.*, n. 5.

[43] Richard Dougherty, "Off-Track Betting Underway in New York, Finds Going Muddy," *Los Angeles Times*, April 9, 1971.

[44] Steve Cady, "OTB: What Makes It So Slow," *New York Times*, May 9, 1971.

[45] Pete Axthelm, "Howie the Horse Is Ahead for the Year," *New York*, 4 (May 3, 1971), p. 42.

[46] "Michigan Studies Gaming Tax Plans," *New York Times*, May 9, 1971.

what's entertainment?"[47] In addition, (as their opponents had mournfully predicted they sooner or later would), the OTB leaders had begun bulling their way into even more disputatious moral territory by proposing to the State legislature that it reduce the age for betting from 21 to 18, that it expand racing and parimutuel betting to Sundays, and that it exclude OTB winnings from State and local taxes.

These early moves and responses, however, hardly talk to the moral implications for the quality of life in a jurisdiction with an offtrack betting program. From California, a group dispatched by the Attorney General to observe the New York effort returned convinced that there was "a possibility of a major scandal in New York." "I predict that this is going to happen," the Attorney General said, apparently basing his views on the fact that the leaders of the offtrack betting system were political appointees, and therefore subject to political pressures, and that too many employees were being allowed to handle betting monies. Such arrangements, the California Attorney General insisted, contain built-in headaches for law enforcement officials. The Attorney General said that California ought not act on offtrack betting until the New York operation had gone on for a much longer period of time.[48]

Among those standing back some and philosophizing on the implications of offtrack betting was one writer who posed some of the important, far-from-answered questions concerning offtrack betting:

> Ultimately, OTB will have to face judgment in four areas: Will it strike a blow against organized crime by draining huge sums away from bookmakers? Will it bring sudden prosperity to the hard-pressed city government? Will it eventually cripple the racing industry by drawing fans away from the tracks, or will it breathe new life into racing by introducing it to millions who never thought of betting on a horse before? And finally, how will the hundreds of projected legal betting parlors affect the quality and pace of life in New York?[49]

RESPONSES TO NEW YORK'S PROGRAM

The Kentucky Derby triumph of New York's offtrack betting program stirred a Michigan legislator, as we have noted, to propose

---

[47] Howard Samuels, quoted in "New Game in Town," *Time*, August 2, 1971, p. 66.

[48] "Younger Expects N.Y. Bet Scandal," *San Diego Evening Tribune*, July 1, 1971; California Department of Justice, *Task Force Report on Legalized Gambling* (Sacramento: June 21, 1971).

[49] Axthelm, *op. cit.*, n. 56, p. 42.

that his State begin moving in the same direction in regard to offtrack betting. Endorsement of the principle of offtrack betting was
far from universal, however. In Minnesota, for instance, a bill to
take a prior step, that is, to legalize parimutuel ontrack betting,
died by a 95 to 32 vote after strong opposition was mounted by the
Minnesota Council of Churches.[50] In California, as we have seen,
the reaction of State authorities was in the nature of a wait-and-see
attitude, tinged with expectations of latent difficulties emerging in
the New York program. But the New York breakthrough had
clearly turned attention in California toward legalized gambling
as a source of State revenue. "Most of the leaders [in Sacramento]
no longer approach this as a moral or ethical matter," a political
observer noted.[51] "It has become largely a technical and economic
question." In this vein, the justifications and rationalizations supporting State-sanctioned gambling were being set into place in
California. There was, for instance, the stress on relativism:

> Most politicians are not . . . fastidious. They figure we are
> all in the business of exploiting human weakness in one form or
> another. And the fact is that money raised through legalized
> gambling is one of the few forms of taxation that people volun-
> tarily and cheerfully pay.[52]

Then there was the comparative assessment of social and personal
costs attached to gambling as compared to other activities:

> But of all the foibles and weaknesses that flesh is heir to,
> gambling must surely be among the least harmful or risky—
> since nothing is lost but money. Drinking, doping, warfare,
> autoracing, boxing, football and politics take an immeasurably
> greater toll on human life, welfare, and happiness.
> It is as if all the primitive instincts that ordinary men expend
> in abusing their wives and children, making war or proclaiming
> their ignorance as infallible truth tend, in the gambler, to be
> concentrated into simple acquisitiveness. Making and losing
> money may not be the noblest activity known to man, but
> neither is it among the lowest and most vicious. And it focuses
> the attention wonderfully.[53]

Also, the seemingly inexorable move in California toward approval
of lotteries and offtrack betting was moved forward considerably by
the critical findings of the San Francisco Committee on Crime on

---

[50] "Minnesota Kills Betting Bill," *New York Times*, May 13, 1971 (AP).

[51] Park Terry, quoted in Myron Roberts, "Gambling in California: Why You
Can Bet On It," *Los Angeles*, 16 (July 1971), p. 30.

[52] Roberts, *ibid.*, p. 30.

[53] *Ibid.*, p. 32.

the content of the laws and the enforcement practices in regard to gambling in that city.

Sarcastically, the Committee noted that betting at tracks on races had been legal in California since 1933 on the spurious justification that racing encouraged "agriculture and the breeding of horses," as if, the Committee noted, "society had any interest in 'the breed' except as a tool for gambling." [54] Particularly galling to the Committee was the allegedly discriminatory manner in which gambling laws were being enforced. During 1969, it found, the police charged 593 persons with gambling in San Francisco. Of these, 67 percent were black. All told, 86 percent of those charged were minority group members, while only 14 percent were white. Nor had the police tactics gone unnoticed by the judiciary. In November 1969, for instance, one trial judge stated from the bench: "I'm sick and tired of seeing only black defendants here on gambling charges. You can't tell me that white people in this city don't do any gambling." [55]

All told, the Committee thought that the attempt to enforce gambling laws when there was no evidence of organized crime control or of exploitative, coercive tactics was a vain and self-defeating process:

> (An) unmeasurable cost is the loss of respect for law when it tries to illegalize what the people largely desire. Certainly much of the reason why gambling laws are not enforced against church bingo games, football pools and private clubs is that *most* people in the community do not want the laws enforced against these activities. It is not simply a matter of whether the police could get evidence. Rather, by refusing to enforce broadly drawn laws to the letter, the police save themselves—and the rest of the legal system—from public ridicule. Antigambling laws still try to prohibit all people from engaging in any activity that *many* people want to pursue. And this has been true since at least Biblical times. There is no way for the law to *prevent* gambling or to prevent people from losing money at it. [56]

This quotation is not, of course, quite to the point. There may be no way to prevent all gambling, but there certainly are ways to see to it that there is less rather than more of it. The issue concerns neither those persons who will inevitably gamble nor those who will never gamble, but rather those who will gamble, and perhaps recklessly, if given the opportunity readily, but will not do so otherwise. There

---

[54] San Francisco Committee on Crime, *A Report on Non-Victim Crime in San Francisco* (Part II: *Sexual Conduct, Gambling, Prostitution*), June 3, 1971, p. 47.
[55] *Ibid.*, pp. 49–50.
[56] *Ibid.*, p. 53.

are other issues too, one of which is the matter of selective law enforcement, which the Committee highlights. But an inability to achieve utopian conditions ought not to be allowed to interfere with attempts to achieve more desirable states than might otherwise prevail. It is only when, by reasonable standards, one set of conditions appears less desirable on balance than another that we ought to opt for the better of the two.

GAMBLING IN NEVADA

Americans who say that we ought to look to Britain for clues to the proper approach to gambling in the United States often hear that Britain has a quite different social system, and that its experiences cannot be relocated in the United States with any hope of similar outcomes. Instead of Britain, they say, persons seeking insight into the consequences of open, legalized gambling ought to look at Nevada gambling.

The history of sanctioned gambling in Nevada is most often cited to indicate the inability of authorities to keep organized criminals from manipulating gambling enterprises once they are legalized. Nevada first permitted gambling in 1931, in large measure to create revenue for a jurisdiction faced with little prospect of otherwise supporting itself. Today, reported gross earnings of gambling enterprises in Nevada are $240 million yearly, taxes on which provides the State with 20 percent of its income. This is well below original expectations, and six States, in fact, realize more money from parimutuel betting.[57] More important, however, are widespread allegations that huge sums of money are regularly drained from Las Vegas and Reno gambling establishments, hidden from tax investigators by a process known as "skimming," and funneled into the pockets of organized criminals, who employ the money to invade legitimate businesses. When Las Vegas needed gamblers who knew how to run big casinos, it is alleged that promoters "went to the training halls of Cicero and other underworld fiefs."[58] Another writer notes that "it is common in Las Vegas Strip casinos that among the shareholders will be some with a background in illegal gambling, bootlegging and horse-books. That is where they sharpened the skills

---

[57] Wallace Turner, "Gambling Reforms in Nevada Win Public's Support of the System," *New York Times* (western edition), May 19, 1963; Turner, "Las Vegas' Gambling Take Creates New Force in U.S.," *New York Times* (western edition), November 18, 1963.

[58] Milton R. Wessel, "Legalized Gambling: Dream and Realities," *The Nation*, 20 (January 18, 1965), p. 47.

and gathered the capital that permitted them to be successful in the competitive atmosphere of the Strip." When such persons enter into traditional kinds of business they are said "to tend to take with them the same business practices they learned in the backrooms in New York, Chicago, Miami, and Los Angeles—the 'fix,' the hard shove, the fast fleecing of the unwary." [59] In summary, it is argued that "Las Vegas is the strangest city in America. It is the source of an infectious immorality that rides out of the desert on a golden flood of gambling wealth to spread across the nation." [60]

The indictments of Nevada gambling come down hardest on the alleged gangster control of the casinos. There are also protests fortified by stories of tragedy as a consequence of gross overindulgence in gambling. One writer observes, for instance: "The temptations are too much for almost anyone. I've seen church bishops playing the slots. Our local Catholic Charities allocates almost its entire budget to getting stranded people out of town—getting them gasoline, food baskets, and cash." [61]

Attention is often called too to the fact that the crime rates in both Las Vegas and Reno tend to be a good deal higher than for cities their size elsewhere. This is said to attest to "the difficulty of maintaining order in a gambling society, in a climate of easy virtue in which all distinctions become blurred." [62]

On the other side, at least two arguments are made. One suggests that Nevada-style gambling is not being offered as the prototype for operations in other jurisdictions. Offtrack betting and lotteries are both conducted under State auspices by State authorities, not by licensed franchisers. It is also alleged that the horrors of Nevada gambling are greatly exaggerated. Most persons report that the games are operated honestly, with their owners being content with the profits accruing through odds offered the wagerer. That organized criminals filter money from the operations is said by some to be a matter of no great consequence. Now that Howard Hughes has bought into so many Nevada gambling operations, such persons ask, does this mean that they have somehow become purer, because Hughes is a legitimate businessman who uses his immense profits

[59] Wallace Turner, "Las Vegas: Casinos' Hoodlums Face A Cleanup," *New York Times* (western edition), November 30, 1963.

[60] Wallace Turner, "Las Vegas: Casinos Get Millions From Teamsters' Funds," *New York Times* (western edition), November 22, 1963. Cf., Turner, *Gambler's Money: A New Force in American Life* (Boston: Houghton Mifflin, 1965).

[61] Ed Reid, quoted in Fred J. Cook, *A Two-Dollar Bet Means Murder* (New York: Dial, 1961), p. 7.

[62] Cook, *ibid.*, p. 93.

only for benign purposes? It is suggested that if Nevada gambling money is legally earned then the only concern of the society ought to be whether it is legally spent by those who earn it. If not, then there are proper recourses to be had, just as there are suitable methods available to see to it that the profits themselves are not controlled by illegal entry into Nevada gambling. Others, contrariwise, find such arguments naive, and say that the public authorities are quite helpless against the power and the monetary suasion of organized criminals, and that creation of an iniquitous den such as they believe Nevada to be represents an inevitable invitation to further corruption of people and politics.

OVERSEAS BETTING ARRANGEMENTS

Proponents of legalized gambling note that British investigatory commissions have consistently supported it. The 1951 Royal Commission, after a 2-year study, concluded that, although gambling "may and does cause poverty," it does so no more than smoking, drinking, and other known human "weaknesses," it does not "seriously" interfere with production, it "cannot be regarded as imposing a serious strain on national resources or manpower," and it has not been a significant factor as a cause of crime. The Commission also claimed of gambling that "many of its forms involve some mental activity, and it has a social value as a general topic of conversation." [63]

All legal gambling in Britain was done by telephone, on a credit system, or at the track, until passage of the Betting and Gaming Act in 1960, which permitted bets to be placed in person at neighborhood shops which, in the words of one observer, range from "seedy holes in the wall and small 'Momma and Poppa' operations" to "rather cushy parlors with bright lights, soft couches, closed-circuit television to display the odds and loudspeakers for race broadcasts." [64] The British law bans live television from betting shops on the ground that it would add too much emotion to the experience. The shops are licensed and the bookmakers are forbidden by law to encourage anyone to bet or to advertise outside their shops. Nor can there be any access through a betting shop to other premises.[35]

Major opposition to the British gambling scheme has come from persons who believe that it undermines traditional British concern with good horses and "pure" sportsmanship or, as a Member of

[63] Great Britain, Royal Commission on Betting, Lotteries and Gaming, 1949–1951 (Cmnd. 8190, 1951), pp. 48–55.

[64] "Offtrack Betting: A World Study," *New York Times*, April 26, 1970.

[65] J. P. Eddy and L. L. Lowe, *The New Law of Betting and Gaming*, 2d ed. (London: Butterworth's, 1964), pp. 80–81.

Parliament put the matter, "Racing should not become the appendage of gambling. The tail must not be allowed to wag the horse." [66]
The initial fears regarding the impact of gambling on horse racing
seem rather well founded. The average daily attendance at the tracks
in Britain, for example, is down from 7,339 10 years ago to 5,200
today. In monetary terms, offtrack betting has a turnover of about
$1.75 billion annually as compared with $144-million bet at the
tracks. The explanation for the decline in track attendance is
stated in the following terms by the head of the National Bookmakers Association:

> Petrol is expensive. The races are sometimes far away from
> home. And many people like to sit in the comfort of their home,
> pop down to the corner or pick up the phone and place a bet,
> and then pop back into the chair to watch it all on color TV.[67]

Today, some 15,000 betting shops operate in Britain (2,000 more
than the number of pharmacies), and it is estimated that 2 percent
of the national income is wagered on racing alone. The attraction
of gambling in Britain is evidenced by the fact that 70 percent of
the population participates in the state-run pool on soccer games,
and that this pool accounts for 10 percent of Britain's domestic mail
during the 9 months that it operates.

According to Geoffrey Gorer, a well-known British anthropologist,
the British gambling law resulted primarily because of the country's
commitment to welfare state principles which insisted that gambling
rights be extended to working class persons and not confined exclusively to credit-worthy individuals able to place bets by telephone.
Gorer believes that part of the abiding British interest in gambling
is related to the equation of money with love. British children, Gorer
points out, rarely receive regular allowances from their parents, but
are indulged with money erratically, usually on those occasions when
they have won their parents' favor.[68]

There remains no definitive judgment on the consequences of the
decade-long British experience with legalized offtrack betting, run
by private operators under state supervision. Prior to legislative
consideration of the subject in New York, analysts there submitted
an 88-page report on England. Its major conclusion was that it was

---

[66] Quoted in Robert S. Kenison, "Off-Track Betting: A Legal Inquiry into
Quasi-Socialized Gambling," *New Hampshire Bar Journal*, 6 (October 1963),
p. 37.

[67] *New York Times, op. cit.*, n. 38.

[68] Geoffrey Gorer, "British Life—It's a Gamble," *New York Times Magazine*,
September 1, 1963, p. 10ff.

preferable to venture into the numbers business than into offtrack gambling. The report's summary was inconclusive, though cynical:

> There is, however, one sure lesson we have learned from our labors in this field; legalized gambling, like illegal gambling, can be a 'sucker's game.' Those who claim, at this point, to know with certainty what the precise consequences of a legislative venture would be are either fools or frauds.
>
> The British experience, we believe, serves to demonstrate the need for caution in dealing with this mercurial legislative issue.[69]

Perhaps the most ominous note from the field of British gambling was the report in mid-1971 that from that time forward gambling club managers and staff members would be required to secure an official work permit. The move was announced as an attempt to lessen the danger that legalized gambling would fall into the hands of "criminal elements." The permit would have to be renewed annually.[70] Obviously, the move would not have taken place without some foreboding that the evil it sought to protect against was at least reasonably possible, if not likely. On the other hand, it is quite clear that there is no significant move to retreat in Britain from the position of sanctioned offtrack betting.

Other countries illustrate primarily that they are a good deal more indulgent—if not downright enthusiastic—about legal gambling than the United States has been to date. In France, the most popular legal gambling pastime is the *tiercé*, in which bettors seek to pick the first three finishers in a designated horse race. The *tiercé* last year involved 75 different races, and five million Frenchmen wagered an average of more than $10 million on each race, with the payoff odds sometimes soaring as high as 20,000 to 1. The *tiercé* began in 1954, and today is described as a "national craze." The French had outlawed offtrack betting in 1891, but restored it in the face of the economic crisis of 1929. Betting cafes in France are said to be "important centers of social life and recreation. People meet there to dope out the races at their leisure and have a drink with friends." [71]

In Poland, a national monopoly controls all games of chance and allows neither telephone bets nor credit.[72] In Australia, the Totali-

---

[69] Arvis Chalmers, "England Has Some Tips on Gambling," *Knickerbocker* (*N.Y.*) *News*, May 15, 1970.

[70] Charles A. Smith, "British Rule—Work Permit for Gambling," *San Francisco Examiner and Chronicle*, June 6, 1971.

[71] *New York Times, op. cit.,* n. 38.

[72] *Ibid.*

zator Agency Board (TAB) system was introduced to channel money away from illegal offtrack bookmakers. The TAB system is said to have been successful in cutting down a prime source of police graft. New South Wales, the most populous Australian State, has 329 TAB agencies to serve 4½ million people. Racing officials say that the TAB program has improved racing attendance because money is put back into the tracks, allowing them to make improvements which attract more customers. Horse owners are also subsidized by profits from the wagering which are used to improve breeding standards. The results of the Australian TAB program, except for its moral connotations, are believed to have been advantageous:

> TAB has not affected oncourse betting. TAB betting has created no new gambling problem. Social and church workers see it as only one more part of the overall gambling problem in a country that has legal lotteries, totalizators and, in New South Wales, slot machines. It has greatly reduced illegal bookmaking and its attendant corruption of the police.[73]

Japan, which has taken something of an in-between position, trying to discourage gambling yet to deal with its realities, may serve as a case example of the futility of such half-way measures. A 1963 governmental inquiry maintained that as a social evil, gambling should not be allowed to spread. No new betting centers were opened therefore, and as a consequence illegal offtrack betting, usually occurring in small bars, restaurants, and private homes, increased greatly. The police make periodic arrests, but they are said to barely touch the tip of the illegal gambling iceberg.[74]

In Argentina, the Government approach has been a good deal more pragmatic. In June 1971, the Argentinian Welfare Minister announced that the Government was opposed to gambling, but that henceforth it would tax it, where it could be found. "You should not gamble," the Minister said. "But if you do, despite our advice, you'll have to pay a fool's tax which will go to finance social projects to benefit all the community." [75]

FURTHER IMPACTS OF GAMBLING

The foregoing materials, in reviewing new and previous patterns in gambling laws and their enforcement, indicate most of the trou-

---

[73] *Ibid.*

[74] *Ibid.*

[75] "Argentine Gaming Tax Will Defray Social Costs," *Los Angeles Times,* June 16, 1971 (Reuter's).

blesome issues whose adjudication is necessary before informed
judgments can be entered concerning reasonable approaches to gambling in the United States. The following items perhaps need
reemphasis in this concluding section.

Gambling and the Individual

Gambling is one of the less serious vices in regard to its direct
harm to the individual. It has no physical consequences except by
indirection. It is not apt to be particularly time-consuming. It may
engender a philosophy rather unrealistic in terms of mundane existence, but it is arguable whether such a philosophy is more detrimental than enabling to an individual. That some individuals who
do not now gamble will become inextricably involved in its operation if it were made legal, to the point that they will be defined as
"problem" gamblers, seems inevitable. It is now estimated that there
are some ten million "compulsive" gamblers in the United States,
and Gamblers Anonymous, begun in 1957, has become the therapeutic force resembling its counterpart for alcoholics in the field.[76]
By some standards, including those of the present writer, it is unfortunate that many persons now without them are apt to develop
gambling difficulties under legalized systems. But I would suggest
that if this problem becomes particularly serious then the society
might care to discover techniques to handle the situation that are a
good deal more effective than those hit-and-miss, haphazard approaches now in fashion when gambling flourishes undercover.

The issue of gambling and class position poses some difficult
dilemmas. Certainly enforcing the gambling laws against the poor
and not against the rich is unconscionable. Would legalized gambling however, as the Governor of California claims, be "the very
worst kind of taxation" because gambling "has a much heavier
impact on the poor than anyone else"?[77] This proposition rests, of
course, on the doubtful estimate that legalized gambling would have
a disproportionately greater involvement of the poor than it now
does. The contrary might rather seem to be the truth—that the poor
now gamble anyway, and it is the richer, more "respectable" citizen
who is somewhat wary of being involved in such things as numbers
and bookmaking activity. If so, then the "drain" of financial resources by legal gambling might fall more heavily on the richer
than on the poorer citizen. Further, of course, some equity can

---

[76] James F. Clarity, "Gamblers Anonymous Bids City Consider It a Safe Bet,"
New York Times, March 16, 1971.

[77] Ronald Reagan, quoted in Tom Goff, "Lottery Urged to Raise School Funds,"
Los Angeles Times, January 14, 1971.

always be introduced into the system, if the fear is that the poor are being unduly burdened, by earmarking sizable portions of the funds obtained for assistance to the poor so that they will not continue to be poor indefinitely.

Perhaps the argument for legalizing betting as an act which cannot be contravened by reference to meretricious consequences to the individual is made in the following quotation. In it, the public relations manager of the New York City offtrack system heavyhandedly compares illegal gambling to the prohibition of liquor, and easily carries his argument. Is there any outcry in the society, he is really asking, for return to prohibition? If not, then why bar gambling?

> Well, look at Prohibition. They took out Prohibition in '33 and people could drink openly and as much as they wanted. So a certain number of people drank who should not have been exposed to liquor. There are always an unfortunate few. At the racetrack, there's a hard core of people whom some scathingly refer to as betting degenerates. People who have got to have action.
>
> But when they made liquor legal in '33, did three-quarters of the people become alcoholics? Are the streets full of drunken, falling-down people? Sure, people get drunk. Some people drink to excess. And OTB, I'll admit, may uncover a latent bettor or two.
>
> But on balance legalizing offtrack betting is a good idea, just as repealing Prohibition was.[78]

Gambling and the Social System

The corruption that sometimes adheres to the coattails of legal gambling and particularly the involvement in such gambling of organized criminals is one of the points raised against State-sanctioned gambling. Yet, the matter seems controllable by relatively simple means. Thomas C. Schelling, a professor of economics at Harvard University insists that gambling is a commodity that will readily respond to usual economic principles once it is removed from the black market. Gambling, Schelling observes, is an enterprise which by its nature forbids monopolization. For Schelling, the most effective method for dealing with gambling would be to place it within organizations already in possession of the resources and the tradition to conduct it honestly:

> The greatest gambling enterprise in the U.S. has not been significantly touched by organized crime. That is the stock market . . . . Ordinary gambling ought to be one of the hard-

---

[78] Irving Rudd, quoted in Charles Maher, "Off-Track Betting: Successful Venture or Frankenstein?", *Los Angeles Times*, May 30, 1971.

est industries to monopolize because almost anyone can compete . . . . If ordinary brokerage firms were encouraged to
take horseracing accounts, and buy and sell bets by telephone
for their customers, it is hard to see how racketeers could get
any kind of grip on it. We can still think gambling is a sin,
and try to eliminate it; but we should probably not try to use
the argument that it would remain in the hands of criminals
if we legalized it. Both reason and evidence seem to indicate
the contrary.[79]

A similar observation has been made by Carl M. Loeb, Jr., President of the National Council on Crime and Delinquency. Loeb
emphasizes that a clear distinction must be made between licensed
gambling and legalized privately operated gambling. In regard to
the former, Loeb notes that "more than 15 countries now operate
gambling with little or no evidence of corruption." Loeb insists
that lotteries and offtrack betting were the poorest fields for New
York State to have invaded with its gambling program. The first,
he notes, does not compete with organized crime's interests, and the
second involves complicated trackside activities. Instead, efforts
should have been made to take bets on numbers and sporting events—
the main sources of income for organized crime and, potentially, for
the government. For Loeb, this would be "a relatively simple process" in which a well-guarded computer could eliminate corruption.
The Government, he suggests, should take its share from a percentage of the total amount bet, not from the winnings.[80]

Perhaps the major objection voiced to date to the Loeb proposal
is that from sporting figures. The head of the National Football
League has said that offtrack betting seems perfectly reasonable to
him, since it merely extends the facilities for legal betting on horse
races. But to expand betting to other sports would, for him, change
their entire scope and nature. "The values of football," it is argued,
"are hard work, disappointment, and honest competition, which
must exist in an honest environment." Gambling would "accentuate"
the pressures on football players beyond a tolerable point, and
change a sporting event into a gambling spectacle, it is insisted.[81]
The football executive, however, fails to include in his analysis a
review of the foreign scene where soccer games are notable events

[79] Thomas C. Schelling, "Economics and the Public Enterprise," *Public Interest*,
7 (Spring 1967), p. 77.
[80] Carl M. Loeb, Jr., "Legal Gambling: Right and Wrong Way," Letter to the
Editor, *New York Times*, January 18, 1971. Cf., Stanley Penn, "Uncle Sam the
Croupier," *Wall Street Journal*, March 26, 1971.
[81] Pete Rozelle, quoted in Maher, *op. cit.*, n. 76; "Legalized Bet Idea Hit by
Rozelle, Others," *Schenectady (N.Y.) Union*, January 20, 1971 (UPI).

for betting but also performances engendering tremendous national pride and enthusiasm and attracting audiences even larger than those which attend professional football games in the United States. The relationship between illegal gambling and police corruption is one that elicits constant comment, and the suggestion that legalizing gambling would assist in putting police work on a more honest basis is a recurring theme. Reports from Australia indicate, as we have noted earlier, that this indeed is one of the consequences of sanctioned gambling there. The argument may be made, of course, that police corruption as a consequence of gambling payoffs has little meaning for the enforcement of the laws against such things as violence, and that it represents nothing more sinister than an easy manner for law enforcement officers to realize more decent incomes. It could be said too that the close relationship between the powerful forces behind illegal gambling and the police permits some sort of control to be exercised in the community over other aberrant behaviors, since, like most vulnerable enterprises, the gambling business generally prefers quiet and anonymity. The counterargument, of course, is that any corruption breeds further deviation, and certainly that it breeds contempt for the corrupted and their total being even in regard to aspects of their activities that are honestly conducted.

The nature of police corruption in regard to illegal gambling is a well-documented subject. One illustration, from a report of the Massachusetts Crime Commission, will suffice by way of example:

> It seems to have been a universal finding by crime commissions that organized illegal gambling could not exist within a community without the knowledge and protection of the local police. For all practical purposes this is a fair statement . . . . The existence of an illegal gambling operation is as apparent as any other type of retail business. The place to which customers come, such as a horse room, the location of a card or dice game or of pinball machines, is more than apparent; it is obvious. The idea that games float to hide from the police is more fiction than fact. Gaming operators have told the commission that they move to avoid complaint, not arrest . . . . Protection is a state that occurs as frequently by the demand of the police as by the offer of the racketeer . . . . The universal complaint among gaming operators is that the demands have been becoming increasingly exorbitant. Some have told the Commission that the price of protection has reached the stage where illegal gambling is police business instead of bookie business.[82]

On balance, it would seem that moves to legalize and thereby to

---

[82] Quoted in Cook, *op. cit.*, n. 72, p. 7.

control gambling offer the most promising method that has been put forward for dealing effectively with organized crime in this field.

Gambling and the Quality of Life

The condemnation by Fred J. Cook of legalized gambling, after his study of both the legal and illegal varieties, is so uncompromising as to give pause to even mild advocacy of a move in such a direction:

> The entire history of legalized gambling in this country and abroad shows that it has brought nothing but poverty, crime and corruption, demoralization of moral and ethical standards, and ultimately a lower living standard and misery for all the people.[83]

The categoric nature of the castigation is probably what makes it most suspect. Gambling may have produced all the ugliness and misery that it is said to have, but one is apt to suspect that gambling alone could hardly have been so potent a force in shaping the quality of human existence everywhere. Nor that the results of gambling have been "nothing" other than those charged by Cook against it. In fact, it seems that a similar accusation—or a stronger one—might be made (presuming there is some truth in the Cook allegation) against illegal gambling.

In any event, it seems clear that public opinion is divided in regard to legalized gambling in the United States, with several surveys reporting widely different results, though with somewhat different samples. A survey by the Opinion Research Corporation of Princeton, for instance, has reported that 47 percent of American men are opposed to legalized betting.[84] In California, one legislator maintains that 91 percent of the population of the Bay Area said that they were in favor of a State lottery if the funds derived from it were earmarked for education.[85] The California Poll reported that for the State more than two-thirds of the population favored offtrack betting or a State lottery as a source of further State revenue and that more than half liked the idea of Nevada-style gambling.[86]

So—as in the manner of the behaviors we have surveyed earlier— the verdict of public opinion and the verdict of history and analysis comes down to a weighing of difficult and complicated ideological issues. For gambling, that decision seems less uncertain than for

[83] Quoted in Cook, *ibid.*, p. 224.
[84] *Schenectady (N.Y.) Union, op. cit.*, n. 79.
[85] Goff, *op. cit.*, n. 75.
[86] "Off-Track Betting Favored, Poll Finds," *Los Angeles Times*, May 27, 1971.

several of the other behaviors. Gambling is a mildly unnerving kind of behavior in a society interested in preserving regularity and predictability. There are dangers to the individual from legalized gambling, but they seem no more intense than those attendant upon criminalized gambling. And, even if they were so, our thesis has consistently been that individuals ought to be allowed to go their way unmolested to the extent that they do not directly harm others or do not place the polity in clearly recognizable and immediate jeopardy. Gambling obviously may be controlled—and must be—in a manner designed to minimize social harm attendant upon exploitation and corruption that might become associated with it. Perhaps the simplest way of saying it all is to observe that democracy, as a form of government, is itself something of a gamble, a calculated risk based on the premise that informed people will behave well in the face of a wide variety of behavioral choices. The opportunity to gamble, it seems to us, is one of those choices that ought to be vouchsafed to people who elect to make it.

VII. Conclusion

No attempt will be made in this final section to return to the specific behaviors we have examined and to again assess facets of their operation. What we have previously said about them will have to suffice as the factual basis in terms of which policy and other decisions may be made.

To set the stage for our concluding observations, we would first endorse the observation of Jerome Michael and Mortimer J. Adler:

> It is clear that laws which cannot be enforced should not be made; hence behavior, the legal prohibition of which cannot be enforced, should not be prohibited legally. If the social consequences of the enforcement of a law are themselves undesirable for one reason or another, it may be difficult to determine whether the behavior in question should be prohibited. The decision may rest in part upon the balance of the disadvantages involved or upon the availability of other than legal means of preventing the undesirable behavior. Empirical investigations are needed to decide questions of this sort. In some cases it may be impossible to answer the question except by the hazard of guesses or opinions.[1]

It is, of course, equally important to determine by some standards whether the behavior in question really is "undesirable," even if it can advantageously be inhibited by recourse to the criminal law. But this too, of course, usually involves a weighing of very subtle kinds of items and a rendering of something less than an obvious and unassailable positive or negative judgment.

In this section I want to put on record some views expressed generally on such matters in the past, and to indicate, briefly, some apparent present trends. Thereafter, to conclude, I would like to examine some of the social and psychological reasons which seem to underlie continuing criminalization of victimless behavior and to suggest advantages, and the way to achieve such advantages, of alternative approaches.

ON VICTIMLESS CRIMES

We have earlier noted the observations on victimless crime recorded by the Wolfenden Committee in Great Britain and, in the

---

[1] Jerome Michael and Mortimer J. Adler, *Crime, Law and Social Science* (New York: Harcourt, Brace, 1933), pp. 356–357.

introductory chapter, some of the ingredients of the debate on this subject by Professor Hart and Justice Devlin. Among writers who have inveighed against the futility and self-defeating nature of attempts to use the criminal law for purposes for which it is neither intended nor those which it can adequately perform particular mention might be made of Baruch Spinoza and Jeremy Bentham.

Spinoza (1632–1677), a Dutch philosopher, advocated the excision from statute books of laws restricting activities that do not injure another party on the grounds that, "he who seeks to regulate everything by law is more likely to arouse vices than to reform them. It is best to grant what cannot be abolished, even though it be in itself harmful." [2] A similar point has recently been made in the following words: "Those who crusade . . . against evil leave the world worse rather than better, for by thinking of evil we create occasions for evil. What is inside us, not around us, causes our corruption." [3]

The same point has been made in recent times by Walter Lippmann in a statement on the underworld: "We find ourselves accepting in their lawless form things which in lawful form we repudiate, having in the end to deal not only with all the vices we intended to abolish but with additional dangers which arise from having turned over their exploitation to the underworld." [4]

The warning of Bentham (1748–1832) was that "imaginary offenses," which he defined as "acts which produce no real evil but which prejudice, mistake, or the esthetic principle have caused to be regarded as offenses may be punished with greater severity than real ones involving a serious manifestation of social destructiveness." [5] Bentham illustrated his theme by reference to fornication and drunkenness, two acts still often regarded as criminal in Anglo-Saxon jurisdictions:

> With what chance of success . . . would a legislator go about to extirpate drunkenness and fornication by dint of legal punishment? Not all the tortures which ingenuity could invent would compass it; and, before he had made any progress worth regarding, such a mass of evil would be produced by the punish-

[2] Benedict de Spinoza, "Tractatus Theologico-Politicus," Chap. XX [1670], in *Writings on Political Philosophy*, ed. by A. G. A. Balz (New York: Appleton-Century-Crofts, 1937), p. 141.

[3] Gordon Davidson, "Do Devils Exist: A Note on the Play," in program for *The Devils*, Mark Taper Forum, Los Angeles, 1967, p. 15.

[4] Walter Lippmann, "The Underworld, A Stultified Conscience," *Forum*, 85 (February 1931), p. 65.

[5] Jeremy Bentham, "Principles of the Penal Code," [1802], in *Theories of Legislation*, 2d ed. (London: Trübner, 1841), p. 245.

ment as would exceed, by a thousand fold, the utmost possible mischief of the offence.[6]

In contemporary times, the same kinds of views appear in the work of F. A. Hayek, who reechoes Mill's sentiments in a number of pointed observations, including the following:

> But where private practice cannot affect anybody but the voluntary adult actors, the mere dislike of what is being done by others, or even the knowledge that others harm themselves by what they do, provides no legitimate ground for coercion . . . .[7]

(The best-known vernacular statement of the same point is that of the actress, Mrs. Patrick Campbell: "It doesn't matter what you do in the bedroom as long as you don't do it in the street and frighten the horses.") [8]

Hayek maintains: "It is indeed probable that more harm and misery have been caused by men determined to use coercion to stamp out a moral evil than by men intent on doing evil," [9] a theme which finds its best-known enunciation in the words of Justice Brandeis in a dissent in a case upholding the constitutionality of wiretapping:

> Experience should teach us to be most on our guard to protect liberty when the Government's purposes are beneficent. Men born to freedom are naturally alert to repel invasion of their liberty by evilminded rulers. The greatest dangers to liberty lurk in insidious encroachment by men of zeal, well meaning but without understanding.[10]

As Mill had, Hayek too takes pains to point out that the absence of criminal sanctions does not necessarily mean that a society is obligated to view all forms of behavior within its midst with moral indifference and to take no stand in regard to them. "Yet the fact that conduct within the private sphere is not a proper object for coercive action by the state," he notes, "does not necessarily mean that in a free society such conduct should also be exempt from the pressure of opinion or disapproval." [11]

Perhaps the most penetrating critique of the irrationality of some legal sanctions is that delivered by a psychiatrist, Thomas Szasz.

---

[6] Jeremy Bentham, *A Fragment on Government and An Introduction to the Principles of Morals and Legislation* [1789], ed. by Wilfrid Harrisson (Oxford: Blackwell, 1948), p. 420.

[7] F. A. Hayek, *The Constitution of Liberty* (Chicago: University of Chicago Press, 1960), p. 145.

[8] Quoted in Theo Lang, *My Darling Daisy* (London: Sphere, 1968), p. 31.

[9] Hayek, *op. cit.*, n. 6, p. 146.

[10] *Olmstead v. United States*, 277 U.S. 438, 479 (1928).

[11] Hayek, *op. cit.*, n. 6, p. 146.

Szasz is primarily concerned with the use of labels of psychiatric aberrance as devices to bring the restraints of criminal law to bear upon persons whose behavior is only different, not harmful. "The state-appointed psychiatrist performs a function similar to that of a priest when he excommunicates a sinner," Szasz has maintained.[12] "Most of the legal and social applications of psychiatry, undertaken in the name of psychiatric liberalism," Szasz believes, "are actually instances of despotism." [13] Szasz observes, for instance, that persons are often proceeded against criminally or otherwise deprived of liberty on the ground that they represent a danger to themselves and to others. First, he disputes the likelihood of such alleged dangers becoming actual; then, he notes that similar allegations are never raised against persons who are obviously a good deal more dangerous. His examples refer to persons other than those whose behaviors we have considered in this paper, but the underlying point is quite on target:

> Drunken drivers are dangerous both to themselves and to others. They injure and kill many more people than, for example, persons with paranoid delusions of persecution. Yet, people labeled paranoid are readily commitable, while drunken drivers are not.
> Some types of dangerous behavior are even rewarded. Race-car drivers, trapeze artists, and astronauts receive admiration and applause. In contrast, the polysurgical addict and the would-be suicide receive nothing but contempt and aggression. Indeed, the latter type of dangerousness is considered a good cause for commitment. Thus, it is not dangerousness in general that is at issue here, but rather the manner or style in which one is dangerous.[14]

The philosophy expressed in the foregoing quotations has, as our earlier review indicated, been gaining favor in the United States in recent years. The legislative debates and other comments that we have reported in regard to specific issues amply document this trend. In the academic sphere, the movement has been marked by the writings of a lawyer-sociologist, Edwin M. Schur of New York University, and two criminal law professors, Sanford Kadish of the University of California, Berkeley, and Herbert Packer of Stanford University. Schur's approach is much the same as has been taken here: a review of relevant literature on some forms of victimless crime and a statement about the apparent meaning of such

---

[12] Thomas S. Szasz, *Law, Liberty and Psychiatry: An Inquiry into the Social Uses of Mental Health Practices* (New York: Macmillan, 1963), p. 85.

[13] *Ibid.*, p. vii.

[14] *Ibid.*, p. 46.

literature. Published in 1965, Schur's *Crimes Without Victims* [15] appeared just before the extraordinary legislative and social developments that began to take place throughout the country in regard to the laws bearing on these offenses.

Kadish's analysis, which appears anonymously as part of the body of the report of the President's Commission on Law Enforcement and Administration of Justice, has been widely cited, in part because of its persuasive and forceful manner of enunciation, in part because of its prestigious source. In the Crime Commission report, Kadish carefully reviewed the operation of criminal law in regard to several victimless crimes. "The criminal prohibitions against some types of sexual behavior," it is noted, "reflect an idealized moral code, not what a substantial percentage of the population, judged by their conduct, regard as beyond the margin of tolerability for the average fallible citizen." [16] In a later article, "The Crisis of Overcriminalization," Kadish observed that the law in regard to victimless crime has three functions, all of them questionable: (1) to enforce public standards of private morality; (2) to provide needed social services because no other agencies exist to do so; and (3) to remove restraints on law enforcement.[17] The concluding remarks in the Crime Commission report are calm and reasonable:

Undoubtedly a great deal of research is needed on the uses and limitations of criminal law as a means of social regulation,

[15] Edwin M. Schur, *Crimes Without Victims* (Englewood Cliffs, N.J.: Prentice-Hall, 1965). Cf., Jerome H. Skolnick, *Coercion to Virtue: A Sociological Discussion of the Enforcement of Morals* (Washington, D.C.: President's Commission on Law Enforcement and Administration of Justice, 1967); Nicholas N. Kittrie, *The Right to be Different: Deviance and Enforced Therapy* (Baltimore: Johns Hopkins, 1971); Eugene Doleschal, "Victimless Crime." *Crime and Delinquency Literature* 3 (June 1971), pp. 254–269. Increasing concern with victimless crimes can be documented by the growing mass media attention to the subject—e.g., Alexander B. Smith and Harriet Pollack, "Crimes Without Victims," *Saturday Review*, December 4, 1971, pp. 27–29; Bill Hazlett, "Victimless Crimes—Does Society Pay the Ultimate Price?", *Los Angeles Times*, October 17, 1971; Eric Pace, "Reform in 'Victimless Crime' Laws Urged at Legislative Hearing," *New York Times*, September 14, 1971; Lewis I. Maddocks, "Crimes Without Victims," *Social Action*, 38 (February 1972), pp. 34–36; "Criminals and Victims," *New Republic*, 166 (April 1, 1972), pp. 7–8; Jonathan Kwitny, "Victimless Offenses Should be Legalized, Some Officials Think," *Wall Street Journal*, August 25, 1971; "Victimless Crimes,"—editorial, *Poughkeepsie (N.Y.) Journal*, January 25, 1972.
[16] President's Commission on Law Enforcement and Administration of Justice, *Task Force Report: The Courts* (Washington, D.C.: Government Printing Office, 1967), p. 106.
[17] Sanford H. Kadish, "The Crisis of Overcriminalization," *The Annals*, 374 (November 1967), p. 159.

on the circumstances in which it is more likely to be effective, and on the situations in which its use overbalances social disadvantages and consequences and those in which it does not. But enough is now known to warrant abandonment of the common legislative premise that the criminal law is a sure panacea for all social ailments. Only when the load of law enforcement has been lightened by stripping away those responsibilities for which it is not suited will we begin to make the criminal law a more effective instrument of social protection.[18]

A definition is offered by Packer of the kinds of behavior that ought to be looked at very closely in terms of their proper place in the criminal law apparatus. These are "offenses which do not result in anyone's feeling that he has been injured so as to impel him to bring the offense to the attention of the authorities." [19] Three conditions ought to be assessed—the gravity, proximity, and probability of the harm—in regard to each offense, Packer notes, if it is alleged that the behavior threatens social life and ought to be condemned by use of the criminal law.[20] Packer further identifies six conditions that should be present before criminal sanctions are invoked against disapproved conduct. It can be argued that none of them are met by the kinds of behavior we have reviewed in earlier sections:

1. The conduct must be regarded by most people as socially threatening and must not be condoned by any significant segment of society.
2. Subjecting the conduct to criminal penalties must not be inconsistent with the goals of punishment.
3. Suppressing it will not inhibit socially desirable conduct.
4. It can be dealt with through evenhanded and nondiscriminatory law enforcement.
5. Controlling it through the criminal process will not expose that process to severe qualitative or quantitative strains.
6. No reasonable alternatives to the criminal sanction exist for dealing with it.[21]

THE DEVELOPING LAW

Specific elements of the legal conditions and statutory interpretations bearing upon each of the behaviors we have considered have been covered in the preceding material. It need only be noted here that principles being developed by judicial interpretation in regard to other kinds of behavior might in time come to be applied to vic-

---

[18] President's Commission, *op. cit.*, n. 15, p. 107.
[19] Herbert L. Packer, *The Limits of the Criminal Sanction* (Stanford, Calif.: Stanford University Press, 1968), p. 151.
[20] *Ibid.*, p. 266.
[21] *Ibid.*, p. 296.

timless crimes. More particularly, the *Griswold* case, which defined the marital relationship as one of privacy, existing beyond the right of the State to interfere with accessibility to contraceptive information, might by extension be brought to bear on several aspects of victimless offenses.[22] *Griswold* was further interpreted by a Massachusetts court which declared that the State had no right to ban contraceptives simply because it considered them immoral.[23] The thrust of these and similar decisions has been aptly generalized in the following terms:

> After years in which American law operated on the assumption that sex was likely to get out of hand unless it was hemmed in by laws, the constitutional right and propriety of governmental interference with the private sexual morals of adults is coming under a broad attack.[24]

Similarly, a 5–4 Supreme Court decision declaring that it was unconstitutional to outlaw "loiterers," who by their congregating "annoy" others, might have some of its reasoning applied to phases of victimless crime. The Supreme Court, in its ruling, noted that the loitering statute under review was unconstitutionally vague because a violation "may entirely depend upon whether or not a policeman is annoyed." Under such conditions, the statute was an "invitation to discriminatory enforcement" since the gathering of certain individuals might be considered annoying "because their ideas, their life-style or their physical appearance is resented by the majority of their fellow citizens." [25]

In sum, the movement of the appellate courts clearly appears, both in terms of the foregoing decisions and in terms of others noted throughout this presentation, to be in the direction of permitting a wider latitude for personal behavior, so long as such behavior does not evidently interfere with the rights of others. Perhaps the broadest underlying principle coming to the surface is that expressed by Henry Steele Commager, at least if we accept the view that interference by the criminal justice system with an individual's behavior is apt to be particularly destructive of human dignity:

> . . . it is becoming increasingly clear that it is respect for the dignity of the individual that most sharply differentiates democratic from totalitarian systems. Granted this basic principle, it

[22] *Griswold v. Connecticut*, 381 U.S. 479 (1965).
[23] *Baird v. Eisenstadt*, 429 Fed.2d 1398 (1970).
[24] Fred P. Graham, "Broad Attack on Attempts to Regulate Morals," *New York Times*, July 12, 1970.
[25] *Coates v. Cincinnati*, 402 U.S. 611, 616 (1971).

follows that any conduct of the state that impairs the dignity of man is dangerous.[26]

WHITHER MORALITY

We have generally tried to avoid the task of assaying the moral temperature of this country as an aspect of determining whether the drift toward "permissiveness" in regard to things such as homosexuality, abortion, and the other offenses we have discussed is sapping the vitality and integrity of the United States. Suffice it to say that overall the issue is extraordinarily complex, and the facts—even when agreement can be had on their nature—admit of diverse, often contradictory interpretations. It should be noted, though, that public opinion polls report that a large majority of Americans today are convinced that the moral character of their country has gone into a serious decline in recent years. And it should further be noted that such a view has long historical precedent. As historian Allen Nevins has noted: "From Juvenal to Voltaire and from Swift to H. L. Mencken, critics have weighed their own lands in the balance and found reasons for denouncing a generation of vipers." For Nevins, "one reason for dubiety about charges of deterioration in national character is that they have reappeared so frequently in history, and have so often been disproved by events." [27]

Today, an unrelievedly dismal portrait has been drawn, for example, by another writer, Andrew Hacker, who believes that we have reached the end of the American era:

> The United States is now about to join other nations of the world which were once prepossessing and are now little more than plots of bounded terrain . . . . Americans no longer possess that spirit which transforms a people into a citizenry and turns territory into a nation. There eventually arises a time when a preoccupation with private concerns deflects a population from public obligations. The share of energy devoted to common concerns gradually diminishes, and a willingness to be governed is less evident.[28]

It should be pointed out, however, that Hacker's pessimism is based not on the view that hedonism has triumphed over asceticism,

[26] Henry Steele Commager, *Freedom Loyalty, Dissent* (New York: Oxford University Press, 1954), p. 5.
[27] Quoted in "What Has Happened to Our Morality?," *New York Times Magazine*, June 10, 1962, p. 12.
[28] Andrew Hacker, *The End of the American Era* (New York: Atheneum, 1970), p. 6. But see Herbert J. Gans, "The American Malaise," *New York Times Magazine*, February 6, 1972, pp. 16–17ff.

which is sometimes said to be involved in developing attitudes toward victimless crime, but on more fundamental structural elements of America's economic commitments. It should also be noted that Hacker's evidence hardly provides an irrefutably conclusive demonstration of his thesis.

The complexity of the matter of interpretations of general American morality was highlighted, for instance, a few years ago when Dwight Eisenhower insisted in a public statement that the early patriots would be appalled were they able to see youngsters doing the twist rather than the minuet and if they were to read today's books "using vulgarity, sensuality, indeed, downright filth." [29]

A panel of experts, responding to Eisenhower's statement, found his interpretation of our moral climate at least doubtful. Nevins, for instance, offered the following observation:

> To suggest that because some works of modern art are silly, and some recent novels evoke charges of obscenity, the nation is in retrogression is as unconvincing as to say that our astronauts, our Peace Corps and our long list of Nobel Prize winners prove that our national life is highly satisfactory. A wider collection of data, a longer perspective, and a more rigorous analysis are required.[30]

In particular, it was Nevins' impression that "our chief need is for vigilance respecting public [i.e., the McCarthyism of the 1950's and the relationship of military and industrial forces to governmental processes] rather than private conduct." [31]

Other panelists were similarly persuaded. One thought that there had been an "impressive shift here from the morality of the social worker to that of the social builder," [32] while a church official took the following view:

> . . . there is a great deal more understanding of those who display certain patterns of undesirable behavior, such as alcoholics, drug addicts, and homosexuals. There is a greater recognition of the psychologically compulsive factors in such persons' makeup. [But note the comment of Thomas Szasz, *supra*.] Thus, there is much more compassion (which is indubitably a moral virtue) for such persons, who in times past were simply written off as "sinners." And there is more eagerness to provide constructive help.[33]

---

[29] Quoted in "What Has Happened to Our Morality?" *op. cit.*, n. 26, p. 12.

[30] Allen Nevins, "A Mixed Picture," in *ibid.*, p. 12.

[31] *Ibid.*, p. 32.

[32] Millicent C. McIntosh, "A 'New Morality,'" in "What Has Happened to Our Morality?" *op. cit.*, n. 26, p. 34.

[33] James A. Pike, "A Moral Person is a Whole Person," in "What Has Happened to Our Morality?" *op. cit.*, n. 26, p. 40.

It can be seen, therefore, that clucking and tongue-wagging about moral conditions is an enterprise that ought to be engaged in only after some preliminary strenuous attempt at much clearer definitions of both concepts and facts than those generally employed. In particular, issues of causality and concomitance need careful attention. Many events may be a response to other things rather than a cause of them. All told, moral evaluations ought to be done with a good deal of tentativeness and intellectual humility. Humor and perspective help too. A Quaker writer offers the following formula for examinations of areas of social concern:

> What we need in our time is a mature realism which makes us understand that the human predicament is with us to stay. We shall not eliminate sin in others and we shall not eliminate it in ourselves. We shall not achieve Utopia in universities or anywhere else, though we can make some things relatively better than they are. Meanwhile, we are wise to learn again to laugh, primarily at ourselves.[34]

In such terms, perhaps our best contribution at this point would be an anecdote which might provide a formula for beleaguered political candidates confronted with public agitation about victimless crimes. There is a story of one such office seeker, who was asked by a belligerent listener at the end of his speech: "How do you stand on gambling?" He replied quickly: "I'm okay on that one. Are there any other questions?" [35]

RESPONSE TO DEVIANCY

There is an important lesson to be learned from experiences in the Soviet Union and its attempts to deal with youthful deviants. The Soviet government, as much as any cosmopolitan nation is apt to be able to do today, has attempted to train its youth into patterns of acceptable behavior and beliefs. The result is that there exists in the Soviet Union today a sizable coterie of strong and intractable delinquents, with their strength emerging and growing as a necessary defense to the concerted efforts of the authorities firmly to bring them into line.[36]

The moral is clear. To the extent that a society thrusts from its

---

[34] D. Elton Trueblood, quoted in "Notable and Quotable," *Wall Street Journal*, June 10, 1969.

[35] Paraphrase of Tom Connally, quoted in *New York Times Book Review*, June 23, 1968, p. 10.

[36] Allen Kassof, *The Soviet Youth Program: Regimentation and Rebellion* (Cambridge: Harvard University Press, 1965).

core nonconformists and then takes harsh measures to repress them, it will create a resistant force in its midst. Obviously, repressive measures will have a certain success, particularly with the weaker elements of the deviating group. But those with some strength will, of necessity, grow stronger, needing the added strength to survive. In addition, of course, by its counteracting measures, the major society will come to label and define elements of itself as alien, different, and undesirable—and such elements will so define themselves—so that the path of return to the mainstream will become for them irrevocably closed.

I would therefore suggest that the most efficacious method of dealing with deviancy is to ignore, to the furthest point of our tolerance, those items which we find offensive. Such response is predicated upon the assumption that there exists in our society a core of values which exert enough appeal to win over the deviant ultimately, or at least to keep him within the society in terms of other aspects of his behavior, provided that he has not been irresolutely shut off from conformant living.

Concomitant with such tolerance is an attitude that stresses those kinds of traits and behavior which it is desired to elicit and to perpetuate.

There is a story which illustrates this theme, found in Theodore Sorenson's discussion of a phone conversation between John Kennedy and his father following a Kennedy-Nixon debate. How had his father thought Kennedy had done, Sorenson asked. He reports the response: " 'I still don't know,' the candidate said . . . . 'If I had slipped and fallen flat on the floor, he would have said, "The graceful way you picked yourself up was terrific." ' " [37]

That is what is meant by positive reinforcement, leading to the creation of self-confidence and the duplication of desired behavior.

The whole idea is wrapped up neatly in a quotation from the book *I Never Promised You a Rose Garden*, by Hannah Green. A mental patient has been asked why it is that one attendant at the hospital is successful with the patients, while the other has so much difficulty.

> Deborah knew why it was Hobbs and not McPherson. . . .
> Hobbs *was* a little brutal sometimes, but it was much more than
> that. He was frightened by the craziness he saw around him
> because it was an extension of something inside himself. He
> wanted people to be crazier and more bizarre than they really
> were so that he could see the line that separated him, his in-
> clinations, and random thoughts, and his half-wishes, from the

---

[37] Theodore C. Sorenson, *Kennedy* (New York: Harper and Row, 1965), p. 697.

full-bloomed, exploding madness of the patients. McPherson, on the other hand, was a strong man, even a happy one. He wanted the patients to be like him, and the closer they got to being like him the better he felt. He kept calling to the similarity between them, never demanding, but subtly, secretly calling, and when a scrap of it came forth, he welcomed it. The patients merely continued to give each man what he really wanted. There was no injustice done.[38]

There is no need to pursue the point further. Suffice it to say that Hobbs, driven to despair, eventually killed himself.

SUMMARY

Three items need to be reiterated in conclusion of this final chapter. The first is that victimless crimes often represent defined deviations singled out for reasons more subtle than those sometimes stated as justification for campaigns against them. The second is that singling out behavioral items and labeling them creates designated groups and pushes such groups toward alienation if their actions are viewed as invidious. Given such a situation, there is the need to emphasize, finally, the vital importance of tolerance and flexibility, combined with attitudes designed to encourage and reward desired behavior.

---

[38] Hannah Green, *I Never Promised You a Rose Garden* (New York: Signet, 1964), p. 66.